PLANNING AND MANAGING

WEB SITES on the MACINTOSH®

The Complete Guide to WebSTAR™ and MacHTTP

Jon Wiederspan
Chuck Shotton

Addison-Wesley Developers Press

Reading, Massachusetts • Menlo Park, California • New York
Don Mills, Ontario • Wokingham, England • Amsterdam
Bonn • Sydney • Singapore • Tokyo • Madrid • San Juan
Paris • Seoul • Milan • Mexico City • Taipei

Many of the designations used by manufacturers and sellers to distinguish their products are claimed as trademarks. Where those designations appear in this book, and Addison-Wesley was aware of a trademark claim, the designations have been printed in initial capital letters or all capital letters.

The authors and publishers have taken care in preparation of this book, but make no expressed or implied warranty of any kind and assume no responsibility for errors or omissions. No liability is assumed for incidental or consequential damages in connection with or arising out of the use of the information or programs contained herein.

ISBN 0-201-47957-5 Copyright © 1996 by Jon Wiederspan and Chuck Shotton

A-W Developers Press is a division of Addison-Wesley Publishing Company.

Sponsoring Editor: Kim Fryer
Project Manager: Vicki L. Hochstedler
Cover design: Watts Design
Set in 11-point Palatino by Carpenter Graphics

2 3 4 5 6 7 8-MA-0099989796
Second printing, February 1996

Addison-Wesley books are available for bulk purchases by corporations, institutions, and other organizations. For more information please contact the Corporate, Government and Special Sales Department at (800) 238-9682.

Find A-W Developers Press on the World-Wide Web at:
http://www.aw.com/devpress/

*To our wives, Renée and Linda,
for their loving support, patience,
and understanding.*

Contents

Preface

Overview of Book and Intended Audience

This book is intended to be a guide for Web site management using WebSTAR or MacHTTP. Most of the material in this book was selected because it appeared often on the MacHTTP-talk mailing list, which for over a year was the center of discussion for Macintosh Web site adminstration. Preference was given to topics that seemed to appear repeatedly on the list, indicating that they were stumbling blocks for beginners. Design issues are not addressed, except where they impact on administering the server; nor are technologies affecting the client side of things, such as the Java language, VRML, and other file types that the server is generally oblivious of. That sort of information is already available in dozens of books (and dozens more to come, I am certain). The book's focus on administration issues is relatively unique, especially for the Macintosh computer.

So who should be reading this book? Everyone! Failing that, though, probably anyone who owns a Macintosh or who works in a Mac-centric environment will benefit from this book, especially anyone running or planning to run a Web site. Even if you just ran your WebSTAR server for the first time last week (or are still planning to find time to run one), this book will be useful to help you gain the skills that will make your site fun to create and useful to others.

You will notice throughout the book that certain topics keep reappearing. We have tried as much as possible to make this book accessible to Macintosh Web developers of all levels. One way we do this is by introducing key topics, such as client-server communications and CGI applications, in phases, first giving the reader enough understanding to see where they fit in, then increasing that understanding as other topics are introduced. We assume a basic level of familiarity with Macintosh computers (about enough to install the operating system), but you by no means need to be a power-user to install and run your own World Wide Web site. That's the whole point of WebSTAR: Take five minutes and join the Web.

Overview of the Companion CD-ROM

The companion CD-ROM has a collection of software and documentation that will be of use in site development. Quite a bit of the software is shareware or freeware; please pay any requested fees for that software if you decide to use it, so that the authors can continue to improve it and release new products. Wherever we were restricted to using demonstration versions (as was the case with most of the commercial software), we have tried to get time-limited versions so that you can use all of the features and get a feel for what the software can really do.

The general structure of the CD-ROM is as follows:

- **WebSTAR Install** This rates its own folder, since that is what the entire book is really about. Directions are included for obtaining a trial key (or purchasing a full version) from Star-Nine Technologies, Inc.

- **Apps** This folder contains shareware and freeware software that will be valuable in administering your site. The shareware software is included on the companion CD-ROM for your evaluation. If you like it and choose to continue to use it, please be sure to pay the appropriate shareware fees to the author. This ensures that these great products will continue to be available in the future. Whenever possible, the disk provides a link to a site that contains the latest version of the software, since updates are a monthly event in some cases.

- **CGI** This folder contains specifically CGI applications that are available as shareware, freeware, or demonstration software for your use.

- **Demo** This folder contains demonstration versions of commercial software that is especially useful for site development and administration.

- **Docs** This folder contains Requests for Comments (RFCs), Frequently Asked Questions (FAQs), and other useful documents gleaned from my Web wanderings. The URLs to these documents are also provided so you can obtain the latest version as well.

- **Code** This folder contains sample code for a number of computer languages. Most of the code is for writing CGI applications, but some is for other related purposes. All of the code provided is for instructional purposes and may be freely used for a personal site or the development of noncommercial products. In some cases there are restrictions against using the code for commercial development (and in some, not).

Author Biographies

Jon Wiederspan

Jon Wiederspan was born in Waco, Texas, and dragged all over the continental United States by the Air Force until his father finally retired and settled in eastern Washington. Jon was introduced to computers in high school in the late 1970s and after three months took second place in a statewide programming contest with a trusty TRS-80. This success naturally led him off to college in search of a degree in medical research.

He graduated from the University of Washington in 1986 with dual degrees in Microbiology and Immunology and Laboratory Medicine. Along the way, Jon managed to land jobs working with an AIDS research group, the Human Genome project, and other cool stuff, all of which convinced him that medical research and laboratory work in general were incredibly dull (sorry, folks). He also managed to make a lot of friends at these jobs by criticizing the design of the software used for processing test results and rewriting whatever he could get his hands on. After a couple of years of this, he received many hints that he should return to college and get his computer science degree and generally get out of the medical field altogether.

Jon accomplished this task in 1990, receiving a B.S. in computer science from the University of Washington. Soon after that he was hired by the Technical Japanese Program at the university as a Research Consultant in Software Design, which involved both writing software and maintaining a network of Macintosh, Sun, and Xerox computers.

In 1993 Jon got his hands on NCSA XMosaic and immediately saw the benefits of using the World Wide Web for advertising the Technical Japanese Program. After several failed attempts to build NCSA httpd on the SPARCstation, he found MacHTTP on an Info-Mac site, and the rest is history. Today Jon is Director of Technical Services for ComVista Internet Solutions, Inc., in Redmond, Washington, where he is actually paid to play with Internet tools, go to conferences, and tell people what he thinks of their software.

Chuck Shotton

Chuck Shotton started life with computers in the late 1970s, sitting on the floor in Radio Shack and playing with one of the very first TRS-80s. Long hours of summer work on a loading dock resulted in an Apple II+, ostensibly for school work. After graduating from the College of William and Mary in 1984 with a B.S. in Computer Science, he spent the next seven years working for a large government contractor, Planning Research Corporation, as a lead software engineer and manager of various DoD and NASA software development projects.

1985 saw the arrival of a Macintosh on his desk. Along the way, he developed several shareware games, some communications software for one of the major online services, and many TCP/IP networking tools for the Macintosh, all distributed under the BIAP Systems, Inc., label. After moving to Houston, Texas, in 1987 for a four-year stint on the Space Station project, he spent 1991 through early 1995 working for the University of Texas, Houston, Office of Academic Computing. As assistant director, he was responsible for investigating new technologies on the Internet. One of these was the World Wide Web.

MacHTTP was started as a spare-time project at home, at the urging of some of the original WWW developers at CERN. During 1993 and 1994, MacHTTP grew into an elaborate, time-consuming development effort. By January 1995, BIAP Systems, Inc., was ready to launch MacHTTP as a full-blown commercial product. In April 1995, Chuck and StarNine Technologies, Inc., worked out arrangements that resulted in the birth of WebSTAR and Chuck's joining StarNine as the senior vice president of engineering.

Acknowledgments

We would like to thank everyone at Addison-Wesley who worked so hard to help us make the book a reality, especially Martha Steffen, who held our hands while we learned how to write a book, and Kim Fryer and Vicki Hochstedler, who made sure that we actually got into print. We also owe thanks to Scott Yoshinaga, who reviewed the entire manuscript for technical accuracy and did a great job on a very short deadline. Additional thanks to Mike Bell for cleaning up all the graphics on extremely short notice. Special thanks go to our wives as well, who worked as hard as we did to keep things going while we wrote WebSTAR (Chuck) and this WebSTAR book (Jon). Finally, we owe great thanks to everyone who has posted to the MacHTTP-talk mailing list. The input from that list, the creative solutions that have appeared there, and the general willingness of everyone to provide help and input have been critical in making WebSTAR the great product that it is today.

Part I

Introduction

This background material will help you to understand how Web-STAR operates, why some of the features work the way they do, and how the existing standards affect features that we want in the future.

1

The Internet

Everything in this book begins with a basic understanding of the Internet. Even if you will be running your WebSTAR server only on an internal network, you will be using protocols that were designed with the Internet in mind. An understanding of what the Internet is, how it came about, and how it was designed will help you to understand some of the design decisions made in WebSTAR.

Definition

The *Internet* is the world's largest computer network. Any definition more specific than that is likely to be somewhat inaccurate or subject to discussion. The Internet is comprised of thousands of individual networks in countries around the world, all communicating via the *Internet Protocol (IP)* to exchange information. Each network operates independently for the most part, with independent sources of funding and sometimes even independent decisions on how best to implement the IP suite. One analogy would be the system of roads in the United States (or anywhere else). Each state maintains the majority of the roads within its borders and makes decisions about what kinds of materials to use, how often to repair roads, and travel restrictions. Since it benefits interstate travel to have the roads in two states meet at the state borders, and since the same type of vehicle (an automobile or truck) can be used on roads in various states, all of the states agree to support this minimum level of cooperation. Try to suggest that they share their road maintenance budgets, though, and watch the fur fly!

Why is it so difficult to describe the Internet? There are three main reasons (and dozens of lesser ones) for this. First, there is no strong, centralized authority running the Internet. The Internet works solely because of cooperation among the people in charge of the various networks that compose it. The closest thing to a board of control or a governing body for the Internet is the *Internet Society (ISOC)* **(http://info.isoc.org/)**, which governs network interactions, sets standards, and investigates possible problems with communications or security. ISOC's authority is relatively limited, though, and it doesn't maintain information on every single computer on the Internet. In fact, given the size and growth rate of the Internet, it would be extremely difficult for anyone to maintain that kind of information.

Second, to be "on the Internet" has no common definition, and any definition of the Internet must depend on a definition of what it means to be connected to the Internet. There are varying levels of communication among the various networks and among individual computers on the networks. Some computers are able to use many different protocols to exchange messages and text and binary files and even to run applications on remote computers. Other computers have connections that allow them to exchange only small messages (mail messages or possibly news postings). There are also *gateways* that allow entire networks that don't use IP for communications to exchange information with the Internet. This is how BITNET used to exchange electronic mail with Internet hosts, and the same method is used for FidoNet, UUCP, MCI Mail, Nifty-Serve, and others. CompuServe, America Online, Prodigy, and their like also began with this sort of connection, although most of them are now migrating toward providing full Internet connectivity. Some networks use a *firewall* to isolate their networks and limit intercommunication with the Internet. A firewall controls what kinds of packets (what information) may be exchanged between one network, typically a company's internal network, and another network, typically the Internet. Firewalls are used primarily for security reasons because many of the information exchange methods that host computers on the Internet have problems that could allow others to break in to the computer system.

Third, the Internet is continually both growing and changing at an increasing rate. New capabilities appear each year for sharing files and other data, and existing software and hardware must then be updated to handle the greater loads or new client capabilities. Computers are increasing rapidly in power; this year's desktop computer has all of the power of the workstation of a few years ago. More and more operating systems are adding native support for IP networking and are rolling client software into the operating system. As a result, any definition that tries to be too specific is likely to be out of date before it can even make it into print.

For the purposes of this book, whenever I refer to the Internet, I am referring to every computer and computer user who at any time has the ability to connect to your World Wide Web (WWW) server using a WWW client. That definition includes users who have dial-up accounts and are not continuously connected to the Internet. It also includes all users of multiuser systems whether they have used the WWW client software or not, as long as they have the capability to do so. These are the people you need to worry about when you are developing your site. The other millions of people who are limited to only exchanging electronic mail or news postings probably do not need to figure noticeably in your planning.

For further clarification, I want everyone to understand that the Internet is not the "information superhighway" (IS) or any of the slang derivations of that term thrown about in magazine and newspaper articles. The "information superhighway" is an analogy that was used to describe a future network that would connect every single person in the world and provide instant access to any imaginable piece of information. Despite all of the hype by politicians, corporate leaders, and the media, the Internet is neither the IS nor even a large subset of it. At best, the Internet is a working prototype of one small aspect of the IS. Since it *is* working, though, it is extremely likely that the Internet will be coerced into growing into the IS, with all of the accompanying growing pains.

Internet History

The Internet began life in 1969 as a project for the Advanced Research Projects Agency (ARPA) of the U.S. Department of Defense to connect the many military, university, and defense contractors that were working on ARPA projects. The original design was made with the assumption that any portion of the network could go down at any time, since potential military targets were involved. This meant that control of network operation had to be distributed so the loss of a key computer would not take large portions of the network down with it.

The solution was a suite of protocols known as the Internet Protocol (IP). The term *protocol* refers to a standard procedure for regulating communications between computers. The Internet Protocol requires every computer to take part in maintaining communications instead of depending on one central server. With this protocol, data is passed around in IP packets, each of which has an address attached for the computer it should go to. Every computer on the network knows how to recognize its address, and it is up to the sending and receiving computers to be certain that the communication was successful. The resulting network became what has been called ARPANet.

In the mid-1980s the National Science Foundation (NSF) stepped into the picture. NSF had created five supercomputing centers around the United States that were to be shared by all universities and colleges for any scholarly research. At first NSF tried to use ARPANet to connect the centers, but problems with the existing bureaucracy and insufficient staff support forced NSF to look for its own solution. The NSF's solution was to create several networks that connected all of the schools in a region, with one connection from the regional network to the supercomputing centers. The resulting network, known as the NSFNet, used 56 Kbps telephone lines for the backbone (56,000 kilobits per second, or 7 kilobytes per second) and the same IP communications as ARPANet.

By 1987 it was clear that the backbone was too slow. The NSFNet now allowed almost universal access to higher education by offering to pay for campus connections if the campus had a plan to spread the access around. Although the network was intended for scholarly communications, it was quickly put to other uses, as students and faculty found themselves only a keyboard away from their peers around the country. Newsgroups, network games, file archive sites, and more contributed until the lines were overloaded. The NSF awarded a contract to Merit Network Inc., in partnership with IBM and MCI, to manage and upgrade the NSFNet. The first upgrade, in July 1988, was to T1 lines (1.5 Mbps, or 190 Kbps), then in 1992 they began to migrate to T3 (45 Mbps), which was completed in December of that year.

The NSFNet project is currently being phased out. Merit's contract ended in April 1995, and the NSF is funding the transition of the POPs (Point of Presence, referring to the largest network providers) to commercial backbones through the end of 1995. As part of this transition, the restrictions against commercial traffic on the Internet have been lifted. Originally the NSFNet was restricted to educational traffic; anything that could be construed as being commercial was not allowed. Several companies had connections to the network, but those connections were primarily to their research laboratories and were not used for promotion or sales. Later on commercial networks appeared and were allowed to have limited interaction with the NSFNet, although the acceptable-use policies still restricted them to support- and research-type activities.

Commercial Web Sites—Go for It!

Coincident with the NSF transfer of authority, the NSF provisions against commercial use of the Internet were lifted from the acceptable use policies. This means that *it is now perfectly acceptable to have sites on the Internet that are intended purely for commercial purposes.* The changes have been made without much announcement, so a strong (and incorrect) belief remains among the older Internet denizens that commercial use of the network is a no-no. That should change rapidly, though, as more and more businesses expand their sales tactics to include the Internet.

It is still true that blatantly commercial use of UseNet (network news groups) and e-mail is frowned on and considered extremely bad form by the general Internet community. People aren't very eager to see junk mail predominate in their electronic mailboxes or their favorite newsgroups. Any company that uses these tactics is likely to face a very hostile response from the users, including e-mail bombs (large messages intended to flood the sender's network) and plenty of bad publicity. Since it is so easy to forward a message to other users, news of such activity spreads quickly and widely. Many service providers specifically warn that such activity is cause for them to stop service because the possible retaliation can harm their networks.

This is why commercial Web sites are a Good Thing. With a Web site, people are actively coming to you rather than passively having advertising dumped on them. They can choose how much of the advertising and sales stuff they want to read and leave when they want. In addition, the usual tactics of giveaways, contests, and special sales work very well for attracting people to your site. The ease of communicating with large numbers of users means that people on the Internet will find out about a really good offer with a speed that puts overnight Express Mail to shame.

At the same time that the NSF was running NSFNet, other countries were joining the Internet, first with educational and major research sites but also later with commercial and personal connections. Western Europe (especially the Scandinavian countries), Australia, Japan, and of course Canada all developed large internal networks that connected to one another and, via transoceanic lines, to the United States. The transoceanic lines were generally 56 Kbps lines and were major bottlenecks to overseas users seeking to transfer files from the popular anonymous ftp sites in the United States, or vice versa. Recently these lines have been improved, but it is still generally true that communications will be much faster within your own country or continent than between continents. This is especially true of file transfers, which require more time and therefore are more susceptible to interruptions or lost connections.

Today the Internet spans almost the entire world, including Antarctica. The large majority of the hosts are still located in North America, Western Europe, Japan, and Australia, but nearly every country is represented to some extent now. This is primarily because of the obvious educational benefits of an Internet connection and is reflected in the fact that, for many of these countries, the only connections are to technical schools or universities.

The Internet Society

In June 1991 a new group was introduced to take charge of the Internet: the Internet Society (ISOC). ISOC was officially created in January 1992 as a not-for-profit corporation with headquarters in Reston, Virginia. Its stated purpose is "to maintain and extend the development and availability of the Internet and its associated technologies and applications—both as an end in itself, and as a means of enabling organizations, professions, and individuals worldwide to more effectively collaborate, cooperate, and innovate in their respective fields and interests." Membership is voluntary and includes individuals, organizations, corporations, and governments.

The Internet Society has several components. The Internet Architecture Board (IAB) handles the definition and approval of standards for communications on the Internet and allocates Internet resources, primarily computer addresses. Membership in IAB is by invitation only. The Internet Engineering Planning Group (IEPG) coordinates Internet operations worldwide.

The Internet Engineering Task Force (IETF) worries about approaching networking problems of all kinds. When a problem is identified as being important, such as the possibility of running out of computer addresses at current Internet growth rates, a working group is created to investigate the problem. If a solution is found, the working group proposes a standard or writes documentation, which is then considered by the Internet Engineering Steering Group, with final approval given or denied by the IAB. Anyone may volunteer to join IETF or to be part of a working group.

Internet security problems are handled by Computer Emergency Response Teams (CERTs) located around the world. They were formed to continually monitor the network for security incidents, serve as a repository for information about such incidents, and develop responsive advisories. The CERTs are coordinated by the Forum of Incident Response and Security Teams.

Although this sounds like an impressive structure for control, ISOC is very new and is not really all that big compared to the Internet population. There are no Internet Police watching every user's moves to "keep things in line"; nor are there any rules and regulations covering the majority of activity on the Internet. In all areas outside of ISOC's control—and that is a lot of area—the only controls are courtesy and peer pressure.

Internet Growth

The growth of the Internet has been a hot topic for several years now and for good reason, because it is simply phenomenal. Although any hard numbers on the rate of Internet growth or the number of users on the Internet can be strongly disputed (because of the difficulty of defining what it means to be connected to the Internet), all of the estimates are quite large, and the growth rate doesn't appear to be declining in any way. There are several ways to estimate these numbers, and each method has its own strengths and flaws, so here is a sampling of what is available.

New Networks

One way to estimate growth is to look at the number of new networks announced. Merit used to keep track of this when it was running the NSFNet. According to Merit data, only 217 networks had been formally announced when it first began keeping records in July 1988. By December 1990 there were 2,190 networks; by December 1993, 21,430 networks. At the last count (in April 1995) there were 50,766 networks.

This is a good way to show that the Internet is definitely growing and doing so at a rapid rate. It is terribly imprecise, though, because there are large variations among networks. Each network could represent anywhere from a few dozen to hundreds of computers. In addition, the more recent numbers are less and less accurate because fewer networks were being formed in areas that Merit controlled, and the backbone that Merit maintained was being converted to a new distributed system that Merit didn't monitor. Finally, the numbers don't show in any way the growth that likely was occurring within the existing networks.

Hosts

A better way to estimate the size of the Internet and how quickly it is growing is to look at the number of computers connected to the Internet. Mark Lottor (formerly of SRI and now with Network Wizards, **http://www.nw.com/**) wrote some software that he used to estimate how many hosts were on the Internet. His software queried Domain Name Service (DNS) servers for their data, with the assumption that each entry in a server represented a host, or a computer connected to the Internet. His study has become the most commonly quoted source for estimates of the size of the Internet, and the results are shown in Figure 1.1.

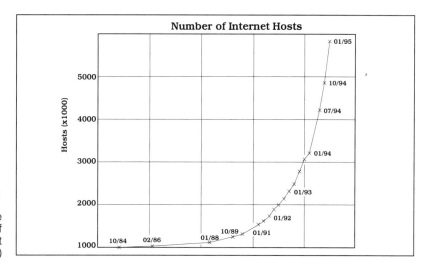

Figure 1.1

Number of Hosts on the Internet (data courtesy of Network Wizards at http://www.nw.com/)

The results clearly show that the number of computers on the Internet is increasing rapidly and at an increasing rate. It is not clear, though, how accurate the numbers are or even exactly what they represent.

Each host in his study represented an entry in a DNS server somewhere on the Internet. There is no guarantee, though, that each of these hosts is reachable by other computers on the Internet. We are therefore stuck with the question of what it means to be connected to the Internet. If the definition involves the two-way exchange of information via TCP/IP protocols, a large number of these hosts do not qualify. On the other hand, if you are interested in how many computers can connect to your Web pages, not only these hosts qualify but also many more that do not have DNS names, which is a common situation in university laboratories and users sharing dial-in IP addresses.

Internet Users

The previous information indicates a tremendous increase in the number of computers being added to the Internet, but it doesn't show the statistic that most people (especially in sales and advertising) want to know: How many *users* are on the Internet?

Tony Rutkowski, Executive Director of the Internet Society, says that a common method of estimating the total number of Internet users is to multiply the number of host computers by 10. This factor is based on the assumption that a large number of the computers connected to the Internet are multiuser systems that have possibly hundreds or even thousands of users. This reflects the situation on many college campuses, which used to make up the majority of traffic on the Internet. There is no evidence, though, whether this factor is still valid or whether it has decreased due to the proliferation of direct microcomputer network connections.

If you use a factor of 10, Fig. 1.1 would indicate about 58 million users with direct connections to the Internet (this does *not* include the millions who can only exchange electronic mail or news postings with the Internet via gateways). John S. Quarterman and Smoot Carl-Mitchell, the two principals of Matrix Information and Directory Services (MIDS), made the news in 1994 when they were quoted out of context as stating that the number of users might be only one tenth of that, since the factor could as easily be 1 as 10. In their FAQ they state that they preferred to use a factor of 7.5 because it was halfway between 5 and 10, which was anybody's best guess as to the lower and upper limits of the probable factor. They also state that the factor at that time might have dropped to 3.5 due to the large influx of single-user systems but might also be climbing because of the addition of systems such as Delphi and America Online, which have hundreds of thousands of users per host, and the increase in the use of Serial Line Internet Protocol (SLIP) and Point-to-Point Protocol (PPP) connections where users often share IP addresses. In other words, it is still anybody's guess. Their FAQ is available at

```
gopher://gopher.tic.com/00/matrix/news/v4/faq.406.old
```

So how many users are on the Internet? In October 1994, MIDS (of Austin, Texas) tried a more direct tactic, surveying roughly 1500 domains for user information. MIDS divided the users into three categories: the Core Internet (users on computers that can be reached from the rest of the Internet), the Consumer Internet (users who can use FTP or WWW client software to reach Core Internet computers), and the Matrix (any users who can exchange electronic mail with other users in the two categories or in the Matrix). According to their study, the Core Internet has 7.8 million users on 2.5 million computers, the Consumer Internet has 13.5 million users on 3.5 million computers, and the Matrix has 27.5 million users. The Matrix estimate includes users of CompuServe, Prodigy, GEnie, and other online services that allow electronic mail exchange but had not yet offered access to other Internet services. As those services become available, those users would be moved to the Consumer Internet category. MIDS reported that the confidence interval for these numbers was 38 percent, which reflects the difficulty in obtaining data with any degree of accuracy about the Internet. The MIDS study is available at

```
http://www.tic.com/mids/pressbig.html
```

Why is it desirable to know how many users, or even how many hosts, are on the Internet? It is more than just a question of how many people can see one's Web page or how large this new marketing audience might be. The Internet has proved to be an extremely flexible system, but there are limits to how much stress it can take. As the number of users increases, there is more traffic across the entire network. The connections between major networks and across the Atlantic and Pacific oceans are communications bottlenecks and are increasingly busy. Famous sites, such as the Umich and Info-Mac archives, have long since become too busy for outsiders to access directly, and even the dozens of mirror sites are kept very busy meeting the increasing demands.

Another problem accompanies this growth. Estimates on growth rates currently range from 85 percent to 135 percent per year, but most have the growth rate roughly doubling every year. This means that this year there are as many *new* users on the Internet as were on the entire Internet the year before. Therefore, peer pressure from long-time users is no longer enough to control activity on the Internet, and abuse of users and servers, whether intentional or not, is likely to increase every year. With large systems, such as CompuServe and America Online, offering Internet access to their users, there is the added problem of millions of users suddenly being unleashed on the Internet and carrying with them preconceived ideas about how things should operate, based on their experience with the online services.

Network Traffic

A different way of measuring the Internet is to look at the *activity* that takes place on it. This is usually done by measuring either the number of packets or the amount of data that is transmitted over the Internet. Because of the distributed nature of the Internet, there is no central point through which all information passes. This makes accurately measuring activity levels impossible. It is possible to get a sampling, though, by looking at the data that is transferred over the backbone, or that portion of the Internet that connects the major networks. There is not even a single backbone, though, so the best that can be done is to look at one and guess that it is representative of activity on the Internet in general.

Merit used to keep track of how many packets were transmitted each month across the NSFNet backbone. This didn't reflect all of the activity on NSFNet, because not all traffic went across the backbone. If you were contacting a computer in your own network or even anywhere in your region, your packets probably never reached the backbone. In addition, traffic in other countries was reflected on this backbone only when a computer in the United States was involved. Still, the level of traffic was high enough that the results are probably representative of what was going in most parts of the Internet. The highlights of Merit's data are given in Table 1.1.

Date	Monthly Traffic (in millions of packets)	Comment
Jan. 1988	85	First count reported
Jul. 1988	152	Merit assumes operation of NSFNet
Mar. 1991	14,906	NSFNet now using mixed T1 and T3 for backbone
Dec. 1992	22,009	All traffic now on T3
Nov. 1994	86,372	Last accurate count as traffic moves to new NAP architecture

Table 1.1

NSFNet Packet Traffic History (from `ftp://nic.merit.edu/`)

As you can see, the growth has been nearly as rapid as the estimated number of users or networks appearing on the Internet. From January 1988 to November 1994 traffic levels increased 1000 times, and the numbers have been doubling for each of the past two years. This kind of growth places a huge burden on those who provide the physical connections that connect the various networks. Many of these interconnections were originally running at 56 Kbps and have since been upgraded to T1 (1.5 Mbps) or T3 (45 Mbps) or multiples of these connections. Even higher speeds are needed, though, to handle the anticipated load in the near future.

Three factors are driving this increase in network activity. The first is obviously the increase in the total number of users on the Internet. When you are looking at total activity, you need to consider the entire Matrix portion, since even those users without direct connections are capable of generating traffic on the Internet through e-mail or news postings. The second factor is the new protocols available for Internet communications. Protocols such as Gopher and HTTP are making it much easier for users to move around on the Internet, to find what they are looking for, and to share files with others. Along the same line, client software is continuing to improve so that users can do more with less experience or understanding of what is going on behind the scenes. The third factor is the push toward multimedia in Internet communications. Users can now share 3 MB

QuickTime files with the same ease as a 3 KB e-mail message. New client-server software is offering real-time audio and video over Internet connections; even with compression, they still take quite a toll on network bandwidth.

This last factor may in fact be more troublesome than the others. Currently most people are unwilling to wait for the time it takes to download a large file from most sites or to put up with the poor quality of Internet audio and video connections. As network speed improves, though, they will begin to make more use of these options. That means that not only will there be large numbers of new users, but also the current users will be increasing their use of the Internet. In addition, most of these new client-server options scale performance back to whatever the connection will allow. When higher speeds are available, the client software will take advantage of that and be sending even more data.

Internet Communications

This section discusses the most common protocols that are used on the Internet. Since space does not permit a thorough discussion of each, I recommend that you purchase one of the several fine books on the Internet that have been published in recent years. If you really need to get in to the nitty-gritty details of these protocols, I cannot recommend a better book than *TCP/IP Illustrated*, Volumes 1 & 2, by W. Richard Stevens (Addison-Wesley, ISBN 0-201-63346-9).

Internet Protocol (IP)

The Internet Protocol is a suite of about 100 protocols that define communications over the Internet. Although the *Transmission Control Protocol (TCP)* is just one protocol in the suite, the term TCP/IP is commonly used to refer to this entire suite and to Internet networking in general. On an IP network every computer can communicate with every other computer. Each computer is given a unique 32-bit number to represent it. This number is called the computer's *IP address* and is represented as four 8-bit numbers (0–255) separated by decimals. The IP address for my old WWW server is 128.95.202.45, for example.

These numbers are not handed out randomly. The numbers define a computer's physical location on the Internet by using a hierarchical structure to organize networks. The leftmost portion of the IP address is the most significant number and indicates a large network "region" that contains your computer. Each number to the right defines a progressively smaller region. The three left numbers together define the exact network your computer is connected to; within that network, your computer is one of no more than 256 total (it is fewer than that, since some numbers are reserved and other addresses are needed for routers and such). Thus my server can be thought of as computer 45 on the network 128.95.202. This is, of course, an extreme simplification of the topic, but it will get you started if you never understood that part before.

In order for a network to be part of the Internet, the computers on the network must communicate using TCP/IP. There are thousands of networks on which only one or a few of the computers on the network speak TCP/IP, and they act as a gateway for the rest. These are not part of the Internet, but they represent a huge and rapidly growing portion of the traffic and therefore are often included as part of the Internet for many purposes. On other networks the majority of the traffic is one-way: Users in the network can connect to hosts on the Internet, but not vice versa. Again, the computers in these networks should be considered as part of the Internet for some purposes (such as when considering how many users might be able to view your WWW pages) and not for others.

There is currently some concern about the use of the IP numbering method for identifying computers. Since the number is 32 bits, it can be used to represent at most 2^{32} (or 4.3 billion) computers. This sounds like a lot of computers (and it is!), but not every number gets used. Some numbers are reserved in every network and some network numbers are reserved as well. In addition, since networks are given entire pools of numbers to use, quite a few of the numbers get wasted. Although the resulting pool of addresses is still quite large, there are valid concerns that it might cease to be sufficient at some point in the next decade.

As a result, ISOC has created a working group to define a new standard called IPng (IP next generation), or IP version 6 (IPv6). This proposed standard is meant to be as compatible as possible with the current IP standard while adding support for many more computers and networks. This proposed standard is outlined in RFC 1752. The main changes are:

- IPng increases the IP address size from 32 bits to 128 bits, to support more levels of addressing hierarchy (currently only four) and a much greater number of addressable nodes.

- Some IP header fields have been dropped or made optional to keep the headers as small as possible despite the increased size of the addresses.

- Changes in the way IP header options are encoded allows for more efficient forwarding, less stringent limits on the length of options, and greater flexibility for introducing new options in the future.

- IPng includes the definition of extensions that provide support for authentication, data integrity, and (optionally) confidentiality.

Domain Name Service (DNS)

Because IP addresses are not very mnemonic, a standard was developed for assigning names to computers. The *Domain Name Service (DNS)* allows one or more names to be assigned to a single IP address. The names have at least two parts: a top-level domain name and a second-level domain name. In the United States the top-level domain is usually "edu" for educational sites, "gov" for government, "mil" for military, "com" for commercial, "net" for networks, or "org" for organizations. In other countries the top-level domain is usually the country extension, such as "no" for Norway, "de" for Germany, or "jp" for Japan. The second-level domain name can be anything, such as the name of a university (washington.edu), organization (isoc.org), or company (comvista.com). Further subdomain names can be assigned by each network as needed. Almost every single computer also has a personal name that distinguishes it from other computers in the same subdomain (only a very few computers have only two parts to their name). My server's name is "www.comvista.com" and my workstation is "jon.comvista.com".

DNS servers maintain databases of these mappings of names to addresses. Every site needs to have a DNS server running that maintains the database of names for that site. These DNS servers work together to maintain a distributed database so that no single DNS server has the information for every single computer on the Internet (that would be huge!). When you type a DNS name (such as "www.comvista.com"), your client software sends a request to a DNS server to have the name translated into an IP address. The names provide more than just a nice way of identifying machines, though. They also provide a level of abstraction. For example, Chuck has had several different machines with the name "www.biap.com" in the last year or two. As he upgraded the server, the name was reassigned to a new IP address. If you were using the DNS name to access the machine, though, it didn't matter. He told the DNS server what the new IP address was, and it told your client software and you never knew the difference.

The most common DNS implementation is called Berkeley Internet Name Daemon (BIND). The BIND server is called *named* and runs primarily on UNIX and UNIX-like operating systems. The latest revision of BIND supports the ability to designate a pool of IP addresses that map to a single name. This is often referred to as "round-robin DNS service" because of the way it handles address resolution. As an example, the name "www.apple.com" could be assigned to four different computers, each with a different IP address (it isn't, but it could be). When a request comes in asking for the IP address that matches that name, named gives back the next IP address in the pool, looping through them in a round-robin fashion. This type of service allows a server load to be distributed relatively evenly across several computers while maintaining the appearance of one server to the user (I'll discuss this in more detail in later chapters). Even as this book was being written, two DNS servers were coming out that will run under the Macintosh OS, and both promise to provide the round-robin service capability.

Common Internet Services

Dozens of different protocols are in use on the Internet today for disseminating messages, files, information, or just for playing games.

The majority of those protocols are based on the concept of a *client* and a *server*. The client is software that interfaces with a user to present information and take requests, such as "get a file" or "search for this item." The server is software that accepts requests from clients and processes them, possibly returning a file or the results of a database search. This method of dividing the labor has two advantages: The client software can run on relatively small computers because all of the heavy-duty processing is done by the server, and data can be made available to many clients from one location, so it is easy to update and maintain.

The following protocols are those you will encounter most often on the Internet. They are also those most often supported by WWW client software. Each protocol has one or more documents that detail what the protocol covers, communications procedures, what is allowed and not allowed in implementing a server or client, and what has been removed from previous versions. These documents are known as RFCs (Request for Comments), and they are important reading if you plan to do any serious work with Web servers. They can also keep you from looking like a fool when you make a comment in a newsgroup. Several sites carry these RFCs (there are a lot of them!) for public access. Depending on where you live, you can find them at

`http://www.cis.ohio-state.edu/hypertext/information/rfc.html`

or

`ftp://nic.ddn.mil/rfc/` or `ftp://munarri.oz.au/rfc/`

or

`ftp://funet.fi/rfc/`.

Telnet

The Telnet protocol defines communications between computers. Using a Telnet connection, a user can issue commands on a remote computer and view the results as if logged directly into that computer.

Simple Mail Transfer Protocol (SMTP)

This protocol defines methods for transmitting electronic mail between computers, via mail servers. It defines how to send a message to a server, how to find the message recipient, and what to do if a recipient or server is unavailable. Another protocol closely linked to this is the Post Office Protocol (POP), which defines mail transfer from a server to a client. POP provides better handling for clients that are not continually connected or that log in from multiple computers.

RFC 821 covers the Simple Mail Transfer Protocol, with some additional information in RFC 974.

UseNet News (NNTP)

The news protocols (there are several) define the transmission of network news articles, which are much like e-mail messages but are directed at group servers rather than at individual clients. The network of all machines that exchange news messages is called the UseNet, and it includes most of the Internet and then some. The *Network News Transfer Protocol (NNTP)* is one method used for computers to retrieve news postings from servers. Some WWW client software now supports reading newsgroups.

RFC 855 covers UseNet.

File Transfer Protocol (FTP)

This protocol defines a method for exchanging files between computers across a TCP/IP network. It is independent of computer type or operating system and works with any type of file.

RFC 959 covers the File Transfer Protocol.

Gopher

The Gopher protocol defines a distributed information system that uses a lightweight protocol similar to HTTP. Users view lists of information; each item links to a file (which may be downloaded), a search engine (external software), another site (a hyperlink), or another menu of information. Since these menus are easily mapped to hypertext links, all WWW client software supports Gopher connections.

RFC 1436 covers the Gopher protocol.

HyperText Transfer Protocol (HTTP)

HTTP is the protocol spoken by WWW servers (thus they should be called HTTP servers). It uses very lightweight processes and is stateless. In other words, connections are made only at the instant that new information is needed and are completely dropped in between. Once a connection is dropped, the server has no memory that it ever existed (no state information is saved). This allows an HTTP server to handle many more connections than an FTP or Telnet server, where the connection is held open by the client until the user chooses to close it.

The HyperText designation does not mean that this protocol is only for transferring hypertext, but rather that it provides the quick and stateless connections that are needed to link elements in a hypertext system.

Wide Area Information System (WAIS)

WAIS is a text search and retrieval system that is accessible over TCP/IP networks. It can search large numbers of documents and return documents containing the search string. In addition, WAIS servers can usually return a quality level to indicate how likely a document is to contain the information that was being searched for.

RFC 1625 covers the WAIS protocol.

Before You Move On

Before you move on to the next chapter, I want to summarize the most important points from this chapter, as well as some other points.

The Internet is not a concrete entity that one can easily define or point to. The definition depends on what your specific need is and is continually changing.

The Internet is relatively young; 75 percent of the people using the Internet today probably were not using it as recently as 1990, and fewer than 10 percent can really be considered "Internet veterans."

The Internet is international. It is not unusual for me to receive e-mail from Japan, Korea, Israel, Norway, Australia, Brazil, Italy, Germany, Canada, and Poland all in the same day. I'm still waiting for something from Antarctica, though.

The Internet is not an association, business, organization, or any other sort of structured unit. Although an organization now oversees a lot of what happens on the Internet, things work mostly because many very helpful and hard-working people and companies make it work.

The Internet is not a toy. It is a communication medium, like a telephone network or the air itself. Hundreds of thousands of people use it every day to do serious work, some of which would not be possible without the Internet. The rest of the people are playing bolo.

The Internet is made of people like you and me. That means that they are not perfect and are prone to impatience, misunderstanding, and fits of random stupidity. There are millions of them, too, so even the most uncommon mistake is likely to happen at least once a month on the Internet.

2

The World Wide Web

The World Wide Web, as difficult to describe as the Internet itself, might best be described as a virtual network spanning the physical Internet (or maybe not). It is certainly aptly named, as any diagram of the virtual connections would resemble a spider web enclosing the earth, especially if you used little silver lines to represent the connections. Similarly, the ease with which users can move from one site to another is very analogous to crawling along such a spider web, as opposed to FTP connections, which are similar to booking a flight to another city (not guaranteed to get through, have to know everything about where you are going, still might lose luggage along the way).

The World Wide Web is not a protocol. Commonly referred to as *WWW*, or *the Web*, it is a virtual network formed by connections between servers running various protocols, such as Telnet, FTP, Gopher, and HTTP. The connections consist of hypertext links, called Uniform Resource Locators (*URLs*), that are embedded in the documents available from the servers. Traversal of the Web is done by using WWW client software, often called a *Web browser*. The client software knows how to communicate with the various types of servers and also knows how to use the URLs to connect to other computers.

HTTP servers are the most common choice to deliver the hypertext files that form the connective tissue of the Web, because the HTTP protocol was designed specifically with hypertext connections in mind. As a result, HTTP servers, such as WebSTAR, are often called "Web servers." This name is erroneous, though, because the same hypertext files could just as easily be served from FTP or Gopher servers or any other protocol designed to deliver files. In fact, the

Web is really formed not by the server software but by the client software. It is the client software that knows how to tie together the various protocols into the Web.

Origins

The World Wide Web, a fairly recent phenomenon even by Internet standards, began in 1988 as a project by Tim Berners-Lee to improve communications about project developments among researchers at CERN (European Laboratory for Particle Physics). His vision was a system that would allow links to be made between files and computers as easily as within files so that new projects and research groups could be added without affecting the existing information. Although the Web soon spread outside the walls of the CERN research laboratories, it didn't really begin to take off until late 1992. The sudden increase in popularity was due to the release of Mosaic by NCSA (National Center for Supercomputing Applications), the first WWW client software that provided a graphical interface and inline images. The latter was the real key to success, since it took the WWW out of the realm of advanced information-sharing systems (dull) and into the world of advertising and entertainment (sexy).

Current Status

The rapid growth of the Web since then made it impossible for CERN to continue to attempt to oversee and coordinate the whole thing. As a result, the W3 Consortium was formed with the mission to promote the Web by providing specifications and reference software. The W3 Consortium is run by MIT's Laboratory of Computer Science, with INRIA (Institut National de Recherche en Informatique et en Automatique) acting as the European host and support from CERN. Financial support is provided by industry members so that all of the results can be provided for free. Current members include almost every company that is doing anything with the Web.

A full public listing can be found at

`http://www.w3.org/hypertext/WWW/Consortium/Member/PublicList.html`

Everyone should be well aware by now that the World Wide Web is the fastest-growing thing on the Internet today. It is very difficult to get hard numbers on that growth, for reasons mentioned previously. If you feel the need to reassure your employer that the growth is really occurring, though, a couple of good sources are shown in Figures 2.1 and 2.2. Figure 2.1 is taken from WebCrawler, a searchable database of servers provided by America Online, Inc. `(http://webcrawler.com/)`. Figure 2.2 is taken from Stephen Collins's Web 66 site. Stephen used the raw data from Merit to track the growth of WWW (actually HTTP) traffic on the Internet in relation to other protocols. You can see that in the space of two years, HTTP outgrew every other protocol except FTP. Although the Merit data does not extend past 1994, growth projections indicate that HTTP should have exceeded FTP at some time during the spring of 1995. This is especially significant because much of the activity increase in other protocols is probably also due to the Web, since most Web clients also handle FTP, Gopher, and now even mail and NNTP communications.

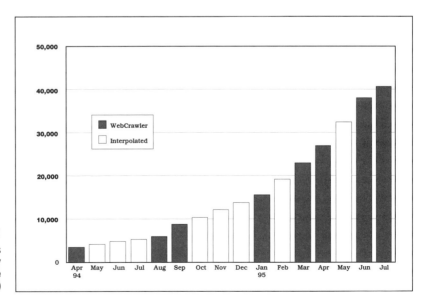

Figure 2.1

Growth in WWW Servers 1/94–7/95 (graph courtesy of WebCrawler, a service of America Online, Inc.)

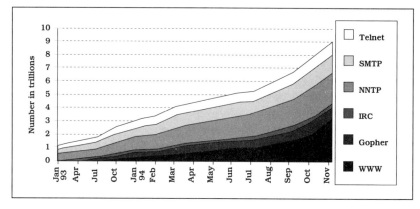

Predictions about the future growth of the World Wide Web range
all over the board, with two exceptions: Nobody really believes that
this is going to suddenly die down anytime soon (the low end), and
there are physical limits to how much activity can occur on the
Internet (the high end). The fact is, there is no proven model for predicting the future of the Web. In fact, there is no way to predict even
what the Web itself will be, as the protocols and standards that
define it are changing as rapidly as everything else.

Learning to Speak "Web-ese"

A few terms pop up frequently throughout the book. Some of
them are covered in depth later, but you need to have at least a
rough grasp of what they mean now so I can use them to discuss
other topics.

Hypertext

This term is used a lot when talking about the World Wide Web, as
are the related terms *hypermedia* and *multimedia*. Hypertext refers to
text that has special embedded links that allow the user to jump
straight from one section of a file to another section or even to
another file. The new section or file might also have links to the
original section or to still other files. The result is a system of links
that can crisscross over an unlimited number of files.

Each link is connected to a word or phrase in the text called the *link text*. The link usually leads a reader to either further information about the link text or information on a related topic. There are very few limits on where a link can go or how many links a file can have. The result is that the links create pathways through documents, allowing users to follow the information in the ways that most suit them.

As an example, User A is reading about the American West and decides to follow links to information on the settlement of California and finally ends up reading about the history of his hometown, San Francisco. User B is reading the same file about the American West and notices a comment about the Western film genre; she follows links from there to information about John Wayne's movie career and ends up checking to see whether *She Wore a Yellow Ribbon* is going to be available on laserdisc any time soon. Although both users began from the same text file, they were able to use the hypertext links in that and related files to move to the information they were most interested in.

Three things are needed to create hypertext. First, you need a way of defining the links in a text file. The links need to be defined in a way that is hidden from the user so that the text can still be easily read. Second, you need a way to let the user follow the links. Graphical hypertext systems usually allow the user to click on the link text to follow the link. Text-based systems might require the user to move a cursor to the link text and press a key to follow the link. Third, there needs to be a way to let the user know when a word or phrase has a link attached to it. Not every word in a document will have a link, and it isn't a good idea to make the user guess where the links are. Typical methods for indicating a link include changing the color of the text; using special character formats, such as underline or italics; and changing the cursor when it moves over link text.

Hypermedia is a marriage between hypertext and multimedia. A multimedia file includes a mixture of multiple media types, such as text, graphics, audio, and video. A hypermedia system contains many multimedia files where the links might lead to any of the media types. A word in one file might link to text in another file to a picture, or to an audio or video file that relates to the topic. As with a hypertext system, there are few limits to the number of connections within a file or between files.

The World Wide Web is a distributed hypermedia system where the links are made between files that can reside on separate servers located anywhere on the Internet.

CGI Applications

CGI applications are special applications that have an interface for communicating with HTTP servers. The purpose of these applications is to provide new capabilities for the HTTP server. CGI applications can be used as gateways between HTTP servers and other applications (such as databases or text-searching software) or other services (such as online banking and purchasing systems). They can also do processing themselves for anything from counting how many times a page has been accessed to taking in form information and sending it off as an e-mail message. CGI applications can also be used to provide improved versions of services that HTTP servers already provide, such as improved security measures or trying to correct problems with bad requests. This will all be covered in much greater detail later in the book.

Hypertext Markup Language (HTML)

HTML is a standard for marking up text so that it can contain links (URLs), styles (bold, large font), and other elements (graphics). Although other data formats could be used by WWW client software (and will be in the future), HTML is the most commonly used format. It is a rapidly evolving standard, with several competing forces at work in defining it. This is covered in more detail later in the book.

Page

"Page" is a term that is commonly used to refer to an HTML document as it is viewed in a WWW client. A page includes not only the entire HTML document but also any graphics that it may have tagged to be shown inline. If the client software has to scroll to show a long document, the entire document is still considered to be one page. This is a derivative of the early concept of the World Wide Web as a new form of online publishing (of course, it is much more than that). This also leads to the term "home page," which refers to the primary document or entry point for a site. People may also refer to their personal home pages, meaning the entry point for their personal information section of the site, or to the home page for a product or topic, meaning the entry point for information about that product or topic on the site.

I will also use the terms *document* to refer to a text page that may be displayed by a WWW client (also to a pdf document, when they become viewable) and *file* to refer to any file at all, including viewable documents. Although many types of graphics files can be displayed by some WWW client software, I do not include these in the definition. Not all pages are documents, since a page might also be made of information returned to the client software by a server (as when an error occurs) or by a CGI application (more on that later) or information generated by the client software itself (such as an FTP server directory listing).

Client-Server

Before discussing the HTTP protocol, it is important to have a good understanding of how client-server computing works (or is supposed to work) and where the various responsibilities lie. If you don't feel like reading this entire section, though, just keep this one statement in mind: Clients are smart; servers are stupid. This is generally true and for good reason.

The Client-Server Advantage

Client-server refers to a system in which computing is split over two packages: the *client*, which provides an interface for users to access the system and interprets responses for them, and the *server*, which processes requests from the client and returns a result of the processing. This system has several benefits. First, it allows large amounts of data or very complex and expensive software to be made available to a large pool of users for a minimal cost. The expensive software and data are stored on only one server machine; all the users need is a relatively cheap client to communicate with that server. Second, it makes it easier to keep a large body of data current by keeping it in one location. Third, it allows the software to be scaled to the capabilities of the computer. The server software presumably needs a very fast and robust computer to run it, but the client software should run on much smaller computers, preferably desktop models.

You're now probably thinking that I got the statement backward. After all, if the server needs the largest computer, it must be the smartest piece of the package, right? Well, I suppose that depends on how I define "smart." In this case I am referring to the flexibility of the software. In general, server software is built to handle a set of commands with a definite, pretty inflexible format. This set of commands might be quite large and might lead to some very powerful processing, but there is little or no tolerance for commands that don't meet the right terminology. In fact, in many cases sending an incorrect command will cause the server to take an action that is completely erroneous, such as trying to search the wrong database or sending the response to an incorrect address.

The client software, on the other hand, has to be quite flexible because there is just no telling what those wild and wacky users will do next. Very few users enjoy memorizing complex instruction codes, so the burden is on the client software to provide some friendlier interface for defining requests. It is also the client's burden to anticipate mistakes that a user might make and try to avoid them or correct them before sending out a request. The client then has to take this variable set of inputs from the user and squeeze them into the fixed set of acceptable commands for the server. The return process is not much better, since the client has to take data that is likely to be nearly incomprehensible to the user and put some nice formatting onto it to make it presentable.

Let's see how this relates to the World Wide Web. As you will see, a Web (HTTP) server accepts only a few types of requests, and they have a very fixed format of what can be requested and how to phrase the request. Other servers (such as FTP and Gopher) are no better, and the various servers completely lack the ability to speak directly to one another. The client software, on the other hand, offers a variety of ways to communicate with the server. Netscape Navigator has five ways just for requesting a URL from a server. The client software is also able to connect to a variety of types of servers and may even be able to hand the processing off to other software when it can't handle things directly. The client has to know how to handle a wide variety of data types as well and has to decode and display everything that is sent down from the server or allow the user to store the information to disk.

This distinction between the relative "intelligence" of the client and server software is important when you are trying to track down problems. In a nutshell, if you have a problem with a connection, look to the client software first. Because the server is so limited in its offerings, it is also less likely to have problems than the client software, which is trying to do everything.

Connection

The whole basis of TCP/IP communications is connections. The client connects to the host, makes some kind of request, then either disconnects or makes another request. How a connection is handled and how many connections are made varies among protocols, however. A Telnet session has one connection between the client and server, with that connection being held open the entire time that you are "logged in," whether anything is happening or not. If you walk away from that terminal to get some lunch and forget to log out, the connection is still held open. With FTP, two connections are in place: one to handle commands for listing and changing directories and another for transferring the files.

Every server has a limited number of connections that it can handle simultaneously, so this becomes one of the primary limits on how many users the server can process. The longer the connections are held open, the fewer users who can be processed; if multiple connections are required for each user, the processing capabilities are decreased even further. This is why many servers, especially FTP servers, automatically close a connection that has been idle for longer than a set period of time, so it can give the connection to someone who really wants it.

HTTP servers make good use of their connections because the connection is opened only when the user actually sends a request, and then it is closed again as soon as the request is processed. In addition, since the server makes no effort to retain any information about the last file the user requested (state information), there is no associated processing overhead. This means that the user can download a file and, while that user is viewing a page, another user (or another 2000 users) can also download files.

It is important to remember that every single file that is transferred from an HTTP server is a different and independent connection. Some client software allows users to make more than one connection simultaneously to the same server. The server doesn't know this, though. As far as the server is concerned, each connection might as well be from a unique client. There is another element to this also. If a page contains an inline graphic, the client software needs to make another connection to get the graphic file, separate from the connection that retrieved the text of the page. Thus if a page contains 10 or 15 graphics, even small ones, 10 or 15 separate connections are required to get them all for displaying in the page. This is something to consider when you use inline graphics, and I will mention it again when I discuss getting more speed out of your server and processing server connection statistics.

Listens

In order to handle connections from client computers, the server keeps a process "listening" at the network port. If anything is sent to that port, the listening process begins a new connection, assuming that the information is from a WWW client. At that point the server needs to start another process listening in case more than one client wants to connect to your system. The problem is that there could be another connection attempt during the short (but measurable) interval between the last connection and the start of the new listening process. To avoid this, a server must have more than one process listening at any one time. Just how many processes you need to have listening depends on how busy your server is and how long it takes to generate another listening process, or rather how likely it is that there will be more connections attempted than processes available to listen for them. For most servers it takes less than one tenth of a second to generate a new listening process, so only three to six listening processes, or "listens," are needed.

Having said that, I have to point out that WebSTAR uses listens slightly differently. Since every connection is handled by an independent thread, WebSTAR begins by creating one listening process for every possible connection. Therefore if you decide that you want your server to be able to handle up to 30 concurrent users, the server will also have 30 listens running at the start. Since each listen requires very little memory and processing time, this is not the performance hit that it might be on a UNIX system.

Logging

Most information servers offer the option of saving information to your disk about every connection that is processed (every file transfer). The file that the information is saved in is called a *log file*, and the act of saving this information is called *logging*. The log file is generally a text file containing one line of information about every connection.

HyperText Transfer Protocol (HTTP)

The HTTP protocol defines a method of client-server interaction that is optimized for the short, fast connections that are necessary for serving distributed hypertext information systems. Its most unique features are that it is generic and stateless and uses very lightweight processes. *Generic* means that the protocol can easily be extended for a variety of types of services, not just hypertext-type transactions. *Stateless* means that in between connections, the server doesn't keep any record that the client has recently been there, so every connection is treated absolutely the same, like a brand new client. *Lightweight* refers to the fact that the client connects to the server only long enough to transfer a file; then it closes the connection. This is very different from an FTP server, where a connection is held open as long as the user wants, whether or not a file is being transferred.

> **Read This Carefully**
>
> An understanding of the HyperText Transfer Protocol is crucial if you want to understand how your HTTP server operates and why some of the features operate the way they do. The information in this section has been checked against the HTTP/1.0 Internet draft of March 8, 1995. Internet drafts are valid only for a maximum of six months, so that draft is certain to have been updated by the time you read this book. I highly recommend that you start by reading this section carefully. Then, after you have been using your HTTP server for a while, read this section again to see whether more of it makes sense. If it does, it is time for you to read the latest Internet draft, which will cover many more topics than I did here, including some that are very specific to writing a server or client.

HTTP Transactions

The HTTP transaction model was purposely made to be very simple, which is one reason that it can be so easily extended to provide other services. A typical transaction works as follows:

1. *The client establishes a connection to a remote server.* The information on what server to contact and what port to use to contact it is part of the hypertext link. The client locates the server and initiates the connection process.

2. *The client issues a* request. Several types of requests can be made, as will be covered in more detail later. The request can include information about such things as what data types the client can handle, what natural language the user prefers, and what type of data is being sent to the server. This kind of information makes it easy to extend the system to handle new data types. It also allows data to be stored in a variety of data types or languages, with each client receiving its own preferred type.

3. *The server processes the request.* An awful lot can happen here. Most requests will be processed directly by the server. Other requests will be passed off to other applications, mostly CGI applications, for processing, and those applications will provide a

response for the server to pass back to the client. The processing could save data to a file, append information to a database, or do a search on a system. Most of the time, the processing will simply be to locate a file to be returned to the client.

4. *The server returns a* response *of some kind.* The structure of the response is very similar to that for the request. It could be returning a file that the user requested, data found in a search, simple confirmation that the request was processed, or an error. Several codes are defined in HTTP and can be returned to tell exactly what happened. These *response codes* are covered later in this chapter. The request can also contain information about the server, such as what nonstandard methods it is able to handle and what type of data it is returning to the client. This is yet another way that the protocol provides for extensibility, since new types of servers can let clients know about their new features or warn new clients about features they lack.

5. *The server closes the connection.* Early protocols, such as Telnet and FTP, were designed with the idea that a user would connect to a single remote system for an extended period of time. The user holds a connection open and issues consecutive commands to the remote computer. This saves time, because later file transfers don't have the overhead of opening a connection, and the client can set options that last through several file transfers or commands, such as using a binary file transfer mode. When dealing with hypertext, though, the user tends to be moving from one server to another quite often, so that the next request is as likely to be directed to a different computer as to the current one. In that case there is little benefit to holding the connection open or to maintaining any information about the client. Therefore, HTTP was designed to release a connection as soon as it has finished processing one request.

HTTP and MIME

Unlike most Internet transaction protocols (such as FTP and Telnet), HTTP includes provisions for a client and server to negotiate the data type of information that is passed back and forth. Both the client and the server have ways to include information about the type of data being sent, how it is encoded or compressed, and how it was encoded for network transmission. They both also have facilities to let the other know what their preferences are for data types, compression methods, and even what natural language the data is written in.

This is done by using some of the features of *Multipurpose Internet Mail Extensions (MIME)*. MIME defines special **media-types** (previously called **content-types**) that identify the data type of the file being transferred. The client software uses this information to determine how to handle the file when it is received: whether to display it, save it to disk, or possibly launch another application to process it. The server can use this information to tell how data sent from the client is encoded. HTTP transactions are not limited to the types defined for MIME use, though. New types can be defined and used if they are acceptable to both parties in a transaction.

MIME is covered in more detail later in this chapter.

HTTP Requests

A client can make several types of requests. The general form of a request from a client looks like this:

```
<METHOD> <URI> "HTTP/1.0" <CRLF>
(<Header>: <Value><CRLF>)*
<CRLF>
<BODY>
```

METHOD is a single word that tells the server what kind of request is being made. URI is essentially the path and file name portion of the URL for the request (see the section "Uniform Resource Locator (URL)" later in this chapter). The multiple Header lines follow the format in RFC 822 and can include optional information, such as the User-Agent (the name of the client software) and multiple Accept headers, which define the MIME content types the client can handle. CRLF is a carriage return (ASCII 13) and line feed (ASCII 10), the indicator of a line ending on UNIX systems. BODY is optional data that may be appended with some requests. A request might look like this, for example:

```
GET /default.html HTTP/1.0
Accept: text/html
```

```
Accept: text/plain
Accept: image/gif
Accept: */*
User-Agent: Netscape 1.1N PPC
<CRLF>
```

Request Methods

The first word in an HTTP header defines what kind of transaction is being requested. Seven methods are currently specified. Only two or three of them are commonly used, and more may be added in the future. Here is a summary of the current methods:

- **GET**   This method is used for requesting information from a server. Whenever a user clicks on an anchor link (for example, **<A HREF="<URL>">text</A>**), the client software sends a GET request for the URL specified in the link. The GET method can also be used to send a request to a CGI application that returns data as a result of its processing. Search requests on ISINDEX documents are also sent using the GET method.

  Any data that needs to be passed to the CGI application can be appended to the URL used in the GET request by placing a question mark (?) at the end of the URL and then adding the data after that (see the section "Uniform Resource Locator (URL)" later in the chapter). The amount of data that may be passed in this way is limited by the defined maximum length for a URL.

  The GET method can be modified to do a conditional request, so that data is returned only if the file has been recently modified. If the request contains the **If-Modified-Since** header, the server returns the data only if the modification date on the file is newer than the date in the header. If the date is older, the server returns a code to indicate that (**304 Not Modified**; see the section "HTTP Response" later in the chapter). Of course, any request to a CGI application should return data, since the data is always generated on the fly.

- **POST**   This method is used to send data to the server that is to be a new subordinate of the file or application specified in the URI. This is most commonly used to pass data to a CGI application, where being subordinate means that the CGI application processes the data in some way, such as entering it in a database or sending it out as an e-mail message. The primary difference between this and the GET method is that the latter appends its data to the URL, which limits how much data can be sent. The POST method sends the data as an attachment (one empty line after the header, then the data) so the data can be quite large, in most instances limited only by the memory available to the server.

Currently the only way to send a POST request is from a FORM element, where the method can be specified in the opening tag. That might change in the future as client capabilities are added to other applications.

- **HEAD**   This method, used to retrieve information about data on a server, performs the same as the GET method but returns only the header, not the contents of the file. This method is useful primarily for checking to see whether links are still valid or for cataloging the files on an HTTP site.

- **PUT**   This method is used to send data to an HTTP server to be saved as a file on the server. This allows files to be created on another computer and then remotely loaded onto the server or to update a file existing on the server. Unfortunately very few servers have chosen to support this method. There are many unanswered questions about verification methods for allowing users to send files to a server, so it is good that this option has been delayed until the integrity of a site can be protected.

   Both the POST and the PUT methods can be used to put data on a server. The difference between the two is that the POST method is intended to place the data as an addition to or subportion of some existing data. The PUT method places the data as a new file or a new version of an existing file.

- **DELETE**   This method is used to delete a file on an HTTP site. Since this is potentially very destructive, most servers have chosen not to support it yet. The same questions about security and establishing authority that exist for PUT also affect the DELETE method.

   HTTP 1.0 allows for delete actions to be delayed, pending approval by the person maintaining the server (or some automated system).

Instead of returning that the file was deleted, the server returns a code that the file is scheduled for possible deletion.

- **LINK**   This method is used to create links between files on an HTTP site or between sites. The link is made by adding a LINK element to the HEAD of an HTML document (it is possible that links could be created in other types of documents as well, but the method is not yet specified). This requires that the server modify the file to add the link data. It is not supported yet by most servers.

- **UNLINK**   This method is used to removes links from files on HTTP servers. Again, this requires that the files be modified and is not widely supported yet.

Request Headers

There is very little strict definition of what headers may and may not be included in an HTTP request. HTTP builds on much of the experience already gained from defining communications for e-mail and news postings and can use most of the headers that are defined for those two protocols. The following are the most common or most useful headers used in HTTP requests:

- **Accept**   The Accept header is used to indicate the list of data types that the client can handle. There can be multiple Accept headers to list the various types. The format of a single header looks like this:

```
Accept: type/subtype; q={0|1|float}; mxb=<size>,
type/subtype
```

The **type/subtype** pair uses the same format as a MIME header. Everything from the semicolon on is optional and is usually not used. The **q** indicates a quality factor, which ranges from 0 (not acceptable) to 1 (most acceptable). The **mxb** indicates the maximum size in bytes that will be accepted of that **type/subtype** pair. The **type/subtype** pair following the quality factor and max bytes is the pair that they refer to.

Generally all you see is something like the following:

```
Accept: text/plain
Accept: text/html
```

```
Accept: audio/*
```

```
Accept: image/gif
```

This example indicates that the client can accept plain or HTML text files, any kind of audio files, and image files that are in GIF format. The assumption is that any other kind of file will not be handled properly by the client.

The more complicated format could be used to indicate something like the following:

```
Accept: text/plain; q=0.5, text/html
```

```
Accept: text/x-dvi; q=0.8; mxb=10000, text/x-c
```

This is interpreted as "text/html and text/x-c are the preferred media types, but if they do not exist, send the data in text/x-dvi if the data is less than 10,000 bytes; otherwise, send text/plain." Not many clients support this kind of specification, but they are likely to in the future. With this kind of differentiation, users with high-end systems can retrieve data appropriate to their systems, whereas users on more limited systems can still have an option for data that they can handle.

- **Accept-Charset**   This header tells the server that the client can handle and prefers character sets other than the defaults of US-ASCII and ISO-8859-1. The listed character sets are comma separated as follows:

```
Accept-Charset: iso-8859-5, unicode-1-1
```

- **Accept-Encoding**   This header allows the client to specify preferred encoding methods. The methods are comma separated, with the highest preferences occurring first in the list.

```
Accept-Encoding: compress, base64, gzip
```

- **Accept-Language**   This header allows the client to specify preferred natural languages for the data. The methods are comma separated, with the highest preferences occurring first in the list.

```
Accept-Language: cdk, en-gb
```

This example indicates that data should be sent in the Danish version if available; otherwise, the British English version should be used.

- **Authorization**   This header is used to pass authorization information, such as a user ID and password, to the server. This is usually in response to a **401 Unauthorized** response from the server. The basic authentication scheme in HTTP 1.0 calls for the user ID to be sent as clear text and the password as BASE-64 encoded text. HTTP also provides plenty of room for implementing more complicated and secure methods, though.

- **Date**   Requests generally include a Date header only for PUT and POST requests, where a date may need to be associated with the data when it is saved. Only one Date header is allowed per message. An earlier version of the HTTP RFC stated that Date should reflect the creation date of the enclosed data, but that is not the case. It should reflect the time at which the message header was generated.

- **From**   The From header usually contains the Internet e-mail address for the user who is running the client software. This information should not be sent by the client without specific approval from the user for each instance, because it may conflict with the user's privacy interests or site security policies. Therefore it is often omitted.

- **Forwarded**   The Forwarded header is for use by proxies to indicate the intermediate steps between the client and the server. The general form is:

```
Forwarded: by <URI of proxy> for <URI of client or
previous proxy>
```

There may be several Forwarded headers if several proxies are involved. If a proxy server is used for computers behind a firewall, the **for <URI of client>** should not be included, to maintain the security.

- **If-Modified-Since**   This header is used with the GET header to make it a conditional request. The header specifies a date. If the data on the server has not been modified since that date, a **304 Not Modified** response is returned without any data. This conditional request form is used most often by client software that caches pages locally to improve response speed.

- **MIME-Version**   HTTP is not a MIME-conformant protocol. It does use many of the MIME headers, though, for sharing information about file types between client and server. This header can be included to indicate what version of MIME is understood by the client. MIME version 1.0 is the default for use with HTTP 1.0.

- **Pragma**   The Pragma header is used to specify directives that must be applied to all servers (including proxy servers) in the request chain, which is from the user machine to the final server. HTTP 1.0 specifies only one directive, **no-cache**, which tells caching proxies not to return its currently cached version of the document specified by the URI. This essentially forces the definitive version of the data to be returned. This could be used to compare the original source with the cached copy or to force the caching server to update an entry for a page that has been corrupted or is known to be stale.

- **Referer**   This header contains the URI of the document from which the request was initiated. That is usually the HTML document that contained the link used to make the request. In almost all cases it refers to the URI of the page that the client software was viewing when the request was made.

    This information is very useful for server management, since it can be used to track documents containing stale or incorrect links or to find unauthorized duplications of your pages.

    The Referer may be a partial URI, in which case it should be interpreted relative to the URI in the request.

- **User-Agent**   The User-Agent header contains information about the client software that originated the request. Usually it contains the full name as specified by the software creator. This is a string in the software itself, not its name on the hard disk, and can contain not only the name and version number but also information on what WWW library was used to create it or another software package it was based on. An example would look like this:

    `User-Agent: Netscape 1.1N PPC-Universal`

    Some proxy servers append their own information to this line. This is no longer recommended, because it makes machine interpretation of the data in the field ambiguous. Instead, proxy servers should use the Forwarded header, as described previously.

HTTP Responses

After receiving and processing an HTTP request, the server returns an HTTP response. There can be several possible responses to a request. It can be successful, as in a found file or a CGI application that returns data. It can also fail and cause an error, for several possible reasons: file not found, a CGI fails to return data, or a CGI cannot be found. It could also be that the request requires a user name and password to be entered or that the user is prevented from completing the request because of other restrictions. Finally, the result could be that the client software is told to look at a different URL for the results (this is called *URL Redirection*).

Whatever the result, the format of the HTTP response that is sent back to the client software is always the same:

```
"HTTP/1.0" <STATUS_CODE> <REASON><CRLF>

(<Header>: <Value><CRLF>)*

<CRLF>

<BODY>
```

STATUS_CODE is a numerical code that indicates what the result of the processing was. **REASON** is a short string that explains the error. **CRLF** is a UNIX-style line-end indicator. These are followed by many optional headers terminated by a line with only a **CRLF**. The **BODY** contains the returned data for the client, if any is required.

Status Codes

The Status code tells the client software what type of response this is and what happened with the processing by the server. The code usually has a reason or short explanation accompanying it, but those should not be used for determining how to process the response and are only recommended, not specified.

Each Status code is a three-digit integer. Five classes of response codes are currently defined, with the class determined by the first digit of the code. The five classifications are as follows:

- **1xx: Informational**   Not currently used but available for future use.

- **2xx: Success**   The request was successfully understood and processed.

- **3xx: Redirection**   The client needs to take further action to complete the request.

- **4xx: Client Error**   The request contained incorrect syntax or could not be understood.

- **5xx: Server Error**   The server failed to fulfill an apparently valid request.

These are the currently defined individual codes:

- **200 OK**   The request was successfully processed and data is being returned (unless the HEAD method was requested).

- **201 Created**   The request to create a new file or subordinate was successful. This response must include the **URI-Header** to specify the URI of the created file.

- **202 Accepted**   The request was understood correctly and will be processed at a later time. This response may be sent for requests that are batch processed or that require approval of the server manager.

- **203 Provisional Information**   The data being returned is not definitive but is a subset or superset of the original verison. Not often used at this time.

- **204 No Content**   The request was successfully processed, but no data is being returned. The client software should let the user know but not change the document being viewed. This is to support processing that doesn't really need to return any data other than that it was successful.

- **300 Multiple Choices**   The file specified in the URI exists in one or more locations, and the preferred location could not be determined. The returning data should contain a list of the locations from which the data could be retrieved and leave selection up to the client. Ideally this could be used for sites that are mirrored on several continents, so the client selects the closest source.

- **301 Moved Permanently**   The file specified by the URI has been permanently moved to a new location. Clients that are able to should edit any existing bookmarks or cache entries for the URI to reflect the new location.

- **302 Moved Temporarily**   The file specified by the URI is currently at a different location. The move may not be permanent, though, so entries should not be permanently changed.

- **303 Method**   This code is obsolete, and clients should treat it like code 300.

- **304 Not Modified**   The file specified in the URI has not been modified since the date specified in the If-Modified-Since header of the request. This response does not return any data. If the requested file has a specified expiration date, that should be included in a header.

- **400 Bad Request**   The request contained incorrect syntax or could not be processed by the server. The client should not repeat the request.

- **401 Unauthorized**   The client has not included the proper authorization to retrieve the data specified in the URI. The authorization must be sent in an Authorization header. The server must include a WWW-Authenticate header in the response to define how the client is to authenticate the follow-up request.

- **402 Payment Required**   The data specified by the URI must first be paid for. This code is not currently supported but is available for future use.

- **403 Forbidden**   The client is forbidden to retrieve the data specified in the URI, and there is no authorization method available to gain access. The server does not need to specify the reason that access is forbidden. This is usually returned when the client has been refused because of its IP address or DNS name.

- **404 Not Found**   The data specified in the URI could not be located because some portion of the URI was incorrect or the data has been moved. Code `403 Forbidden` may be returned instead if the server was unable to find the file and does not want to let the client know, as an added security precaution. The code `410 Gone` should be used if the server knows that the file has been permanently moved but no forwarding URI is available.

- **405 Method Not Allowed**   The method specified in the request is understood by the server, but the client is not allowed to use it. This might be returned from a DELETE or PUT request. The server is required to return an Allow header that defines what methods the client is allowed to request.

- **406 None Acceptable**   The server found the data requested in the URI but not in a form that satisfies the limits identified in the **Accept** and **Accept-Encoding** request headers. The server's response must include the **Content-Type**, **Content-Encoding**, and **Content-Language** headers that define the found data, but the data itself is not returned. The client must issue another request including the proper **Accept** header to retrieve the data.

- **407 Proxy Authentication Required**   The client must first authenticate itself with the proxy server. This is included for future use and there is no existing means to support this in HTTP 1.0.

- **408 Request Timeout**   The request could not be processed in the maximum amount of time allotted by the server. This usually occurs with CGI application processing.

- **409 Conflict**   The request could not be completed, due to a conflict with the current state of the resource. This should be returned only when the user is likely to know how to resolve the conflict and resubmit the request. The server should return all information that it can related to the conflict.

  This is most likely to occur in relation to a PUT request when another user has the file checked out or the file has changed in the meantime.

- **410 Gone**   The file specified in the URI is no longer available on the server and no forwarding URI is available. If the server does not know whether the condition is permanent, it may choose to return **404 Not Found**.

- **500 Internal Server Error**   The server encountered an unexpected condition that prevented it from completing a valid request.

- **501 Not Implemented**   The method specified in the request is not understood or not implemented on this server.

- **502 Bad Gateway**   The server received an invalid response from a gateway or another server it accessed in attempting to complete the request.

- **503 Service Unavailable**   The server is currently unable to handle the request, due to temporary overloading or incapacity of the server. This might be used during server maintenance activities. The implication is that this condition is temporary, and the client should try again. The server should return a **Retry-After** header that indicates to the client how long to wait before automatically resending the request.

- **504 Gateway Timeout**   The server did not receive a timely response from the gateway or another server that it accessed in attempting to complete the request.

Adding New Codes

HTTP allows for the addition of new codes, and there is no requirement that they be approved before being put into use. Using a new code requires two modifications, though. First, the server must be modified to send the code in the appropriate situations; then the client software must be modified to process the code correctly. If a client does not understand a code it receives, it should treat the code as if it were equivalent to an $x00$ code, where x is the class of the code received. Thus a response of **540 Mars Not Online Today** could be treated as if it were **500 Internal Server Error**. The REASON string is arbitrary and may be changed, if needed, without affecting the client's ability to process the response.

Although individual codes may be developed and used without prior approval, the code classes are fixed. New numeric classes must not be put into use without approval of the HTTP working group. Clients that have not been specifically modified to process the new codes will not have a mechanism for handling the responses and may exhibit unpredictable behavior as a result.

Response Headers

As with the request headers, there is very little strict definition of what headers may and may not be included in an HTTP response, and many of the available optional headers are taken from e-mail, newsgroup, and MIME definitions. The following are the most common or most useful headers used in HTTP requests:

- **Public**   This header lists the set of nonstandard methods supported by the server. The purpose is to inform clients of the added abilities that are available. The header should not include any of the methods that are predefined for HTTP 1.0.

- **Retry-After**   This header is used with the `503 Service Unavailable` response to indicate how long the client should wait before trying the request again. This allows clients to automatically retry a server, especially if the delay is short. The time to wait can be returned as a full date and time (Greenwich Mean Time) or as an integer representing the number of seconds to wait:

  `Retry-After: Wed, 21 Apr 1995 13:14:03 GMT`

  `Retry-After: 120`

- **Server**   This header contains information about the software being used to provide the service. This is analogous to the User-Agent field.

- **WWW-Authenticate**   This header must be included as part of a `401 Unauthorized` response. The value consists of a challenge that indicates the authentication scheme that the server is using and the parameters of the expected reply.

Entity Headers

Some request methods and reply structures are able to transfer an entity (data to be transferred to the client or server) as an attachment. The most common examples of this are the GET method (server returns entity to the client) and the POST method (client sends data to server). When an entity is involved, there are separate headers that should be added to the request or reply structure to provide information about the entity. Many of these headers are very similar to those for the request or reply itself, and those will be covered only in the barest detail. Some others are not very common and will not be covered at all. For detailed information, see the RFC or the Internet draft provided by the HTTP working group.

- **Content-Encoding**   This field is used to indicate what additional encoding mechanism, if any, has been applied to the data. This is separate from the Content-Type header, which tells the type of the data before it was encoded. This uses the same structure as the Accept-Encoding request header.

- **Content-Language**   This header describes the natural language of the data. It uses the same structure as the Accept-Language request header.

- **Content-Length**   This header indicates the size of the data (in decimal number of octets). In the case of the HEAD method, it indicates the size of the data that would have been sent had the request been a GET.

- **Content-Transfer-Encoding**   This header indicates what, if any, type of transformation has been applied to the data to ensure that it is transferred safely between the sender and the recipient. This differs from the Content-Encoding because the transfer encoding is a property of the message itself, not of the original data. This header is used only by gateways that modify the message for transmission.

- **Content-Type**   This header indicates the type of the original data before encoding or any changes made in transit.

- **Expires**   This header can be used to indicate an expiration date for the data. The date should be expressed in Greenwich Mean Time, but some servers incorrectly send the time in seconds until the data expires. A value of 0 or an invalid date format should be treated as meaning that the data expires immediately.

  This header cannot be used to force client software to update its display or to reload a page. It is intended for use only by software or servers that cache pages.

- **Location**   This header is an earlier form of the URI header and should be considered obsolete. However, HTTP 1.0 servers should continue to support the header in order to properly interface with older applications. The purpose of Location is the same as that for URI, except that no variants can be specified and only one absolute URL is allowed. As an example:

```
Location: http://www.w3.org/hypertext/WWW/TheProject.html
```

Note: Netscape 1.1N recognizes only the Location header, not the URI header. Be sure to test clients to make sure that they accept the latest standard before relying on it.

- **Title** This header defines the title for the data and should be considered isomorphic with the `<TITLE>` element in HTML.

- **URI** This header may contain one or more Universal Resource Identifiers (URI—see the section "Uniform Resource Locators" later in this chapter) by which the resource origin of the data can be identified. There is no guarantee that the data can be accessed using the URIs specified. This header is also able to carry information on data that exists in several media types or several languages or encodings. In the following example, the document at that URL is available in multiple media types and multiple natural languages:

```
URI: <http://www.w3.org/hypertext/WWW/TheProject.multi>;
vary="type,language"
```

This can cause trouble for caching servers, because they need to keep track of the fact that the document is available in multiple versions. If a request is received for a version that the server has not yet cached, it must check with the original server instead of serving a different version from its cache.

- **Version** This header contains information on version numbers and modifications for the data. This information is intended for use by a group of people working simultaneously on a single file or set of files. The information will help to track modifications by the group.

Problems with HTTP 1.0

The HTTP method has several benefits when dealing with pure hypertext systems where only one connection is required to get an entire page of information. The addition of inline graphics and now embedded animations and downloadable options, such as Java components, are changing the way the World Wide Web works, though. It is very common now for a hypertext page to have one or more embedded graphics. Each of these graphics requires an extra connection for retrieval. Thus a page with two graphics in it will require three separate connections before the entire page of information is ready to be displayed for the user. As HTTP servers are put to new uses and serving new data types, the protocol needs to be modified to meet the demands. Simon Spero explains all of the following problems in his paper "Analysis of HTTP Performance Problems" (available at **http://sunsite.unc.edu/ses/**).

Redundancy

Because connections are stateless, all of the information about the client and the server needs to be exchanged with every connection. If you look at the model transaction cited earlier, you can see that a lot of information is the same for transactions that occur relatively close together, such as the MIME content types that a client accepts or the User-Agent name. When the client software is retrieving a page with inline graphics, the connections tend to occur in very quick succession, or even simultaneously with some clients. In these situations, which are quickly becoming the norm for Web pages, an HTTP server could reduce the total transaction time by saving some state information, even if only for a very short period of time.

Connection Overhead

Compared to other transfer protocols, such as FTP and Gopher, which tend to deal with large files, HTTP tends to work with smaller files (typically <10 KB). This means that the overhead of establishing a connection is a more significant portion of the total connection processing time. This overhead comes from the way that TCP initiates client-server communications. TCP is a somewhat pessimistic protocol and uses a process called Slow Start to determine when it is safe to send segments.

In TCP communications a sender is allowed to send segments to the receiver even though previously sent segments may not have been acknowledged yet. To prevent the sender from completely flooding the receivers' buffers, the receiver adds a tag onto the end of every acknowledgment telling the sender how much data it is prepared to receive without acknowledgments. This value is called the window size. Because neither the sender nor the receiver knows how busy the network is between them, it is not wise for the sender to assume that it can send a window's worth of data, because that might make an already busy network even busier so that the acknowledgments would be delayed for quite a while. The optimum transmission rate occurs when the sender is sending segments at the same rate as the receiver is sending acknowledgments (both parties using the available bandwidth equally).

The Slow Start process uses a second window called the Congestion window, to help calculate when the optimum transmission rate has been achieved. The Congestion window begins with a setting of 1, meaning that only one segment may be sent at a time without acknowledgment. When a segment is acknowledged without loss, the Congestion window is increased; when a segment is lost or times out, the window is decreased.

This process hurts HTTP connections in two ways. First, because the connection is relatively short to begin with, the overhead of the Slow Start process is more pronounced. The connection is often just getting "up to speed" by the time the data is completely sent. Second, the HTTP headers sent by the client to begin a request are too large to be sent in one segment, and the Slow Start process allows only one segment to be sent without acknowledgment at the start. This means that there has to be one full round of transmission (segment sent and acknowledged) before the rest of the header can be sent and the connection really begun.

TIME_WAIT Data

Very busy HTTP servers are also likely to run into a different TCP-related problem. When a server closes a TCP connection, it is required to keep information about that connection available for a short period of time. This prevents problems in case a delayed packet suddenly shows up after the connection has been recycled for someone else to use. The recommended length of time to keep this information is 240 seconds (4 minutes). This means that a server needs to keep some resources allocated for retaining information about every connection processed in the last four minutes. Since a busy HTTP server processes many more different connections per minute than most other types of server, it can get stuck allocating a large pool of resources to maintaining that information.

HTTP-ng

A new protocol, named HTTP-ng (for "next generation") proposes to address these problems through several changes to the original

HTTP protocol. It proposes using a binary data type instead of text, which would allow for much more compact data files. It also proposes a method for requesting many files as one single request, which would minimize the overhead of negotiating a connection and remove the redundant header information without requiring the server to retain state information.

Multipurpose Internet Mail Extensions (MIME)

The MIME protocol extends the original Internet mail protocol to support the sending of electronic mail with multimedia data. The MIME protocol defines several new headers for mail messages: telling whether the mail is in one or multiple parts, how those parts were separated, and what type of data each part contains. A MIME-compliant mail client can use this information to reassemble files and either display them directly or find another application to display them.

MIME headers can be added to any client-server protocol that involves the transmission of various data types. UseNet news was a natural for adding MIME support, since the news message headers are so similar to those for e-mail. Not all protocols are using MIME, though. FTP doesn't transmit file type information, counting on the user to know what the file type is and how it would best be transmitted. Gopher implements its own method of sharing file type information.

The MIME protocol is defined in RFC 1521. You can get a good summary of it posted by Earl Hood at

`http://www.oac.uci.edu/indiv/ehood/MIME/MIME.html`

How HTTP Uses MIME

HTTP was designed to use the MIME standard to communicate information about data types between the server and clients. This removes a large burden from the user, because the software knows how most files should be handled. HTTP servers and clients should not be considered MIME-compliant, though, because HTTP uses only some of the headers and ignores the rest.

One MIME header that the HTTP protocol uses is the Content-type header, which is used to tell what type of data is in a message part. The Content-type header specifies the data by *type* and *subtype,* using the format:

```
Content-type: type/subtype
```

The **type** is one of several general types, such as text, image, audio, video, and application. The first four are used for those types of known data; the application type is used for data that requires special processing. The **subtype** is a more specific designation of what the data is. There are hundreds of these, since each general category has dozens of subtypes or more. Common subtypes that you might see in HTTP headers include **text/html, image/gif** and **application/x-www-form-urlencoded**.

Because new file types and formats are always appearing, there is no fixed set of content types (type and subtype pairs) for use. New content types can easily be defined by using the type **application** and a subtype that begins with "**x-**", which indicates an experimental type. If you wanted to share bolo maps from your HTTP server, you could create a new content type, such as **application/ x-bolomapedit,** which says that the bolo map is a special file that should be processed by an application that handles the file type of **bolomapedit.**

HTTP servers need some method of determining what type a file is. In most cases the server uses the filename extension to do this, so that files ending in **.gif** are assumed to be GIF files and those ending in **.html** are HTML text documents. If the file does not have an extension or the extension is not recognized, the server will use a default setting, usually **text/html** or **text/plain**. These type mappings are usually kept in a file that provides a mapping of one or more filename extensions to a content type. Servers running on top of DOS or Windows are limited to three character file extensions, so they often have slightly different extensions than other systems, such as using **.htm** instead of .html for HTML documents.

The WWW client software maintains tables on the other end, for the opposite purpose. When the client software receives a file, it matches the MIME type to a file type in its table. This tells the client whether it can display the file directly or needs to hand it off to another application. When the client software receives a file with a content type that it doesn't recognize, it has a couple of options on what to do. Some clients try looking at the filename extension (if one exists) to guess what kind of file it is. Other clients simply use some default processing, usually trying to display the file as text (which results in a really weird-looking page when the file was a binary). Some will also try to guess whether the file is an HTML document by looking to see whether the first character is a < (indicating the possible beginning of an HTML element).

If you are serving files with experimental or uncommon MIME content types, it is a good idea to indicate that fact somewhere on your site (somewhere obvious, folks). If you can distribute some software for handling the experimental type, that should be included as well, so users can download and install it. Most WWW browsers have the ability for users to add new MIME types and define an application to handle them.

Uniform Resource Locator (URL)

A Uniform Resource Locator, or URL (pronounced "U - R - L," not "yurl" or "earl") is a text string that contains all of the information needed to specify the location of a file or directory anywhere on the Internet. URLs are used in hypertext links to specify the target of the link. A complete URL can specify the protocol to use, a user name and password, the server to contact and the port number to use on that server, the path and filename, and a label within the file. If the file specified is an application, the URL can also have data appended to it that can be sent to the application for processing.

The URL Format

The first item specified in a URL is the protocol to use to contact the server containing the target file. Each protocol has a slightly different format for its URLs. There are several common elements, though:

- **Server** The IP address or DNS name of the server that is serving the specified file or directory. The server must be running the protocol listed in the URL for the link to work.

- **Port**   The port to use to connect to the server. If no port is specified, the assigned port number for the protocol is used (for example, 80 for HTTP). If an alternative port number is used, it should
  be greater than 1024, all numbers below that being reserved for
  well-known services, such as FTP, Gopher, and Telnet.

- **Path**   This looks exactly like a UNIX directory path, but it isn't.
  Technically it is a hierarchical listing of directories delimited by
  the slash **/** character, with the higher level in the hierarchy located to the left of the slash. Treat it like a UNIX path, though,
  and you won't hit any snags.

- **File**   This can be any file on the server, including an application.
  It does not matter whether or not the file was made on the same
  kind of computer as the server, because it is up to the client software to determine how to transfer the data.

  If the file specifies an HTML document, it may also contain a *fragment identifier* specifying a location in the document:

  filename#frag_id

  In this format, **filename** is the name of the file (including any filename extension), and **frag_id** is an alphanumeric identifier marking a point in the file (using the NAME attribute of the Anchor
  element). Fragment identifiers are used *only* by the client software,
  never by a server. Sending a request to a server that specifies a
  fragment identifier will usually result in the entire page being
  returned again with the fragment identifier ignored.

A listing by protocol of the various URL formats follows.

FTP

> **ftp://[username[:password]@]server[:port]/[path/][file]**

The default port is 21.

A user name and password are not required for accessing anonymous FTP sites. If only a user name is provided, the client software
should query the user to provide a password before trying to use
the URL to link to the FTP server.

A trailing slash (**/**) in an FTP URL indicates that the client software
should use the FTP directory list command to return a listing of the

directory contents to the user. If the URL ends with only the name of a directory and no trailing slash, the intent is ambiguous, and a **File Not Found** error should be returned to the user.

FTP servers do not return any type data about the file, so the client software will have to guess the type. See the notes on this in the section on MIME.

File

```
file://[server]/[path/][file]
```

This URL is provided primarily to access files on the user's computer, although it can also be used to specify files on a server. The documentation on the NCSA site has led many people to think that this is an alternative form for accessing files via FTP. That is not its intended use, however, and many clients will fail when attempting that.

The path is the *absolute path* to the file from the root of the file system. This allows files to be accessed from volumes on other systems as long as they are currently mounted on the HTTP server. There are no facilities for passing a user name, password, or port number for the connection.

If a server is specified, the file is presumed to be located on the server or some volume that the server currently has mounted. This is intended to work only with HTTP servers. If no server is specified, the file is presumed to be located on the user's computer. In that case the client software is responsible for locating and displaying the file, and no server software is involved at all. This allows files to be viewed in the client without the need to run a server, which can be useful for developing Web pages or making local demonstrations.

This URL requires that a file be specified. If the file is an HTML document, the file portion of the URL can also contain a fragment identifier.

There is no way for any type data to be returned about the file, so the client software will have to guess the type. See the notes on this in the section on MIME.

Gopher

```
gopher://server[:port]/TYPE[gopher_selector]%09[search
_string]%09[gopher+_string]
```

The default port is 70.

Gopher URLs have something that looks like a path but isn't. Unlike FTP and HTTP sites, Gopher resources are accessed through a combination of resource types and selector strings. The resource type is a single-digit field that denotes the Gopher type of the resource to which the URL refers. The selector string is a string describing the resource on the Gopher server. Note that some selector strings also begin with a resource type, so the type may be listed twice. The selector string may also be empty, since this is how Gopher clients refer to the top-level directory on a Gopher server. See Table 2.1 for a list of the Gopher resource type codes.

Code	Resource Type
0	Text file
1	Directory
2	CSO Name/Phonebook server
3	Error
4	Binhex file
5	DOS binary file
6	UNIX uuencode file
7	Full text index search
8	Telnet session
9	Binary file

Table 2.1

Gopher Resource
Type Codes

If the URL refers to a Gopher search engine, the **search_string** is required. Otherwise, it is an empty string (not optional—the %09 is still present). Any occurrences of a carriage return, line feed, or other nonprinting character in the **gopher+_string** must be encoded in the URL.

If the server is a Gopher+ server, the **gopher+_string** can be used to send a request for a Gopher+ item.

HTTP

```
http://server[:port]/[path/][file][$dir_data]
[?search_data]
```

The default for the HTTP protocol is port 80.

The file name may specify any kind of file, including applications. If an application is specified, the data extensions may be used to pass data directly to the application for processing: **dir_data** is data that can be passed to the application as a direct parameter; **search_data** is data that can be passed to a CGI application by using the search parameter. The use of the dollar sign (**$**) to delimit **dir_data** is specific to the WebSTAR and MacHTTP servers. Other servers may use a different character as a delimiter for this data.

Mail

```
mailto:address@host
```

The **address@host** is a complete e-mail address as defined in RFC 822. Clients that support this URL will present some interface for sending e-mail with the **Rcpt:** preset to the **address@host**. This could also be done by launching an external mailer application and passing the **address@host** information to it.

Any use of the percent sign (**%**) in the address, as when a gateway is specified for mail forwarding, requires the **%** to be encoded to **%25** in the URL.

News

```
news:newsgroup
```

The **newsgroup** is the complete name of a valid UseNet newsgroup. This URL requires that the client software have a news server specified that it can access and that the news server be carrying the specified newsgroup. The client software may be able to display the news messages directly or launch an external news application.

Telnet, Rlogin, TN3270

`scheme://[username@]server`

The scheme is one of **telnet**, **tn3270**, or **rlogin**. Only the **rlogin** scheme allows a user name to be sent (in fact, it requires the user name).

All three schemes require an external application to handle the connection. Most clients use a Telnet client to emulate the **rlogin** URLs as well.

Several other protocol schemes are available as well, although they are not as often used and may not be directly supported by most clients. New schemes can be added by using the "**x-**" experimental prefix, but it is unlikely that any client would be able to handle the new URL scheme, so this should be reserved for use in developing new client software.

Notes on URL Paths

The paths used in a URL to specify a file look very much like paths used in the UNIX operating system. The two are not exactly equivalent, however. In almost all cases, you can treat them the same, especially with URLs for FTP and HTTP servers, but don't expect every trick you can do with UNIX paths to work with URLs.

The path in a URL should be thought of as follows: It is a hierarchical description of how to locate a file, with each element of the hierarchy delimited by slash characters and the higher-level hierarchical elements located to the left of the slash. If you are dealing with UNIX paths, it is very easy to map them onto this structure. That is not all that you can do with it, though. As one example, it could be used to describe an object in which each element in the path is a refinement of the description. All that is needed is a way of mapping a unique description of a file or some data onto the URL path structure.

One thing that confuses this for many people is the way that most UNIX servers have been modified to support some Unix-like path structures, specifically the "~" character for jumping directly to a subdirectory. This type of path is specific to certain server software and is not generally supported by HTTP servers.

Virtual URLs

Many times the URL that is returned does not specify a physical file. This might be the case when the data is returned from a database search or when a page is created on the fly by a CGI application. It is quite possible in such cases that using the URL at a later time would not return the same data or even any data at all. This can be a very useful technique for hiding data on a server.

Partial URLs

So far we have been discussing the URL standard, which defines what a complete URL will look like. When writing a hypertext link to pages on the same site, though, it is often desirable to use only a portion of a URL, or a *partial URL*. A partial URL is one that lacks the definition of the method and server to use. Only the path and file name are provided.

The path in a partial URL does not need to be the complete path relative to the server root. If desired, it can be given as a path relative to the document that embeds the hypertext link. In these cases it is up to the client software to use the partial URL to create the complete URL needed to make the hypertext connection. The client does this by assuming that any information not provided in the partial URL is the same as that provided in the previous URL. Thus since the method and server (and server port) are not specified, the values for these are assumed to be the same as before.

This is an important concept to understand because it can be used to make a site portable so that it can be moved from one server to another without changes. The first link that a user uses to connect to a site will contain the method, the name of the server, and any other necessary information. The client software stores this information for the current connection. Then, if the user clicks on a link with a partial URL, the information is used to form the complete URL.

Partial URLs do not apply to every connection method. They can be used only with file transaction services that have hierarchical organization that can be reflected in a path structure. In addition, it is important to remember that partial URLs are used only by the client software. The client must create a full URL before it can send a request to a server.

In order to talk about partial URLs, we'll need to use some terminology. The *current URL* is the complete URL for the page currently being displayed in the WWW browser. The *server portion* of the current URL is everything before the third slash (the first two being useless). That includes the method, server name, and optional port, user name, and password. The *path portion* contains the path to the file, meaning everything between the third slash and the last one. The *file portion* is everything after the last slash. This is the name of the file that is currently being displayed in the WWW browser.

Relative to Root

If a partial URL begins with a slash (/), it is assumed to be specifying a path relative to the server root. The location of the server root will vary with different server types. An FTP server usually has one root directory specified for anonymous users. If you enter with a name and password, though, you are likely to have a different root directory specified. HTTP servers have no facility for providing a user name or password in the URL, so the root directory is the same for all users.

In order to rebuild the complete URL, the client software simply adds the proper method, server name, and port number to the partial URL. As an example, if the current page is located at `http://www.comvista.com:8001/sales/reports95dec.html` and the partial URL in the next link is `/tech/bug23.html`, the new complete URL will be `http://www.comvista.com:8001/tech/bug23.html`. The general method that the client software uses to figure the complete URL from a partial URL relative to the root is

```
server portion + partial URL
```

This type of partial URL is very useful for two purposes. The first is when you are not sure where the file will be that will contain the partial URL. It might be that you are pasting the same URL into many files (such as a header graphic in `/grc/header.gif`) or that the partial URL is in a virtual file (like the results of a database search) or that the file containing the partial URL was accessed through a file alias. The second is when the file being specified is located very close to the server root, such as a CGI in the `/cgi-bin` directory or even a file in the root directory itself. In these cases it is much shorter to type the URL this way rather than relative to the current file.

Relative to File

If a partial URL begins with something other than a slash, it is assumed to be the path to a file relative to the current URL. The client software uses the following formula to create the complete URL:

```
server portion + path portion + partial URL
```

In this case if the current page were **http://www.comvista.com/ products/overview.html** and the partial URL were **software/ MacSoftware.html**, the complete URL to the new file would be **http://www.comvista.com/products/software/ MacSoftware.html**.

Dot Notation

Most client software also supports a special notation that indicates that the partial URL is referring to a directory at a higher level than the current file. This notation uses two period characters (**..**), or "dots," to refer to the next higher directory. Assume that the current URL is **http://www.comvista.com/products/software/Mac Software.html** and you want to refer to the file **/sales/report 95oct.html**. You can create a URL relative to the current file that does this by using the dot notation in the partial URL **../../../ sales/report95oct.html**.

In general, the way to apply this type of partial URL is to remove the rightmost element and slash mark from the current URL's path portion for each occurrence of **../** in the partial URL. After that, the remaining portion of the partial URL is appended to the remaining path.

Since the complete URL uses a path relative to the server root, it is impossible to use this notation to reach any directories at a higher level than the server root. If you look at the method preceding for using this type of partial URL, you can see that it can remove information from the path portion of the URL only until it runs out of information. At that point it is up to the client how to handle things. The best thing for the client to do is generate an error, but it could choose to use the remainder of the partial URL to form the new URL or remove all of the extra occurrences of **.. /** and use the remaining path as the full path to the file.

URL Encoding

Many characters require special encoding if they are included in a URL. There are two reasons for this. The first is that some reserved characters serve special functions in a URL for delimiting data. If any of these occur as part of a directory or file name, they need to be encoded so they are not mistaken for the special delimiters. The second reason is that not all networks are safe for transmitting 8-bit characters. To be certain that the characters are not corrupted by imperfect gateways and will be printable, they should be encoded in a 7-bit-safe format.

The URL encoding scheme is quite simple. Any characters that are to be encoded are replaced with the pattern

%XX

XX is the hexadecimal representation of the character. Since the percent (**%**) character is also encoded where it occurs naturally, it can be assumed that a **%** in a URL always indicates the start of an encoded character. This means that the client and server can choose to encode any characters that they want without worrying that they will not be understood on the other end. The only exception is the short list of special characters. Those characters must *always* be encoded when they occur in a URL except when they act as delimiters. The list of special characters and their encodings is provided inTable 2.2.

Character	Encoding
TAB	%09
SPACE	%20
"	%22
<	%3C

(Continued)

(Table 2.2 Continued)

Character	Encoding
>	%3E
[	%5B
\	%5C
]	%5D
^	%5E
`	%60
{	%7B
|	%7C
}	%7D
~	%7E

Table 2.2

Reserved Characters
That Must Be
Encoded in URLs

Several other characters should also be encoded in URLs. These characters are not specifically reserved by the URL standard, but they are so often used for special purposes that it is a good general practice to encode them. These characters are listed in Table 2.3.

Character	Encoding	Explanation
%	%25	Used to indicate an encoded character
/	%2F	Used to indicate hierarchical structure in URLs
#	%23	Used to delimit file markers in a URL
$	%24	Often used to pass data in a URL to an external application
?	%3F	Used to pass data in a URL to an external application
=	%3D	Used to delimit form data
&	%26	Used to delimit form data

Table 2.3

Special Characters
That Should Also Be
Encoded in URLs

Let's look at an example. If you wanted to write a URL to point to the file `50%Reductions.html` in the directory `1995 Corp Budget`, the URL would look like:

```
http://some.server.com/1995%20Corp%20Budget/50%25
Reductions.html
```

You can see from this how the spaces are replaced with the encoding `%20` and the percent sign itself encoded as `%25`. The result is a string that should be acceptable to any computer system and able to be transmitted over any network.

Common Mistakes

A common mistake is forgetting to encode spaces in a URL. This happens more often with Macintosh users because the Macintosh operating system allows spaces in file and folder names. These spaces may not be easily detectable, especially if they occur at the start or end of a file or folder name. If you have trouble with this, it is a good idea to get an HTML editor that can do the encoding for you. Several editors allow you to highlight a stretch of text and have all 8-bit and reserved characters encoded.

Another common problem is the fact that people forget to use a slash mark (/) to end a URL when no file is specified. The source of this problem might lie not with the users, though, but with the client and server software. In general, client software must be very forgiving of user mistakes, because people will switch to new client software before they will admit to making a mistake. This tends to reinforce mistakes, though, until the mistake is so common that it must be made part of the standard.

As an example of this, almost all WWW clients allow the user to type just the scheme and server name without including a slash at the end. That is not a legal URL, but the client can easily figure out what was probably wanted (the home page) and add a slash before making the request. This mistake is especially prevalent in print, where presumably the editors are trying to save the space that a slash mark would take up on the page.

There is a related problem when a URL specifies a path but not a final file name, and the user forgets to append a trailing slash mark to the path to indicate that no file name is included. In this case the client software is not always able to solve the problem. It would be a bad mistake to assume that any name that doesn't have a filename extension (such as `.html`) is a directory, because only DOS and Windows systems are tied to that naming convention. The Macintosh OS and most UNIX systems do not require filename extensions and may also allow the period (`.`) character to be used in a directory name.

In this case it is the servers that have been causing problems. The NCSA httpd server has built-in error correction so that URLs that specify a directory and do not end in a slash mark are still treated as proper URLs to the directory. Since the majority of early Web sites (and a large percentage of those running today) are using NCSA httpd, this kind of error tolerance has allowed users to become lazy about writing URLs, with the result that every other server (including WebSTAR) must follow suit or face angry hordes of rejected users. WebSTAR 1.2 added this error correction capability.

Why, you may ask, does this even matter? If the server and client can fix problems, why shouldn't they? The problem lies in the time it takes to process a connection. When a client is solving the problem, it doesn't matter, because the delay affects only the user. However, when the server is the one doing the error correction, everyone connecting to the server must wait for connections that have the added processing time of fixing a bad URL. If many users make the same mistake, the overhead of error processing can begin to be a significant fraction of the total processing time.

URLs in Plain Text

The standard does not formally define how a URL should be handled outside of HTML or other formats that use URLs. There are some suggestions, however, that have gained support from quite a bit of software, including many e-mail and news readers.

In general, if you are going to include a URL in a plain-text document, the URL should be encased in angle brackets. There should not be any space between the left angle bracket and the start of the URL or between the end of the URL and the right angle bracket. As an example, the following might be part of an e-mail message (especially if it is from me):

> You can find my directory of Macintosh WWW software at
> <http://www.comvista.com/net/www/mac/> and another
> good listing from Ian Andrew Bell at <http://cosmo.
> arpp.sfu.ca/tools/>.

Limitations of URLs

The primary limitation of the URL is the fact that it is a static specification. It tells where to look for a file, without any guarantee that the file will be there. In fact, the file might be there, but if the name has been changed, or the server's name or any of the directories, it still will not be found. URLs also tend quite often to be somewhat lengthy and to include many special characters, both of which increase the likelihood that someone will make a mistake when typing them in.

Alternatives to URLs

A number of specifications are in development for naming and finding resources on the Internet. The URL is just one and has become widely known because it was selected as the method for defining a resource's location in HTML links, but because of the reasons cited, it is not likely to last as the sole method for identifying resources on the Internet. Designing a replacement that addresses the issue of dynamic locations has been a nontrivial task, though, so for the time being the URL is the key.

The class of all naming specifications is the *Universal Resource Identifier (URI)*. It includes URL and all other methods for identifying how to find a resource on the Internet. The two methods currently in development are the Uniform Resource Name (URN) and the Uniform Resource Citation (URC). URNs are dynamic identifiers that should be able to track files even when they have been moved or renamed. This is likely to work something like DNS does. The IP address is a static specification of a machine and may or may not refer to the same machine or any machine at all from day to day. The DNS name, on the other hand, can be reassigned as needed so that it continues to refer to the same computer even when the computer has been moved or its IP address has changed (or both). A URC is intended to provide extended information about a file. In addition to the file's URL or URN, the URC might also include information about ownership, encodings used, access restrictions, and how long the file will be valid.

WWW Client Software

Dozens of clients are now available for almost every computer in use today. Even handheld systems, such as the Newton, are getting Web client software. There is no possible way for me to cover every client available, and if I did it would be out of date before you read this, anyway. Instead I am going to cover a few important issues when dealing with clients and a few that you might use on your Macintosh.

Graphics versus Text

One of the biggest debates on the Web today is the struggle between text and graphics on Web sites. Originally the Web was entirely text-based, so there was no problem. With the release of NCSA Mosaic, though, came the ability to include graphics that would appear right in a page (inline graphics). These graphics are typically much larger on disk than the text files, meaning that they take longer to download, especially over modem connections. In addition, the newer HTML standards include many more variations for changing the text display, so even the text itself is being treated like a graphic, with variable font sizes, tables, and other elements that not all WWW clients can handle.

The result is that it is nearly impossible now to design an HTML page that looks the same to every client and yet is still considered attractive by most users. Some sites solve this by creating several variations of most pages; the user selects a variation on the basis of the amount of graphics desired. This can hardly be considered an elegant solution, though. In addition, not all clients handle graphics exactly the same, so some graphics formats such as JPEG (Joint Photographic Experts Group) are not usable by all clients, and there may be tremendous variations in what colormap is used or how dithering is handled.

No clear solution is in sight, and the problem is only getting worse as new binary formats are added to the list of those that can be supported by WWW client software.

Multiple Connections

Newer WWW clients have begun using multiple simultaneous connections in order to retrieve pages more quickly. This doesn't do much for a page that has no graphics in it, of course, but when one or more graphics are used inline, the client can fetch several of them at once from the server. It is not at all clear, though, that this is a good thing for a client to do because of two problems. The first problem is for the server. Since clients are now making more than one connection at a time, it is more likely that there will be several nearly simultaneous connections to a server so that three or four clients can use up a dozen or more connections, which could lock out other clients. The second problem is with the client. The client tries to grab everything at once, but the server may not be able to handle that many new connections. Therefore some of the connections may fail, and they are probably more likely to fail than if they had come in sequence. The result is that pages containing many graphics are more likely to have a failure when the client tries to retrieve them all at once.

Therefore, it is important that the client software offer the user the means to restrict how many simultaneous connections will be attempted. It is likely that servers will also attempt to alleviate the problem by implementing load balancing based on IP address, so each client will be limited to a maximum number of connections at one time. This would probably require that another code response be added to the HTTP standard to indicate to the client that it had exceeded its maximum allowed connections. The client would then, presumably, know not to keep trying for more connections until it had let some earlier ones go.

Netscape has a special problem with this, due to its interpretation of when a connection is "finished." With Netscape 1.1 and earlier, the client does not always act the way that is expected. If Netscape is set to use no more than four connections at once, you would expect that no more than four connections are open at any one time. What it really means, though, is that no more than four connections are *being opened* at one time. Once a connection starts receiving data from a server, Netscape considers that connection "finished" and starts to open a new one to take its place (if needed). The result is that it is possible for Netscape to have many more connections open at once than the number specified. I recommend never setting Netscape above two connections. This will decrease the number of failed connections you get and make life easier on the servers while still benefiting from the apparent speed increase of downloading multiple items simultaneously.

Caching

Many of the new WWW clients use some form of page caching to speed up the apparent response for the user. The client checks the server to see whether the page has changed since it was cached. If not, the page is displayed from cache, which can save significant time, especially over modem connections. The problem is that the cache may become damaged in some way or the server may respond incorrectly that a file has not been updated when it has. In these instances the only resort is often to force the software to flush its cache and start over again. There is also somewhat of a problem because the software usually doesn't allow the user much control over the cache beyond simply stating how much disk space the cache can have. There is usually no way to temporarily suspend the cache or to give certain kinds of documents a higher priority than others.

Standards

This is probably the single largest problem facing the makers of WWW client software today. Several different standards are being developed to provide the same capabilities to all clients and improve the uniformity of access, which was one of the original attractions of the Web. However, some companies do not wish to wait for the standards to be fully defined, and these companies are implementing their own features that are not supported by other browsers. Most of these features are desirable to users (which is why the companies do not want to wait), so the problem is enhanced because the features are being put into widespread use despite the recommendations of the standards groups.

The solution is difficult, though. There is tension between those who want to see more features in their Web sites and those who want to remain true to the original intent of the Web design or some standard that they have in mind. Both sides need to make compromises before a solution can be reached. For the Web developers, the best solution is to think carefully before using any features that are not part of an existing standard and to be ready to support the standards when they are released, even if it means extensive changes (this applies to anyone who implemented tables based on Netscape 1.1 or NCSA Mosaic, both of which are not likely to match the final table element definition).

This sort of problem is not unique to Web software, of course. Modem users have been experiencing this same problem for years, as modem manufacturers continually try to second-guess where the standards are going and release hardware that does not strictly meet the final standards.

The Client Software

Several WWW clients have already been mentioned by name. Here is a quick summary of those that will affect your site the most and the main things to keep in mind about them. Remember that the only thing changing as quickly as the Web is the Web clients, so any "facts" that I provide here may possibly be out of date before you read this.

NCSA Mosaic for Macintosh

This was the first big Web client for Macintosh, but its use has declined in the past year. The loss was probably due to three factors: several developers leaving NCSA to work for Netscape Communications Corporation; the NCSA Mosaic software being prone to crashing; and the fact that NCSA Mosaic was still in alpha release (and still buggy) when Netscape was headed to its third new version. NCSA has licensed its code to other companies for the development of commercial clients, the most common one being Enhanced Mosaic. Personally, I think that NCSA XMosaic is still pretty good stuff, but the Mac version is not highly recommended.

MacWeb

MacWeb, from EINet Technologies (now TradeWave Corporation), was the next big client to be released. It had several advantanges over NCSA Mosaic (which at the time was version 1.03) because it ran in much less memory, was more stable, and supported forms. The advantage of running in a small memory footprint cannot be overstated. Fancy graphics, inline movies, and all of that are very nice, but the real meat of the Web is still information contained primarily in the text. If you are using a portable computer or stuck on a low-memory machine, MacWeb is the best way to go. Another nice feature is its strict adherence to the HTML 1.0 and 2.0 standards. The developers chose not to support HTML 3.0 while it was still wildly fluctuating and are not quite as forgiving of really bad HTML tagging as some other browsers. As a result, viewing your document in MacWeb is an excellent way of checking for errors in your pages.

Netscape Navigator

Netscape Navigator, a product of Netscape Communications Corporation, was originally code-named Mozilla, and the name was well chosen. Much the way Godzilla rose out of the ocean to stomp all over Tokyo, Netscape has taken over the Web client market. Netscape Navigator is the client everyone loves to hate. On the positive side, it supports many extensions that users have obviously been wanting, judging by their widespread use. Netscape was also the first client to offer secure communications with equipped servers, which made the Web much more palatable to many companies. On the downside, Netscape implemented new features with little apparent regard for the existing standards, the client is a memory hog, and many bugs in the basic operation still have not been addressed (as of version 1.1).

Although there is no way yet to accurately determine what client software everyone is using, it is very likely that Netscape is the most-used browser on the Web and unlikely to lose that position any time soon. In addition, whether or not you approve of implementing nonstandard HTML elements, it is clear that the users wanted this and will continue to support it. Please, though, let's have no more of the `<BLINK>` tag.

Lynx

Although Lynx does not technically run on a Macintosh (unless you are using Telnet to a UNIX machine), it does represent an important portion of the Web community. Thousands of people are able to access the Internet only via text-based connections, and these people are primarily using Lynx. Although there still have not been any good studies on what kinds of users are using what browsers, it is my guess that most Lynx users are either college students or people using public accounts. If your site plans to attract these people, you will want to keep in mind a possibly large population that will not be able to read your graphics.

Of course, there are dozens of other Web clients out there that weren't mentioned. The InterCon browser that is now used by America Online, and PSI is becoming a major player. Most of the problems reported with it do not stem from the browser, though, so much as the proxy servers that America Online is using. There should also be a Hot Java browser out from Sun Microsystems that will support both HTML and Java extensions. I don't know how quickly this will take off, since (1) there really aren't many sites using Java and fewer still that need it, and (2) I have no idea how it will perform over slower connections. It should be fun, though.

Proxy Servers

You need to be aware of one other service regarding running a Web server: proxy service. A *proxy server* is an intermediary program that acts as both a client and a server in order to forward requests from one network to another. The proxy server acts as a server to receive a request from one network, then acts as a client to resend that request on the other network. Proxies are often used to provide restricted access to protected networks by masking out what machines are on that network. A *caching proxy* is a proxy server that keeps a local cache of the responses for requests that it previously served and uses them to respond to later requests. It can be used to speed up access to sites that are often used because those pages can be served from the local cache instead of going to the site. A *gateway* is a proxy server that translates between protocols when it is forwarding requests. Thus an incoming HTTP request might be translated to a Gopher transaction and sent to a Gopher server. The reply is then translated back into an HTTP reply before returning it to the user. One example of this is MacProxy+, a gateway for Macintosh servers that translates all incoming Japanese text to use the Shift-JIS encoding before returning it to the user.

As you can see, these servers affect the data that is coming from your site. This can cause a couple of problems. The most common problem—in fact, a classic by this time—is with the CERN proxy server, which is the most commonly used proxy server on the Internet. The CERN proxy converts all instances of a dollar sign (`$`) in a URL to a special representation called a "URL encoding" that looks like `%24`. This is not wrong, because there is a lot of flexibility in what should and shouldn't be encoded. As you'll see in later chapters, though, this can really mess up some of your CGI applications with versions of WebSTAR before 1.2 or with MacHTTP. The problem is solved in WebSTAR 1.2 and later.

A much lesser problem is with caching servers. Since they are serving your pages, it is possible that they are falsely lowering the number of hits on your site. The HTTP/1.0 standard provides a way for the client to specify that it wants the original document and not the cached copy, but there is not yet a way for the server to specify that its pages are not available for caching. This is certain to be added in the future both to give sites more control over who is viewing their pages and to reduce wasted cache space, since there is little point in caching a page that will change often (or that comes from a virtual URL).

Robots, or Spiders

Once the Web began growing rapidly, many people started creating automated clients that would attempt to track or catalog what was happening on the Web. These clients, often called *robots*, or *spiders*, are intelligent software agents that autonomously explore some portion of the Web by recursively following links in documents that are encountered. A complete summary of the topic is available at:

```
http://web.nexor.co.uk/mak/doc/robots/robots.html
```

Uses for Robots

A robot has several uses. The basic process (find page, grab URLs, do some processing, get next page) is pretty similar for all of them, with their function defined by what processing they do on the resources they find.

WebStatistics

Some robots exist only to count the number of Web servers. These robots take no action on a document other than to extract the links in a search for new servers. More advanced statistical agents might also track the number of documents per site, the average size of documents, and numbers of specific file types or even search for the occurrence of specific tags in documents on a site.

Searching

The more famous robots are those used to create databases of documents and files available on the World Wide Web. These include such search engines as Lycos and WebCrawler. Several variations are available. Some robots catalog the entire text of a document, others catalog only the title, and still others attempt to create an abstract for the document. Some robots do only active searches and don't keep any static catalog.

Maintenance

Several robots are specifically tuned for site maintenance. The purpose is to test the integrity of links within the site and links from pages on the site to other sites. These robots are usually limited so that they will go no more than one link away from the site. They may also have features to check the last modification date of a linked document or to check for radical changes in file size or contents. A site can quickly grow beyond the capabilities of a human agent to track all of the links, so this type of agent is needed to keep from accumulating too many dead or stale links.

Mirroring and Indexing

Some robots are used for mirroring or indexing other services. The few available are primarily for mirroring Web directories and are not very sophisticated. More advanced robots would be able to limit updates to only the files that have changed and also be able to scan the documents for URLs that might need to be updated to match the new location. Robots would also be useful for sites that index an FTP site on Web pages, since the robot could match file names to entries in a database to provide file descriptions, contact information, and more.

It is possible that a robot could perform more than one of the tasks described here, especially when combining very similar services, such as statistical data gathering and searching. A summary of the currently known robots and their various functions is provided by Nexor at **http://web.nexor.co.uk/mak/doc/robots/active.html**

Problems with Robots

The use of Web robots involves a number of problems both for the site running the robot and the sites to which the robot connects. The most commonly mentioned problem with robots is the possibility that they will tie up your server with requests. A poorly designed robot can fire off requests much more quickly than any human users. If the robot is also threaded, it could use up dozens of connections at a time doing a recursive search of your site. Luckily most robot authors have caught on to the problem and are using breadth-first search methods. This means that one request is placed to each server being searched before any server receives a second request, so that there should be a measurable delay between successive requests to any one server.

Another problem with robots is their effect on network bandwidth. If the robot is able to retrieve files in parallel, the robot could use up quite a bit of the local network bandwidth, which affects all users between the robot and its connection to the network backbone. Since there is no facility for a network to load-balance certain machines or protocols, it is up to the robot author to make sure that the software avoids pounding the network to death.

For some companies there is a question about whether they want robots to be archiving their pages at all, no matter how nicely designed the robot is. Although there is advertising benefit in being listed by a major search site, many companies do not want or need this benefit and do not want to pay for the extra network and server load that robots use up. This might also be a problem if you have documents that are not meant to be made too widely known.

The use of CGI applications has created some complications for using robots as well. It is not desirable for robots to waste time archiving references to virtual URLs, the results of database searches, or other resources that are either extremely large or unlikely to exist in the near future. Some of the more popular search robots are working on methods to determine which files are most interesting to their users and to avoid others.

A final problem with some robots, specifically those that provide searchable databases, is an increase of users linking to URLs that no longer exist or that are badly formed. Robots that focus on locating and cataloging resources will tend to focus on getting new material into the database before updating the existing entries. This means that users could still be getting references to pages months or more after the documents have been moved. Robots that make assumptions about the servers they are contacting, such as those that forget to retain the trailing slash in a directory URL, can cause similar problems by repeatedly generating errors on servers that do not support automatic error correction.

Solving Robot Problems

Luckily several solutions are available for those who find robots to be unwelcome visitors. The first and best solution is to use the standard for robot exclusion, as described at

`http://web.nexor.co.uk/mak/doc/robots/norobots.html`

This "standard" is just a consensus reached by several robot authors and irritated Webmasters on a method for letting robots know that they should not connect to certain sites. The key to this method is a file named `robots.txt` that is located at the root of a WWW site. If the file is found, a robot (a well-behaved one, that is) will look inside the file to see whether it has permission to access the site. If the file is not found, the robot assumes that the whole site is fair game and proceeds to strip the site of every last bit of information it can find.

Not all robots are designed to use this file, though, so stronger methods may be required. The list of all known robots provides some information on identification tags and home machines for many of the robots so that you can refuse them access to your site through the security measures your server provides. If a particular robot is not listed there, you can check your log file to try to get the information. If your log doesn't keep that kind of information, you may be able to get more information about the robot from other users on a newsgroup, such as `comp.infosystems.www.misc.`

Part II

WebSTAR Manual

Sure, WebSTAR comes with a user manual. But who do you think helped to write it? Here is a good basic manual straight from the horse's mouth. Now you need to read only one book to run your server.

3

WebSTAR

The whole book is about WebSTAR, of course, but this is the first chapter to introduce WebSTAR itself.

Origins

In 1993, just as the entire World Wide Web craze began to take off, a developer named Chuck Shotton (sound familiar?) at the University of Texas decided that it would be cool to have a good WWW client for the Macintosh. He contacted CERN for more information but was advised instead that what was really needed was an HTTP server for the Macintosh. Being already thoroughly disgusted with UNIX, he ignored the common knowledge of the time ("The Macintosh OS can't handle network services.") and leaped into the project. The product was dubbed MacHTTP, and the first version came out in June 1993. It wasn't pretty and didn't have the functionality of the NCSA and CERN servers available at the time; in fact, it was able to handle only one connection at a time. On the other hand, it was easy to install and used very little memory or disk space.

Over time the new releases gained features and increased in power, culminating in the 2.0 release in late 1994. That release could do anything that UNIX servers could (and some things they couldn't), thanks to Chuck's clever implementation of CGI applications, and yet it was still very easy to install. By the time of this release, MacHTTP had gained a large and loyal following, a conference was being planned, and there was already a long list of new features that users wanted in the next release. Long discussions were appearing

85

on mailing lists and in newsgroups asking why anybody would want to run a server on UNIX, with all of its associated maintenance and security headaches, and commercial CGI applications began to appear. Things were clearly getting out of hand.

Realizing that one person was no longer sufficient to handle the popularity of this product, Chuck began looking for a company to take over marketing so he could focus once again on great software. He didn't have to look very long, though, and soon found himself beset by eager bidders. When the dust settled, the winner was Star-Nine Technologies, which already had experience with Macintosh networking and was readying its own mailbox for the Macintosh. A new version of MacHTTP was started with more power, faster connection processing, and several new features. The new version was dubbed WebSTAR, and version 1.0 was released in April 1995.

The rest you probably know.

Current Status

This book is current through version 1.2 of WebSTAR and version 2.2 of MacHTTP. MacHTTP is currently marketed by StarNine as a shareware product, meaning that no technical support is available, and it lacks many features that WebSTAR has. Several add-ons for WebSTAR are now available from StarNine, including the Commerce Kit and the Security Kit. These kits generally may not work with MacHTTP, and there are no plans to work on MacHTTP-compatible versions.

If you have been a long-time follower of MacHTTP and WebSTAR, some points should be cleared up. First, there never was a version 3.0 release of MacHTTP. Plans for that were killed when the product was moved to StarNine. MacHTTP and WebSTAR share common roots, but WebSTAR is a complete rewrite of several key portions of the server and should not be considered just another name for MacHTTP 3.0 (which never existed, remember?). Next, original plans had WebSTAR being released in both "regular" and Pro versions, with the Pro version including the commerce and security capabilities. That has changed; only one version of WebSTAR exists, and the various additional capabilities can be added as needed by purchasing the desired kit. This makes things much simpler and will fit with some features planned for later releases.

The companion CD-ROM contains a complete listing of StarNine products, including all of the currently available kits for WebSTAR.

Features

If you have looked at other commercial servers, you have doubtless received a brochure listing all of the features of that software. WebSTAR, of course, shares all of those features that are common to a good HTTP server:

- HTTP/1.0 compliance
- CGI/1.1 compliance
- Site-based security options
- Document-based security options
- Logging to disk (NCSA standard log files are an option)
- Threaded connection processing (not included in MacHTTP)
- Secure connections (optional purchase) (not included in MacHTTP)
- Online transaction support (optional purchase) (not included in MacHTTP)
- Ability to run multiple servers on one machine
- User-definable error handling
- User-definable response to authorization failures

WebSTAR also has many features that are not included in most HTTP servers (including MacHTTP), such as:

- Preprocessing of connections by external applications (optional)
- Postprocessing of connections by external applications (optional)

- User-definable Actions (preprocessing based on file name, type, or creator)
- Logging directly to databases or other external applications even over a network
- Completely scriptable and recordable (write your own administration software)
- Complete control and monitoring of server activity via a remote application (with a nice graphic interface to boot)
- Server push support
- Direct return of RAW! data files
- Availability as a faceless background application for added security

And if that isn't enough, you can pull out the big guns, as described next.

Instant Installation

If you use WebSTAR right after installation (which is a one-button operation, by the way) without changing any settings at all, you are already configured with settings that will match the needs of 80 percent or more of the sites on the Web today. This means that you can test your site and begin publishing instantly and worry about the settings later, when your site becomes more popular.

Apple Event Support

Since WebSTAR uses Apple events to communicate with CGI applications, you can pass data from your Web pages to literally any application on your AppleTalk network. No matter what applications you have been using in-house—whether it is WordPerfect or Excel or FileMaker or 4D (or whatever)—you can automate the actions of that application to be controlled by your Web server. This means that your WebSTAR server is not some alien that you have to fit into your company but an interactive addition to your existing Macintosh network.

Wide Platform Support

You will hear many companies touting the speed of their servers and how many thousands of connections a day they can process. WebSTAR can do that as well, if that's what you need. But for the majority of Web sites, that kind of processing is overkill. Most sites receive fewer than 50,000 connections a day; in fact, most probably receive fewer than 10,000 per day. With WebSTAR, you have the flexibility of choosing a platform that matches your budget and your processing needs. If you are running a small site for your business, or school or for personal use, you can run that site on any Macintosh that will run System 7.1 or later. I have personally run a site that got more than 10,000 connections per day on an SE/30 with 8 MB RAM (and that was with MacHTTP!). WebSTAR will run on almost any Macintosh made (even the MacXL and PowerBooks), as well as all Apple-certified clone machines (such as Power Computing computers).

Macintosh Security

This cannot be overstated. UNIX types may sneer at the Macintosh because it doesn't have the widespread support for networking that UNIX does and it can't pipeline application input and output. The fact is, though, that those "features" are what makes a UNIX server a security risk. You don't need any of those features to run a good Web server, so they are added fluff and added risk. WebSTAR is one of the most secure servers on the market because of the lack of other capabilities that would provide a back door for hackers. This is obvious when you run the SATAN program against your Macintosh server and see the pathetically short list of possible problems that it checks (like leaving an out-of-date copy of NCSA Telnet running). Run SATAN against your typical UNIX server and you could get several pages of warnings!

While I have your attention, let's take a look at one of the bogus claims that some companies make about their servers. You will often see companies advertising that their servers have "Support for HTML 3.0!" If you read the section on HTTP, you should have realized that *every* HTTP server has support for HTML 3.0. In fact, every

HTTP server can serve any kind of file at all, because HTTP is file-type independent. That was one of the big design requirements for the whole thing. HTML is the document type that is currently used for hypertext, but it might as well be Word 6.0 documents or Post-Script files for all that the server cares. It just pumps the data out and lets the client software worry about file types. This will also apply when companies start advertising that their servers can serve VRML documents or whatever other new format comes along. Mac file, Windows file, UNIX file—it doesn't matter to WebSTAR.

4

A Quick Tour of WebSTAR

This chapter takes you quickly through all of the windows, menus, and dialogs that you will encounter when using WebSTAR or WebSTAR Admin. Some of the more obvious features will be covered completely here, but most of them are covered in greater depth in later chapters. This section uses some vocabulary that was introduced in previous chapters. If you run into an unfamiliar term, take some time to go back and read about it first.

WebSTAR

The WebSTAR server has very few interface options. If you are running the background-only version, none of these interface options are available, and you must use WebSTAR Admin to monitor and change the server.

The Status Window

Figure 4.1 shows the window that the server displays when WebSTAR is launched. The title bar of the window contains the version string for the server that is running, as well as the port number that the server is running on (to help differentiate multiple servers on the same computer).

The Status window is divided into two panes: one showing current statistics for operation and the other showing recent connections (logging). The window is resizable to the extent of your monitor, and the window size is stored across restarts of the server. This may cause a problem if you size the monitor for a large monitor and then switch to a system with a smaller monitor.

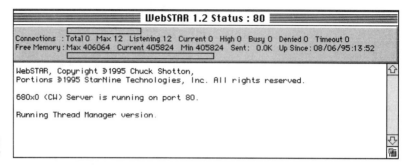

Statistics Pane

This is the top (gray) portion of the window and is packed full of statistical information about the server. All of this information is reset each time the server is launched.

- **Connection bar** The bar at the very top is a graphical representation of connection statistics for the server. The length of the bar represents the maximum number of simultaneous connections available (it gets longer as you raise the Max Connections setting). The left of the bar is the zero setting. As the number of connections increases, the bar fills to the right. The dark gray portion of the bar represents the maximum number of simultaneous connections that have been encountered since the server was last started. The black portion of the bar represents the number of current connections.

- **Connection stats** The line of text below the Connection bar displays the same statistics in text form, as well as some additional information:

  Total The total number of connections since launch.

  Max The maximum number of concurrent connections allowed.

  Listening The number of open processes that are listening for new connections.

  Current The current number of connections being processed (the black bar).

High   The highest number of concurrent connections encountered since launch (the dark gray bar).

Busy   The number of connections refused because the server was too busy.

Denied   The number of connections denied because of IP address or DNS name restrictions.

Timeout   The number of connections that were dropped because the client stopped responding to the server.

- **Memory stats**   The next line of text displays some statistics for memory management:

  Max   The maximum amount of memory available for connection processing. This is not equal to the amount of memory allocated to WebSTAR, because some of the memory is taken up by operation of the server itself at startup.

  Current   The current amount of memory not being used.

  Min   The lowest amount of memory that has been available to the server since it was launched. If this amount ever drops below 200K, you should allocate more memory to the server; otherwise, your CGI applications may crash due to lack of memory.

- **Other stats**   The same line also displays some other statistics:

  Sent   The amount of data sent since the server was launched (measured in tenths of a kilobyte). This is an important statistic, since the amount of data transferred is as good a measure of a server's performance as the number of connections processed.

  Up Since   The date and time of the server's last launch.

- **Memory bar**   This bar provides a graphic display of the memory statistics. As with the Connection bar, the Memory bar displays the total memory (total bar length), high memory use (dark gray bar), and current memory use (black bar) values.

Log Pane

The lower portion of the Status window is used to display information about the clients connecting to your server. This is essentially the same information that will be written to a log file on disk, unless you have logging disabled. The log pane stores only about 200–300 of the most recent entries (roughly 24K of text), so it is useful for a quick look at recent activity, but on a busy server that may extend back only a few minutes. The data continues to be written to this log pane whether you have logging enabled or disabled. The log pane also displays messages that are never written to the disk log, such as server notices about changes in status (such as the startup diagnostics) and the verbose data that is displayed when Verbose Messages is on.

File Menu

Figure 4.2 shows the File menu. The menu has only one option, **Quit**, which obviously quits the application. WebSTAR does not wait until all current connections are finished, so it is advisable to use the **Refuse Connections** option (see following) to make sure that no connections are being processed before quitting.

Figure 4.2
The File Menu

Edit Menu

This is a pretty standard Edit menu (Fig. 4.3), except for two configuration options at the bottom. The first of those options brings up the window for setting passwords for the server (Fig. 4.4). Every password is associated with a user name and a realm. To add a new entry, type the user name and password into the fields at the bottom of the window and click on the **Add** button. To delete a user name/password combination, highlight the correct line in the top part of the window and click on the **Delete** button. Once you have entered a user name and password, you can use the **Realm** pop-up menu at the bottom left of the window to assign the password to an existing realm.

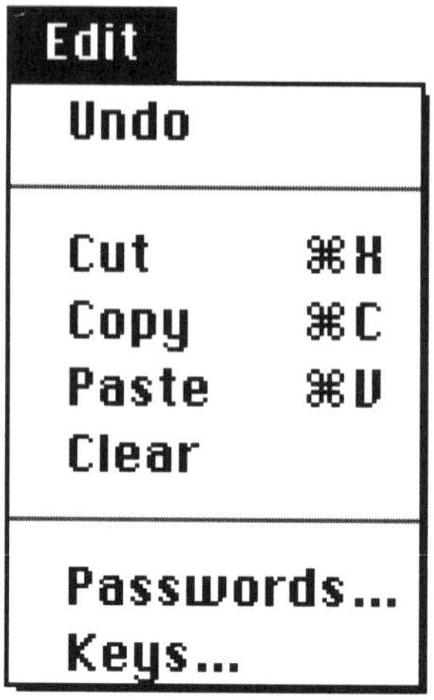

Figure 4.3
The Edit Menu

Edit	
Undo	
Cut	⌘H
Copy	⌘C
Paste	⌘U
Clear	
Passwords...	
Keys...	

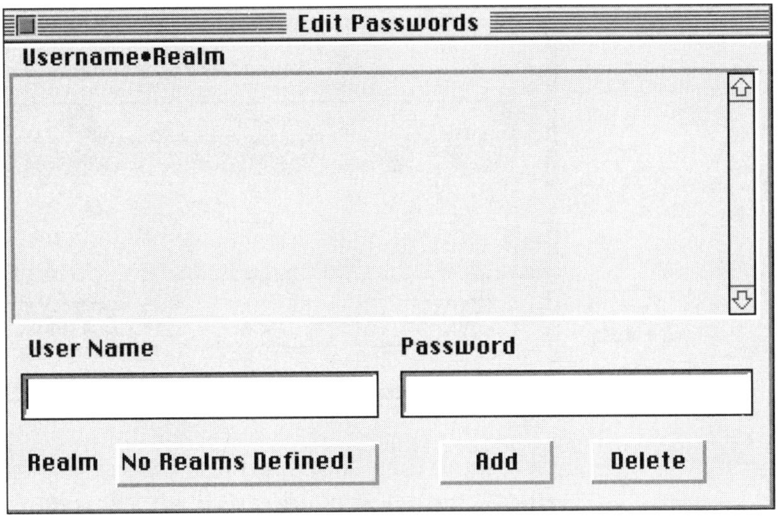

Figure 4.4
The Edit Passwords
Window

The second option is for entering registration keys (Fig. 4.5a). You get one key for each license that you purchase to run a server. You must have at least one key (coded text string) in order to launch the server. The keys are stored in the Preferences file, so you don't have to reenter your license key each time you restart the server. The registration keys control what features you have access to with your server. Demonstration keys will cause the server to operate for only a short period of time and then quit. Basic service keys allow the server to run but don't provide access to secure connections. Professional server keys enable all features. WebSTAR allows the set of all features that are enabled by all keys in the file, so you do not need to delete one key to add another.

This key server is accessible by other applications through Apple events. That means that programmers who write CGI applications could use the same interface to handle key registration for their applications and avoid the overhead of running the same monitoring in their own software. If this becomes popular (and it should), you could conceivably have several keys in this database.

To enter a new key, click on the **New...** button. A dialog box will appear asking you to type in the new key or paste it from the clipboard (this is the same window that appears on startup to ask for the initial key). To get information about one of the keys (you can

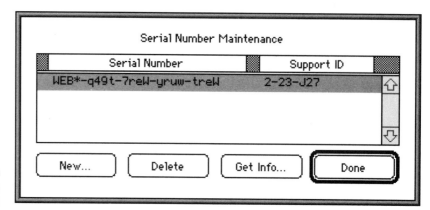

Figure 4.5a
The Registration
Key Dialog

have more than one), highlight the key line and click on the **Get Info...** button. A window will appear (Fig. 4.5b) displaying the information about that key, including its expiration date. To delete a key, highlight its entry in the upper portion of the window and then click on the **Delete** button. Clicking on **Done** accepts the changes and closes the window.

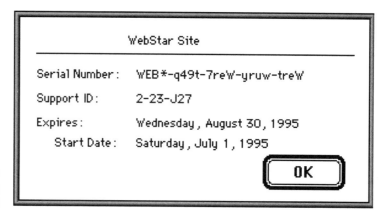

Figure 4.5b
The Key Information
Dialog

If you want to get information on what features a certain key enables, you can double click on the key entry in the list of Key IDs. This will show a dialog listing the features enabled by the key and the expiration date (if any) for the key.

There is no option for canceling, so any changes made are permanent as soon as you click on a button. Be sure that you have a license number written down somewhere before you delete it, or it is gone forever.

Options Menu

The Options menu contains the most commonly needed settings for the server (Fig. 4.6). Each of these items toggles the setting that it describes. A check mark next to the menu entry indicates that the setting is on (true).

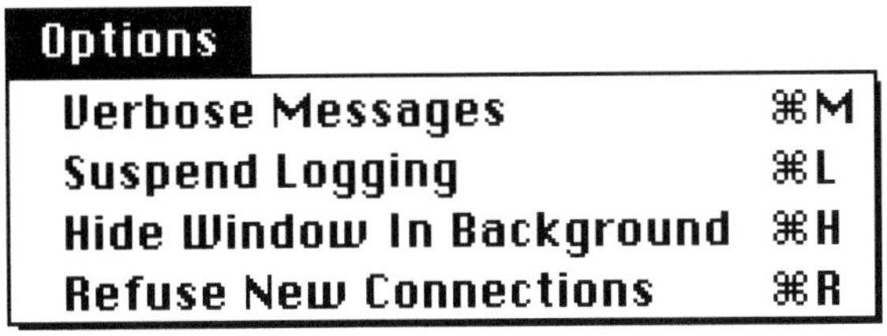

Figure 4.6
The Options Menu

Options	
Uerbose Messages	⌘M
Suspend Logging	⌘L
Hide Window In Background	⌘H
Refuse New Connections	⌘R

Uerbose Messages

This toggles the server in and out of verbose mode for logging connections. In verbose mode, the log pane will contain additional information about MIME typing and connection processing for every connection. Running in verbose mode slows the server down a bit because of the extra information being displayed, but it is very useful for diagnosing problems with file types or CGI applications. The information saved to the log file on disk is the same regardless of whether verbose messaging is on or off.

If you read the section on the HTTP standard, you will recognize much of the data that is displayed when **Uerbose Messages** is on as being the request that the client sends and the response that the server returns in a transaction.

Suspend Logging

When this option is checked, no log information is saved to the log file on disk. The most common use of this option is to temporarily suspend logging so that WebSTAR will close the log file, which allows you to move or rename the file. For daily maintenance, a common method of switching logs would be to (1) send a message to WebSTAR setting the log file name to a new name, (2) suspend logging, (3) unsuspend logging (this starts a new log using the new name), and (4) move the old log somewhere else for processing.

Running a server without logging will improve its performance only slightly.

Hide Window In Background

When this option is checked, the Status window will be hidden whenever WebSTAR is not in the foreground.

Refuse New Connections

When this option is checked, WebSTAR will finish processing all current connections and refuse any new ones. WebSTAR will also display the text **Refused** in bright, red letters in the top left of the Status window to remind you that nobody is getting in. Don't be fooled by this display. It will look as though new connections are still being processed, because it still registers every connection that it is refusing. Sometimes you just have to guess when all of the current connections have finished. One key is when the number of total connections stops increasing even though the connection meter is still operating.

WebSTAR Admin

The WebSTAR Admin application is the main interface for making changes to your WebSTAR server. Many settings can be modified only with this application and are not accessible on the server itself. In addition, WebSTAR Admin duplicates all of the performance-monitoring features that your server displays in the Status window. This allows you to monitor several WebSTAR servers from one remote machine.

Those features that are identical to the WebSTAR server interface are not covered again here. Please read the previous pages for information on those features.

Connection Window

Figure 4.7 shows the window that is displayed for a new connection to a WebSTAR server. The title bar of the window contains the

DNS name and port number for the server being monitored. The connection statistics shown in the top right (gray) portion of the window are identical, with one exception, to those in the WebSTAR server Status window. The Version: information tells what version of WebSTAR server is being monitored.

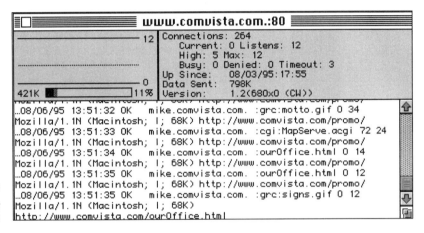

The top left of the window provides a graphical display of the same connection information, as well as memory statistics. The strip chart at the top shows connection statistics. The height of each bar indicates the number of connections at that time (updated every 15 seconds, with newer entries to the right). The dotted line indicates the highest number of concurrent connections since the server was launched, and the top line indicates the maximum number of connections available.

Below this strip chart is a bar graph identical to that on the server for displaying memory usage. The only change is that the number to the left shows the current memory available (in kilobytes), and the number to the right shows the percentage of memory currently being used.

The bottom portion of the window is a log pane that shows exactly the same information as is displayed on the server. If the server is set for verbose messages, they will also be displayed in this window. This log information cannot be saved to disk, and only the last 200 entries or so are kept in the window. For more information, see the section "Log File" later in the chapter.

The window may be resized to the limit of your monitor. The log information will use as much width as is available, although the strip chart remains a fixed size. The window may also be reduced to entirely hide the log information and display only the chart itself. This allows many machines to be monitored from a single remote machine.

File Menu

The File menu has what you would expect: commands to open and close connections and to quit the application (Fig. 4.8).

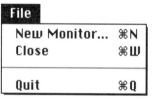

Figure 4.8

The File Menu

The **New Monitor...** command will walk you through making a link to the server. The menu command will display a dialog (Fig. 4.9) for selecting a WebSTAR server on your AppleTalk network. In order for a server to be displayed, it must have Program Linking enabled for the user. This is discussed in Chapter 5.

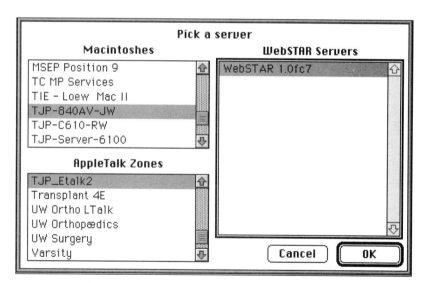

Figure 4.9

The New Monitor Dialog

First, use the bottom-left box (labeled **AppleTalk Zones**) to select the zone that the server is running in. Select a zone by clicking once on the name of the zone. When you have selected a zone, the upper-left box (labeled **Macintoshes**) will display all of the machines in that zone. Select the Macintosh that the server is running on. When you click on the machine name, all copies of WebSTAR running on that machine will be displayed in the right-hand box, labeled **WebSTAR Servers**. Select the WebSTAR server that you want to monitor by clicking on it, then click in the **OK** button to accept the selection. If you are not able to find the server you want or change your mind about making the connection, click on the **Cancel** button to close the window without opening a new connection.

The **Close** menu item will close the frontmost window and its connection. WebSTAR Admin does not save any information about the connections after they are closed. There is no way for WebSTAR Admin to save the settings to reach the server, because of limitations in the way the Macintosh OS implements program linking.

Edit Menu

Edit

Can't Undo	⌘Z
Cut	⌘H
Copy	⌘C
Paste	⌘V
Clear	
Select All	⌘A

Figure 4.10

The Edit Menu for WebSTAR Admin

This is a pretty standard Edit menu (Fig. 4.10). The editing commands can be used when entering data in one of the configuration dialogs (or copying data out of them) or to copy data from the log window. The log information cannot be directly edited, deleted, or pasted into.

Options Menu

Options

Verbose Messages	⌘M
Suspend Logging	⌘L
Hide Window in Background	⌘H
Refuse New Connections	⌘R
Ignore Status Updates	
Ignore Log Updates	
Quit WebSTAR	

Figure 4.11

The Options Menu

The Options menu (Fig. 4.11) contains the same information as the Options menu on the server itself, but it also adds three new items, *all of which affect only the server that is being monitored in the frontmost window.* There is no way to change more than one server at a time (unless you write your own administration application).

The first four items are identical in name and action to the first four items under the Options menu on the WebSTAR server. The remaining three items are useful only for remote administration.

Ignore Status Updates

This tells WebSTAR Admin to display only the log information and to ignore the connection statistics (status updates).

Ignore Log Updates

This tells WebSTAR Admin to display only the connection statistics and to ignore all of the log updates. This is useful if you want to reduce the window to minimal size and just make sure that the server is still running.

Quit WebSTAR

This allows you to quit the server remotely. This will also close the connection immediately, since there will no longer be a server to monitor. As on the server, this command does not wait for all current connections to be processed, so you may want to turn **Refuse New Connections** on before quitting.

Configure Menu

Figure 4.12
The Configure Menu

| Configure |
| Suffix Mapping... |
| Actions... |
| Realms... |
| Allow/Deny... |
| Misc. Settings... |
| Log Format... |
| Add Password... |

This menu (Fig. 4.12) provides interfaces for viewing, editing, and adding information for the server. *All of these items affect only the server that is being monitored in the frontmost window.* Each menu item will bring up a window for editing the type of data specified.

Suffix Mapping...

This item opens a window (Fig. 4.13) that allows you to change the suffix mapping, file type, and file creator information that is used by WebSTAR to decide what MIME type to use for a file it is serving. This is also where the Action is set for a file type.

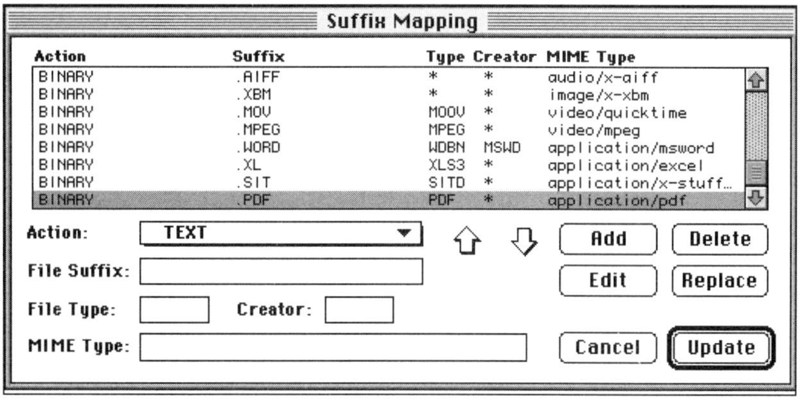

Figure 4.13
The Suffix Mapping
Window

The upper portion of the window displays the current mapping information (see Chapter 2 for information about how WebSTAR uses this information). Each mapping has five pieces of information:

- **Action**　This is a classification of the file used by WebSTAR to decide how to process the file (see **Actions...** following).

- **Suffix**　This is a filename suffix that will map to the MIME type listed. The suffix is used to determine the MIME type only if the type and creator cannot be matched. If the filename has more than one period in it, only the text following the last period will be considered to be the suffix. The suffix is case insensitive, so **.gif** is the same as **.GIF**.

- **Type**　This is the four-character filetype that maps to the MIME type listed. If a * character is entered, any filetype will match.

- **Creator**　This is the four-character file creator that maps to the MIME type listed. If a * character is entered, any file creator will match.

- **MIME Type**　This is the MIME type that should be used for a file matching the previous settings.

The lower portion of the window is used to add to, delete from, or edit the settings. To *add a new setting,* fill in the text areas at the bottom of the window with the information you want to add. Then click on the **Add** button to have it added to a new entry in the list.

To *edit a setting,* highlight the line representing the setting and click on the **Edit** button. This places the information from that line in the text areas at the bottom of the window. Make the changes that you want to that area. Then click on the **Replace** button to add the changed information to the list.

To *delete a setting,* simply highlight the setting (by clicking on it once). Then click on the **Delete** button.

The arrows are used to move lines higher or lower in the listing. WebSTAR does matching by checking from the first (top) item in the list to the last and using the first match it finds. Moving a line up higher in the list will make sure that it is encountered before the others below it.

None of the changes that you make will be sent to the server until you click on the **Update** button. This button will send the changes to the server and then close the window. If you do not wish to keep the changes, click on the **Cancel** button, and nothing will be sent to the server.

Actions...

This menu item brings up a window (Fig. 4.14) that allows you to define new Actions and the CGI application that will process files of that Action type.

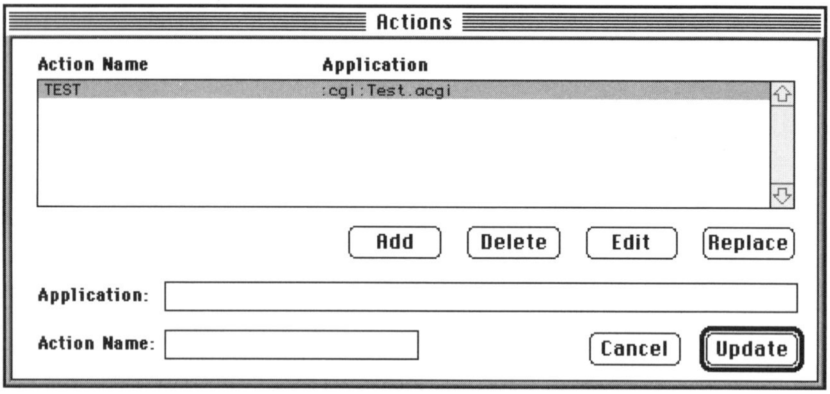

Figure 4.14
The Actions Window

The interface is very similar to that for all of the other windows. Current Action mappings are listed in the top portion of the window. To add a new Action to the list, fill in the two text fields at the bottom of the window (**Application** and **Action Name**), then click on the **Add** button. To delete an item from the list, highlight the item (by clicking on it once), then click on the **Delete** button. To edit an existing entry in the list, highlight the entry, then click on the **Edit** button. This will place the information for that entry into the two text fields at the bottom of the window. Make the changes you want to these two fields, then click on the **Replace** button to update the entry. If you click on a different line in the list and then click on the **Replace** button, the different line will be the one updated, so be certain the correct line is highlighted before updating an entry.

The two arrows are used to move lines higher and lower in the list. To move an entry, first highlight the entry you want to move, then click on the up arrow to move it higher or the down arrow to move it lower. The Actions are checked in order from the top of the list, so those occurring higher in the list are not only found more quickly but also take precedence over later Action mappings.

As with the other windows, the information is not sent to the server until you click on the **Update** button, at which point the window will also be closed. If you click on the **Cancel** button, no changes will be sent to the server (and the window will be closed).

Realms...

This menu item opens a window (Fig. 4.15) that allows you to define text strings and a name for the realm that the string represents.

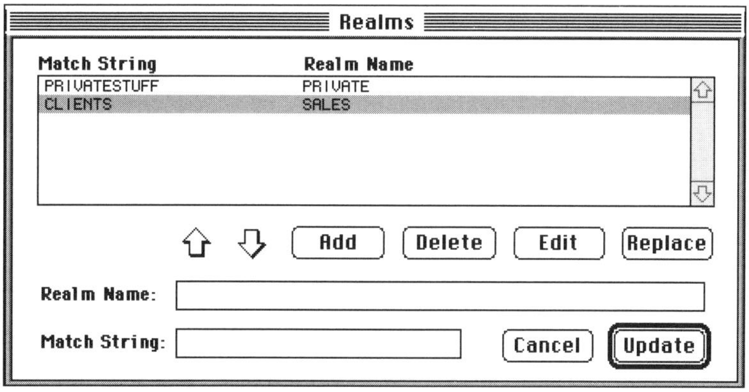

Figure 4.15
The Realms Window

Again, we see the same interface for managing the Realms information as we saw in the previous two windows. Current Realms mappings are listed in the top portion of the window. To add a new Realm to the list, fill in the two text fields at the bottom of the window (**Realm Name** and **Match String**) then click on the **Add** button. To delete a Realm from the list, highlight the line (by clicking on it once), then click on the **Delete** button. To edit an existing entry in the list, highlight the entry, then click on the **Edit** button. This will place the information for that entry into the two text fields at the bottom of the window. Make the changes you want to these two fields, then click on the **Replace** button to update the entry. If you click on a different line in the list and then click on the **Replace** button, the different line will be the one updated, so be certain that the correct line is highlighted before updating an entry.

The two arrows are used to move lines higher and lower in the list. To move an entry, first highlight the entry you want moved, then click on the up arrow to move it higher or the down arrow to move it lower. The Realms are checked in order from the top of the list, so those occurring higher in the list are not only found more quickly but also take precedence over later Realm mappings.

As with the other windows, the information is not sent to the server until you click on the **Update** button, at which point the window will also be closed. If you click on the **Cancel** button, no changes will be sent to the server (and the window will be closed).

Allow/Deny...

This menu item displays a window (Fig. 4.16) that allows you to edit the settings for sites that are allowed or denied access to your site. These restrictions are absolute and cannot be bypassed with a user name or password.

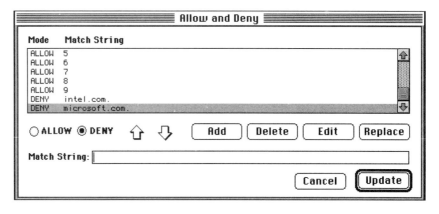

Figure 4.16

The Allow and Deny Window

Current restrictions are listed in the top portion of the window. To add a new restriction to the list, fill in the text field at the bottom of the window (**Match String**), select either the **ALLOW** or **DENY** radio button, then click on the **Add** button. To delete a restriction from the list, highlight the line (by clicking on it once), then click on the **Delete** button. To edit an existing entry in the list, highlight the entry, then click on the **Edit** button. This will place the information for that entry into the text field at the bottom of the window. Make the changes you want to the data in this field, then click on the **Replace** button to update the entry. If you click on a different line in the list and then click on the **Replace** button, the different line will be the one updated, so be certain that the correct line is highlighted before updating an entry.

The two arrows are used to move lines higher and lower in the list. To move an entry, first highlight the entry you want moved, then click on the up arrow to move it higher or the down arrow to move it lower. The restrictions should proceed from least restrictive (top) to most restrictive (bottom). This allows you to isolate single sites in a network or single networks in larger networks by first specifying a general Deny then a more specific Allow. This is covered in more detail later.

As with the other windows, the information is not sent to the server until you click on the **Update** button, at which point the window will also be closed. If you click on the **Cancel** button, no changes will be sent to the server (and the window will be closed).

Misc. Settings...

This menu item opens a window (Fig. 4.17) that allows you to edit a variety of settings on the server. When the window first opens, it will display the current settings for the server you are editing.

Here is a short description of the meaning of each item in the window. Each item is covered in greater depth in other portions of this book.

- **Timeout: 5–120**   This is the number of seconds WebSTAR will wait before declaring a connection to have "timed out." It is also the number of seconds WebSTAR will wait for a reply from a CGI application.

```
╔═══════════════════════ Miscellaneous Settings ═══════════════════════╗

    Timeout:    [60 ]   Seconds      Index:        [default.html        ]
    Max Users:  [12 ]   Users        Error:        [:error.html         ]
    Max Listens: [12 ]               No Access:    [:noaccess.html      ]
    Port:       [80 ]                Log File:     [:WebSTAR.log         ]
    Pig Delay:  [30 ]   1/60 Sec.    PreProcess:   [:secure.acgi         ]
    Buffer Size: [3500]  Bytes       PostProcess:  [:pageLogger.acgi     ]
    ☒ Use DNS                        Default MIME: [text/html            ]

                                            ( Cancel )  ( Update )
```

Figure 4.17

The Miscellaneous
Settings Window

- **Max Users: 4–1000**   This is the maximum number of connections that will be allowed at any one time. Although 1000 is the technical limit, if you are using MacTCP, you are limited to 64 maximum connections.

- **Max Listens: 4–1000**   This is the maximum number of processes to spawn to listen for new connections. If you are running WebSTAR 1.2 or later, this number should be equal to Max Users. If you are running older versions of WebSTAR without the Thread Manager, this number should be in the range of 3–6 (and you should get the Thread Manager!).

- **Port: 80, >1024**   This is the port number that the server will be listening on. Port 80 is the standard for HTTP servers, but you can also use any number higher than 1024 (all lower numbers are reserved for well-known services).

- **Pig Delay: 0–60**   If you are using the Thread Manager (required for WebSTAR 1.2 and later), this setting is not used at all. If you are running unthreaded, this number determines how many ticks WebSTAR will use for each connection before allowing other processing. Higher settings give WebSTAR more processing time at the expense of other applications on the server.

- **Buffer Size: 256–10240**   This is the number of bytes that WebSTAR will hand out in each packet. In general, larger values should result in faster performance, but actual performance will depend on your site. The most network-friendly setting is 4096

(4K). If you have it set higher than 8K, it may cause problems for some Windows machines. Some TCP/IP stacks for Windows are unable to handle packets larger than 8K. If you have it set to less than 2K, though, the overhead of processing each packet will become a measurable part of your processing time.

- **Use DNS: False**   This checkbox tells the server whether to resolve IP addresses to DNS names when logging connection information. If DNS is on (box is checked), the server will run a little more slowly while it converts the IP address of every connection it receives to a DNS name.

- **Index: Default.html**   This is the name of the file that will be considered the Index file for each folder. *Only a file name is specified, not a path.* When an incomplete URL is received (one that specifies only a directory, not a file), WebSTAR checks the folder specified. If a file with this name is in that folder, that file will be returned as the default for that folder. Otherwise, the Error file will be returned.

- **Error: :Error.html**   This is the name of the file that will be returned when a `401 File Not Found` error occurs. If a URL is received for a file that does not exist, this file is returned instead. There is only one Error file for an entire site, so the path to the file relative to WebSTAR is required as well. If the file is in the same folder as WebSTAR, use a colon before the name to indicate that.

- **No Access: :NoAccess.html**   This is the name of the file that will be returned when a site is refused access because of Allow/Deny settings (`403 Refused By Rule`). There is only one No Access file for an entire site, so the path to the file relative to WebSTAR is required as well. If the file is in the same folder as WebSTAR, use a colon before the name to indicate that.

- **Log File: :WebSTAR.log**   This is the name of the file that will contain the connection information on disk. There is only one active log file for a site, so the path to the file relative to WebSTAR is required as well. If the file is in the same folder as WebSTAR, use a colon before the name to indicate that. When logging to disk is on, WebSTAR has this file open, so it may not be moved or copied. If you change the name of the log file to use, the change will not take effect until either logging to disk is turned off (then on again) or the server is relaunched.

- **PreProcess: [none]**   This is the application that will be used to preprocess files. Only one preprocessing application is allowed per site at this time, so you need to specify the path to the file relative to WebSTAR. If the file is in the same folder as WebSTAR, use a colon before the name to indicate that.

- **PostProcess: [none]**   This is the application that will be used to postprocess files. Only one postprocessing application is allowed per site at this time, so you need to specify the path to the file relative to WebSTAR. If the file is in the same folder as WebSTAR, use a colon before the name to indicate that.

- **Default MIME: text/html**   This sets what MIME type will be used if a file does not match any of the settings in the Suffix Mapping window. The default is to assume that the file is an HTML file.

- **Update Button**   As with the other windows, none of the changes you make will be sent to the server until you click in the **Update** button. This will also close the window.

- **Cancel Button**   This will cause the window to be closed without sending any changes to the server.

Log Format...

This menu item presents a window (Fig. 4.18) that allows you to set what information will be logged to disk and the order of each item in each log entry. The default setting for WebSTAR is identical to the standard NCSA server format.

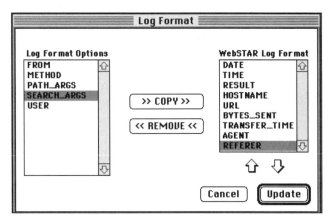

Figure 4.18
The Log Format Window

The scrolling list on the left displays the loggable items that are not currently being logged. The scrolling list on the right shows those items that are currently being logged. To add items to the current list, highlight the item on the left that you want to add, then click on the **Copy** button. To remove an item from the current list, highlight the item in the current list, then click on the **Remove** button (this places it back in the left-hand list). The chevrons next to each button indicate in which direction the data will be transferred when you click on that button.

The up and down arrows are used to determine what order will be used to log the items. The top item in the list will occur first in each line of the log, then the next item in the list, and so on to the bottom of the list. To move an item up or down in the list, highlight the item that you want to move, then click on the up arrow to move it higher or the down arrow to move it lower in the list.

Any changes you make will not be sent to the server until you click on the **Update** button, which will also close the window. If you use automated software to produce log reports, you may want to switch to a new log file before changing the format so you don't have a change in format occurring in the middle of your log file. To close the window without saving any changes made, click on the **Cancel** button.

Add Password...

This menu item opens a window (Fig. 4.19) that allows you to add user names and passwords to the server and assign them to a Realm. At least one Realm must be created before you can create any passwords, since they must be assigned to a Realm for use.

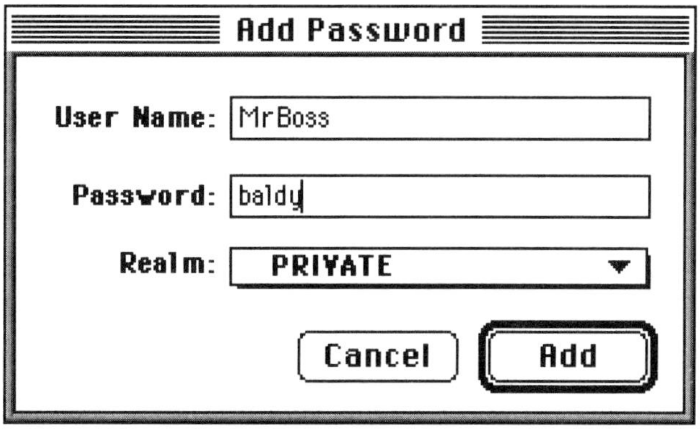

Figure 4.19
The Add Password
Window

To add a new entry, first fill in the two fields (**User Name** and **Password**) and select a Realm from the pop-up menu. When the information is entered, click on the **Add** button to add it to the server's internal database. Remember that the password will be added only to the server that is currently being monitored in the frontmost window. There is no facility for adding passwords to several servers at one time. If you want to close the window without entering any information, click on the **Cancel** button.

When you set up your password system, remember that the user name and password are not allowed to contain any spaces.

5

Installation

Hardware and Software Requirements

WebSTAR has very few requirements: It requires System 7.1 or later and will run on any Macintosh that can run System 7.1. WebSTAR 1.2 also requires the Thread Manager, which can be added to System 7.1.x or is part of System 7.5 and later. The computer also has to have some sort of full-time network connection to the Internet or be configured properly to run independently on a simulated network (see "Running Without an Internet Connection" in Chapter 8). WebSTAR needs a minimum of 1.5MB RAM to run (in addition to system software requirements), although more memory will allow more simultaneous connections to be processed, up to a maximum of 6MB RAM for 48 connections. WebSTAR also needs at least 1MB of hard disk space, plus whatever space is needed for the files that it will be serving and space for a log file if you enable logging (it is on by default).

The minimum requirements will leave you with a server that can handle several thousand connections per day with acceptable speed. If you need additional performance, you need to weigh the various factors in purchasing or upgrading a computer to be your server (discussed later).

Selecting a Proper Server

In general, my advice is to buy the faster, biggest server you can afford, so that you always have room to grow. If you are trying to balance a tight budget, though, and need to find the minimal server that will meet your needs, this section may help. You will also want to read "Improving Single Server Performance" in Chapter 8, which will discuss what factors in software and hardware purchases most affect the speed of your server.

The first thing to do when trying to decide what server hardware to purchase is to decide what software you will be running on the server. If you will be running only WebSTAR, the decision is slightly different than if you will also be running a database, several CGI applications, a mail or list server, or any other server software, such as AppleShare or a DNS server. If you plan to have the machine as an AppleShare server as well as a Web server, you need to decide which is more important and to purchase accordingly. Similarly, if you plan to offer a database via the Web or if your WebSTAR server will also be a central database server for your company, you need to take that into account in selecting a computer.

Now let's look at the various hardware decisions you need to make.

CPU

Selecting a CPU may be the toughest part of the decision. Faster CPUs are generally more expensive, and it is not clear that they will always produce the fastest server. The problem is with the fact that the Macintosh operating system is still in transition from supporting the 680x0 line (commonly call 68K Macs) to supporting the Power-PC line (or PPC Macs). WebSTAR is a fat binary application, meaning that it has code for both 68K and Power Macintosh computers. Unfortunately, a lot of what WebSTAR does depends on the operating system, which runs mostly in emulation on Power Macintoshes. If you are using MacTCP, the network interface is also running in emulation. The result is that a fast 68040 computer may actually outperform some PowerPC computers when the majority of processing involves the file system or network interface. Some software (such as the Butler SQL database) takes advantage of this by supporting both, so that calls to the file system or network use 68K code, but all else uses PowerPC code. Still, there is quite a bit of overlap in performance between the 68040 and PPC 601 line.

I still recommend purchasing a PowerPC server if you can afford it, though. The reason is that the 68K Mac line has ended and will not see much more improvement in processing speed, whereas the PPC line is just getting going. OpenTransport is the successor to the MacTCP and will provide PPC-native interfaces for networking, which should improve speed quite a bit once the server software is converted to use it (and the PPC-native Ethernet drivers are available). Copland is the fully PPC-native release of the operating system that is expected in late 1996 or 1997. Even before that, various portions of the file system will start being converted to PPC-native code. Each change will increase the speed of your WebSTAR server and of any other PPC-native software you are using that makes file system calls. Therefore, your PowerPC server should have a longer useful lifespan than a 68K server.

Another consideration is your CGI applications and external applications. If you plan to run a CGI application for map processing, form processing, or an external database, the Power Macintosh is again a better choice. Almost all commercial and shareware CGI applications are available as fat binary applications, so they will perform much better on the Power Macintosh and return data much more quickly. In addition, if you will be mounting Netware or AppleShare volumes on the server, the Power Macintosh will provide a tremendous speed boost in accessing files on those volumes. And if you plan for your server to also be an AppleShare server, you need a PowerPC to run AppleShare 4.1 or later (which is much faster than earlier versions).

Disk Size and Speed

Disk access speed and data transfer rates aren't much of a factor in your WebSTAR server. I'll cover this in more depth later, but in general your network cannot pump out data as quickly as you can get it from even a slow disk. Thus that the main concern is buying a disk large enough to hold all of your data. I recommend being very generous here. If you think that your site will take 100MB, buy a 500MB or larger disk, as Web sites tend to keep growing until they run out of disk space. New features are always appearing, and suddenly you find that you're trying to squeeze a few large animation files onto your server disk. You will also begin to accumulate additional software to use with your server, and that will take quite a bit of space. Considering how quickly disks are dropping in price, there is little reason not to get at least a 1GB disk and set your storage worries aside for a while.

Another thing to keep in mind is the need to back up your server disk. Nothing is quite as tragic as a disk crash on a site that has never been backed up. I hate to see a Webmaster cry. Therefore it is a good idea to consider purchasing a second disk for data mirroring (using RAID software—it's pretty cheap now) or adding a tape or optical disk backup to your site. You will also need some good software for archiving the site (Retrospect by Dantz Development Corporation is my preference). Dragging files by hand is too cumbersome; without an automated backup, you are likely to forget to do it, and that, of course, is when your system will choose to crash.

When purchasing a disk, keep in mind that the Macintosh file system places some hard limits on disk formatting and space. Every disk can hold a maximum of about 65,000 files. Whether you have an old 80MB Seagate drive or a new 2GB Micropolis, they both are limited to the same total number of files. What happens is that the space allocated for files is broken up into larger chunks on a larger disk. On an 80MB disk, each file takes up about 2K of disk space. On a 2GB disk, each file takes up closer to 30K. Therefore, if you plan to serve thousands of small files (and most text files are small), you are better off getting several smaller disks or partitioning a larger disk so it appears to be several smaller disks.

> **Note:** In order to use multiple disks, you need to make aliases to the disks and add the aliases to the WebSTAR folder. *You cannot do this with MacHTTP 2.2.* MacHTTP is unable to access aliases to other disks and folders, so all of the files need to reside on the same physical disk and partition, or you have to have a separate alias to each file on the remote disk.

Memory (RAM)

WebSTAR uses very little memory, especially in comparison to UNIX servers (some recommend as much as 128MB RAM!). By default, it provides up to 10 simultaneous connections, which requires about 1.4MB of memory. To have 25 simultaneous connections, you need to give it about 3MB of memory and for 48 connections (the maximum under MacTCP) you would need only 6MB at the most. The rule of thumb for determining how much memory is needed is

```
n * 100/K + 750/K
```

where n is the number of concurrent connections the server will support (MaxUsers).

You will need additional memory for the system software, of course, and also for any CGI applications or other software that will run on the server. It is a good idea to avoid letting the server get down to less than 500K of free memory to avoid possible low-memory problems with running CGI applications. If you are planning to run only WebSTAR and possibly one or two small CGIs, you can get by with only 8MB RAM (with a minimal system installation—no speech recognition). Even if you have a lot of software installed, 24MB is probably the maximum you would need. If you need more than that, you probably need another server to run some of the software, anyway.

RAM Disks

There have been suggestions that working off of a RAM disk (a disk image that is kept entirely in RAM) would speed up a server. This doesn't seem very likely, for the same reasons as stated for high-speed disks. There are a couple of areas where a RAM disk might help, though. One would be with CGI applications that read information from disk, such as something that searches files or a database or something that rewrites files before handing them to WebSTAR, such as doing inline includes. Another would be with a very large external application that would run faster if it were all loaded in RAM. Keep in mind, though, that any changes made to data on a RAM disk will be lost in the event of a server crash. This solution is really useful only for serving static data.

Other Hardware

No other hardware is really required for a WebSTAR server, although a CD-ROM is a good idea, since much of the software is distributed that way now. It is not important what kind of monitor or graphics card you have on the server, since that has no effect on performance. In fact, since you can run and modify the server entirely from a remote server, you might want to consider running it without a monitor at all. If you decide to go with that option, there are a couple of things to keep in mind. First, some Macintoshes need to have a monitor attached, or they decide that they have only a 9 inch screen. If you are connecting to the server using Timbuktu (by Farallon Computing), that can be an annoyance. You can get around that by keeping a monitor cable connected to the monitor port. The cable will trick machines that have internal graphics display support into thinking that a 14 inch monitor is attached. Second, although WebSTAR can be run and modified remotely, you will still want to be able to launch or quit other applications and control them as well. For this, the best solution is Timbuktu Pro. Timbuktu brings up an exact copy of the screen and menu bar from your server on a remote machine, and you can run your server as if you were connected to it. The Pro version works over both TCP/IP networks and AppleTalk. The connection is a little bit jerky, especially over modem connections, but it is very workable for most situations.

Sharing Connections

If you are planning to run other Internet services besides WebSTAR on your server, you need to consider how this will affect the available pool of TCP/IP connections. MacTCP limits a computer to a maximum of 64 simultaneous TCP/IP connections. If you plan to have WebSTAR using 40 connections maximum and then want to have FTPd running also with 30 connections, you will run out of connections. Since WebSTAR grabs all of its possible connections when it launches (part of the way it is threaded internally), only 24 connections will be left after it launches.

OpenTransport does not have any limits on the number of connections, so this should only be a temporary problem. It may be a while, though, before OpenTransport is very stable with all network applications, because many of them are written to specifically take advantage of some special "features" of MacTCP. If you are curious about how your TCP/IP connections are being used on the server, get a copy of MacTCP Monitor by Chris Johnson (**http://gagravarr.cc.utexas.edu/**). It will give you a graphical display of what is happening with the connections.

Selecting a Network Connection

You must have a TCP/IP network connection of some sort before you can even launch WebSTAR, even if it is just a loopback connection to your own machine. Unfortunately there just isn't room here to cover a topic like deciding on a network connection. There are dozens of options in selecting a network connection, and the proper choice depends on available funds, where you live, what other services you want to have, and much more. There are a couple of books on this topic already, but if you don't have a connection and want one, the best thing to do is find some people in your local area who recently got connections and ask them about it. You will also find useful information in your local newspaper on occasion or a local computer newspaper/magazine/journal, if one exists.

Having said that, I will tell you that the network connection may have more effect on the speed of your server than anything else, because the network connection determines how quickly you can dump data out to clients. If you are on a 56 Kbps connection, your maximum is 7KB per second of data. This is actually plenty for many WWW sites, especially if you avoid large binary files. It will not be enough, though, if you decide to offer people QuickTime videos. A 630KB QuickTime file (not large for QuickTime) would take at least a minute and a half to download, during which time nobody else is able to use the connection. In practice, that user would be sharing the network with other users and resources, so the download could easily tie up the connection for 10 minutes or more.

One last thing to keep in mind: Many people misunderstand how network bandwidth (or speed) affects the ability of others to connect to their server. Whether you have a 28.8K modem connection or a T3 line, you can still have hundreds of people connecting to your servers. The best analogy is to think of the users as if they are dividing the network into fairly equally sized chunks. As you get more users, they aren't prevented from connecting, but their share of the network bandwidth gets so small that it takes forever to get any data. This means that if you have a slower network connection, you might want to limit the number of simultaneous connections so that the people who do connect are able to get good response speed. A faster network connection means that you can provide quality connections to a larger number of users simultaneously.

Installing from the CD-ROM

WebSTAR cannot be run directly from the CD-ROM, because it will be unable to modify its Preferences file or write to a log file. It must be copied to a writable disk before running it. Luckily installation of WebSTAR is incredibly easy:

1. Open the CD-ROM disk and locate the folder called WebSTAR Install.

2. Double-click on the Installer application and click on the **Install** button.

WebSTAR is now installed. There is nothing to drag into the System Folder and no special configuration files to edit. Everything that WebSTAR needs (and that's not much) is in its folder. If you later want to move the folder, simply quit WebSTAR, move the folder, and relaunch. WebSTAR doesn't care where its folder is on the server.

Required Files

If you object to easy installations and for some reason want to do your own installation, there are only six files that WebSTAR needs in its folder:

- **WebSTAR**   Things don't work too well without the server.

- **WebSTAR Admin**   This is required to change many of the server settings.

- **WebSTAR Settings**   This is the Preferences file for WebSTAR. It stays in the same folder with WebSTAR, so you can run multiple WebSTAR servers if you want.

- **Default.html**   This is the page that will be returned as the home page for the site. You can change this by using WebSTAR Admin (instructions follow).

- **Error.html**   This file is returned to the client when an error occurs. You can change the file or set a new name to use through WebSTAR Admin (see following).

- **NoAccess.html**   This file is returned when access to the site is refused because of a client's IP address or DNS name. This can be modified or set to a new name using WebSTAR Admin (see following).

Everything else in the folder is provided as examples of what you can do with your Web site.

The Root Folder

WebSTAR treats whatever folder it is in as the *root folder* for your site. It doesn't matter what the name of that folder is, so if you don't like WebSTAR, you can change it to anything you like. It won't matter, because WebSTAR never looks at that name, only at things within the folder. I will be using the term *root folder* throughout this book, and in all cases I mean the folder that WebSTAR is running in.

Program Linking

In order to use the WebSTAR Admin application to monitor or change WebSTAR, you must have Program Linking enabled for WebSTAR. Program Linking is a feature of System 7 that allows applications on other computers to control an application on your computer. There are three different places on your computer that you need to set to enable Program Linking.

- Enable Program Linking for your entire system (Fig. 5.1). Open the Sharing Setup control panel and click on the button labeled **Start** in the Program Linking portion of the dialog box (at the bottom).

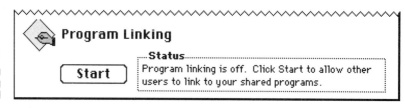

Figure 5.1

The Program Linking
Portion of the Sharing
Setup Control Panel

• Enable Program Linking for WebSTAR (Fig. 5.2). You can control program linking separately for each application on your computer. By default, WebSTAR ships with Program Linking enabled. To check this, highlight the WebSTAR icon (click once on it) and select the menu item **Sharing...** from the File menu. If the checkbox labeled **Allow remote program linking** is not checked, check it now.

Figure 5.2

The Sharing Menu Item
Window for WebSTAR

• Allow Program Linking for a specific user (Fig. 5.3). You need to use the Users and Groups control panel to create a user who has permission to link to applications on your computer. The process for creating new users is detailed in the *User's Guide* that came with your Macintosh computer. Double click on the icon for the user that you want to give access to, and a dialog box will appear. Check the box labeled **Allow user to link to programs on this Macintosh** in the Program Linking area of the dialog box and close the dialog, saving all changes.

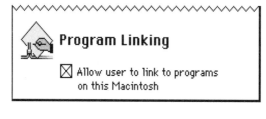

Figure 5.3

The Program Linking
Portion of the User Dialog

This control over who may and may not connect to your server is part of the security for your server, so be certain that it is working properly before you release your system to the public. If it is working properly, only the user name and password for the user that you selected should be able to make a link to your WebSTAR server.

Program Linking is an AppleTalk-only method of controlling a server. There is no access to this through TCP/IP, so your server's Internet security is not compromised at all.

Launching the Server

WebSTAR comes preconfigured for operation on most systems. If you do not have enough memory available for the default configuration, it will let you know how much more memory is needed and then gracefully quit. You can reduce the memory requirements a bit by reducing the maximum number of connections allowed, but a base of about 320K is required for WebSTAR to operate at all.

When you first launch WebSTAR, it will ask you to enter a key code (see Fig. 5.4). Instructions for obtaining a trial key from StarNine are located in the Web-STAR folder on the companion CD-ROM, as well as instructions for purchasing the full server package. WebSTAR will not launch until you type a key code into the key dialog. Once the key is entered, WebSTAR will check to see whether it has enough memory to run with the configurations that have been selected. If not, it will let you know how much more memory it needs and quit (so you can increase the memory partition).

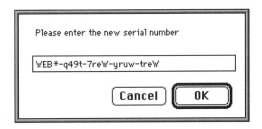

Figure 5.4
The Key Request Dialog
During Initial Startup

When you first launch WebSTAR, it is initially configured for public access. Only the files that are in the root folder will be available to the public, though. If you plan to create any restricted areas on your site or to restrict which sites may access yours, it is best to experiment with that, using the sample files that are supplied, before moving data files onto the site.

Installing Site Files

Now you are ready to add your own files to your site. Any files copied into the root folder or into any subfolder of that folder are accessible from your Web server. You can make files on other disks available by making an alias of the disk and placing that alias in the root folder. You can do the same thing with folders on other disks, by placing aliases of the folders somewhere on your WebSTAR site. If the alias points to a remote volume or a disk on a remote volume, you *must* have that volume mounted before WebSTAR can handle requests for its files. WebSTAR will not automatically mount the disk, because of restrictions in the way the Macintosh OS handles mounting disks.

As mentioned, the file **Default.html** is the default home page for your site. That means that requests to **http://your.server.name/** will return this file. If you already have a home page designed, you can test it by replacing the **Default.html** file with it:

1. Rename **Default.html** to **OldDefault.html**.

2. Rename your home page file to **Default.html**.

Your home page is now the default home page. Later on we will get into how to designate a different name in WebSTAR for your home page file.

Testing the Site

Before you open your site to the public, you will want to have some testing done to find any dead links or other problems that might be embarrassing. There are several ways to do this. For checking links, it is useful to have some software to help. An AppleScript app, called "WebSTAR Link Checker," by David Habermann, can help with this. Commercial products are also available for this purpose. You can find more (and up-to-date) information on these on my Web site at `http://www.comvista.com/net/web/HTMLhelp.html`

For other problems on your site, the only real solution is to have one or more people check your site out. You can ask a pool of friends or other knowledgeable users to test the site for a short period of time. Posting requests like this to a general mailing list or newsgroup may not be a good solution, though. As more and more sites are added to the Web, and with increasing frequency, people get tired of checking out every new site. It is likely that the people checking your site will not be those with the most experience, and the feedback may therefore not be of much value. For a commercial site, the best option may be to hire a consultant to review the site and make a report of any problems found or suggestions for key improvements. Any good consultant will not only report the problems but also be available to help with fixing them, which can be very useful if this is your first site.

Announcing a New Site

Once you have your site working well, you will probably want to announce it to the rest of the Internet. The best place to begin is Brad Schrick's listing of Macintosh WWW servers. The form for adding yourself to this listing is at

`http://brad.net/webstar/mac_server_reg_form.html`

Brad offers listings of registered sites by geographical location, network speed, and CPU type, so it is easy to compare your site's performance with equivalent sites.

The next place to register is the "Submit It!" page at

`http://www.cen.uiuc.edu/~banister/submit-it/`

This page offers a one-stop interface for adding your site to any or all of the most popular search sites, including Lycos, Webcrawler, Yahoo, EINet Galaxy, JumpStation, and more.

There are some key sites that it doesn't interface with, though. The W3 organization has taken over from CERN for the registration of new WWW sites. This might be the closest thing to an official registration available on the Web, located at:

```
http://cuiwww.unige.ch/meta-index.html
```

NCSA's "What's New" page is still very popular for listing new sites. The page, cosponsored by GNN, is at

```
http://www.ncsa.uiuc.edu/SDG/Software/Mosaic/Docs/
whats-new.html
```

Finally, another popular site for searching is the AliWeb resource discovery system, which is made available at Nexor:

```
http://web.nexor.co.uk/public/aliweb/aliwebhtml
```

Once you have registered with the major sites, it might be time to send a notice to key newsgroups. If your site is directly pertinent to a specific newsgroup (such as a site containing the FAQ for a newsgroup), you should post a notice about it to the newsgroup. In general, it does not bother people to see announcements if the content is related to the group, although it is nice to set the subject to something like "NEW WEB SITE: xxxxxx," so people can avoid the message if they wish. The main newsgroup for announcing new sites is:

```
comp.infosystems.www.announce
```

There might also be some mailing lists that you should announce to. In general, though, people prefer not to get these announcements in mailing lists, because there is no choice about getting the mail message. Be very sure that your announcement is valuable to most of the readers of the list *and* pertinent to the topic of the list. It doesn't matter how important your site is: If it doesn't pertain to the list, you will justifiably be flamed.

Another good way to announce your site is to ask related sites to add a link to yours. If your site is about a programming language and you know of some good programming language sites (other than your competitors), you may want to write to the Webmasters of those sites, requesting that they add a link to your site. Remember, though, that it is entirely optional whether they want to add the link or not. There are no laws about this sort of thing.

Finally, you will be announcing your site in an off-hand way by not refusing to allow robots to visit the site. Several smaller robots do not keep local databases, and new robots keep appearing every month. Allowing them to visit your site adds your site to their reports. There are very few badly behaved robots left, so it generally doesn't add much of a load to your site to allow them in.

6

Server Configuration

These options control the operation of all aspects of the server. Some of them can be changed directly from within the WebSTAR server. For most of them, though, you have to use the WebSTAR Admin application, a custom AppleScript, or some other method of interfacing with the Apple events that control these options.

Special Files

The files listed here are special in that they should never be requested directly by a user. They are returned in response to special situations. In each case a file name is specified for the file to be returned in response. There is no limit on what the file name can be, as long as it is a legal Macintosh file name. These settings can be changed only from the WebSTAR Admin application or via an Apple event to the WebSTAR server.

Error

Default: :Error.html

This designates a file to be returned when a URL is received that specifies a nonexistent file. The HTTP error code for this situation is **404 File Not Found** and occurs when a URL is received that specifies a file that cannot be found on the server. In your server log the connections register as an ERR! Only one Error file is designated for an entire site. The file can be placed anywhere on the site, but there is little reason not to have it in the root folder. The full path to the file, relative to WebSTAR, must be provided. Colons are used to delimit folders, and there must be a leading colon to indicate the root folder.

In most cases the Error file will be an HTML document. A good recommendation for a beginning site is to have the file list the most commonly accessed pages for the site, since it is likely the user was trying to reach one of these. It is also useful to include contact information (a Webmaster page or e-mail address) so the user knows who to report the error to.

It is also possible for the Error file to be a CGI application. This very powerful option allows you to create an Error file that tries to correct the error or at least provide more useful error information. Since the CGI application receives the path and file name portion of the URL request from the server, you can use this to test for common mistakes, such as a file that has been moved or renamed, a misspelled folder name, or the wrong file extension (`.htm` instead of `.html`).

One thing to consider when you are handling errors in this way is your two options. You can use URL redirection to just send the client to the correct file. That is easy and produces the fastest response for the user. It doesn't let the user know that an error occurred, though, which means that the same mistake will probably be made again. Therefore it might be a good idea to instead return an HTML document that tells the user that an error occurred and provides a link to the correct file. Since it is likely that the user was following a link from another site, it is also a good idea to ask the user to inform that site of the error so the link can be corrected.

NoAccess

Default: `:NoAccess.html`

This setting designates a file to be returned when a client is refused because of the Allow/Deny settings (because of the IP address or DNS name). The HTTP error code for this situation is **403 Forbidden**. In your server log the connections register as a PRIV. Only one NoAccess file is designated for an entire site. The file can be placed anywhere on the site, but there is little reason not to have it in the root folder. The full path to the file, relative to WebSTAR, must be provided. Colons are used to delimit folders, and there must be a leading colon to indicate the root folder.

In most cases the NoAccess file will be an HTML document. It is nice to give the user some indication of why access was refused and a contact e-mail address, in case there has been an error. It is also possible for the NoAccess file to be a CGI application. This could be useful if you want to return specific warnings or explanations to different clients. It might also be useful if you run several sites and want to redirect the client to a different site for access.

Index

Default: `Default.html`

This setting specifies a file that WebSTAR will look for in a folder when only a folder, not a file, is specified in a URL. With a URL for an FTP server, a trailing slash mark (**/**) indicates a request for a directory listing. Many UNIX servers have added this functionality to their HTTP servers as well, but this can be a big security problem. If you are trying to protect some files, it is not a good idea to let other users know that they are there at all. WebSTAR, therefore, lets you decide whether you want to return information from these requests and what information you want to return.

When a URL is received that ends in a slash with no file name specified, WebSTAR looks in the directory indicated by the URL to see whether there is a file there with the name specified in the Index setting. If such a file is found, it is returned to the user. If no such file is found, an error is generated and the Error file is returned instead.

The Index file is a little bit different from the other two special files. Instead of specifying a single Index file for an entire site, you are specifying only the name that an Index file will have if it exists in a folder. There will be a separate Index file in each directory that you want to have respond in this way. Therefore *there is no colon or path in the Index setting.* Only a file name is entered.

File aliases can be very useful as Index files. If you have a file in the folder that can be the entry point for the folder, you can make an alias of that file and give the alias the name of the Index file. That saves you the trouble of renaming key files. The Index file can be any kind of file, including a CGI application. There are several useful things that could be done with a CGI, such as registering information about users when they enter a folder or creating client-sensitive folder listings on the fly. If you are returning the same folder listing to everyone, you might as well build it in the background and save the listing as an HTML file, which will be returned more quickly by WebSTAR.

The requirement that every Index file have the same name (and therefore must be the same type of file) can be limiting if you want to use HTML files in some cases and CGI applications in others. The easiest way around this is to create an Action (perhaps called "Index") that handles this. The Action could send all Index files to a CGI that looks at the URL that was requested and redirects the client to either an HTML file or another CGI application based on that URL. It would also be possible to put the name of the file to redirect to in the Index file that is passed to the CGI, but that would make processing a little slower, since the file has to be read by the Action CGI application.

Log File

Default: `:WebSTAR.log`

WebSTAR offers you the option of saving information to your disk about every connection that it processes. The log file is a text file containing one line of information about every connection. Every WebSTAR server has at most one log file, and each of multiple servers on one computer must keep its own logs. The log file usually is kept in the root folder for the server site, although you may want to designate a log folder instead to avoid cluttering your site with old log files.

Three options may be set regarding logging: whether to log, the name to use for the log file, and what information to log on each connection. To turn logging on or off, use the menu item **Start/Stop Logging** in the Options menu from the server or WebSTAR Admin. The name of the menu item will toggle, depending on the current setting of the server. To change the name of the log file and select which information to save to the log file, you must use WebSTAR Admin or write your own administration interface.

The following data is available for logging. If any of the data is not available for a given connection, that column is left empty. This happens often with user names and the FROM field. The tab-delimited data is easy to export into a database or spreadsheet:

- DATE: The current date in short format (**mm/dd/yy**).

- TIME: The current time as **hh:mm:ss** .

- RESULT: The result of the request, which is one of:

  OK: The request was processed successfully. This includes requests to CGI applications that are properly processed.

  ERR!: An error occurred in the processing. This could be an incorrect URL, an error with a CGI application, or an unrecognized request type.

  PRIV: The user tried to access a document but lacks privileges to view it.

- HOSTNAME: The IP address or DNS name of the client computer. The value returned depends on whether **Use DNS** is on or off. If **Use DNS** is on, the DNS name will be logged.

- URL: The path and file portion of the URL in the request. Remember that the client software doesn't send the scheme or server name portions of the URL to WebSTAR (everything before the first slash), only the path and file name (everything from the first slash mark on).

- PATH_ARGS: The path arguments, if any, that were sent in the URL (everything after a dollar sign [**$**]).

- SEARCH_ARGS: The search arguments, if any, that were sent in the URL (everything after a question mark [**?**]).

- METHOD: The HTTP method of the request, usually GET or POST, although support for new methods, such as PUT and DELETE, may be added to WebSTAR.

- BYTES_SENT: The number of bytes transmitted in the request. This does not count the size of the headers sent, only the data being returned. Thus an **If-Modified-Since** request from a client may show a 0 for bytes sent, because no file is returned, only headers telling that the file has not been modified.

- TRANSFER_TIME: The number of ticks required to complete the transmission. Each tick is one sixtieth of a second.

- AGENT: The identity of the WWW client software being used. This is usually the name and version of the software, as well as some data on what libraries were used to make it. CERN proxy servers modify this line to indicate that the message went through them, although this action has been discouraged by the HTTP working group for more than a year now.

- USER: The name of the remote user, if authentication was required.

- FROM: The contents of the "From:" field in the request. If it is not empty, this will usually contain the user's e-mail address.

- REFERER: The full URL of the document that originated the request. This could be a page that contains a hypertext link that was clicked on or simply the page that was being viewed when the user typed a URL into the client software. This field can be very useful for tracking the source of bad requests, such as sites that have links to stale URLs.

This information is all very useful, but remember that every additional field logged adds to the total size of your log file. REFERER and AGENT fields can get very long and will add as much as 20 percent to the size of your log file. When my site was getting 15,000 connections per day and I was logging all of this information, the resulting log file for one month was over 45MB!

Log information in WebSTAR is assigned as low, medium, or high priority. Low priority is for messages about changes in server status, such as the information posted when WebSTAR first launches. Medium-priority messages include the extra information shown when you have Verbose Messages turned on and notices about the source of a connection error. Neither low- nor medium-priority messages are ever written to the log file. High-priority messages contain the key information about each connection. These are the lines that are saved in the log file. Therefore on screen you may see verbose information and you may get extra warnings about things such as changes in server settings, but in the log file all you get is the information about each connection.

WebSTAR Admin is able to receive log information from WebSTAR. The log information is sent to the Admin app differently, depending on its priority. Low-priority messages are never sent to the Admin application. High-priority messages are always sent as soon as they are logged. Medium-priority messages are queued up in a 10K buffer and then sent either when the buffer gets full or when a high-priority message is ready to go, whichever occurs first. This is why the log data seems to come in bursts when you have Verbose Messages turned on. WebSTAR Admin is not able to save the log data to disk, though. Only the server can do that, unless you write your own application to replace the logging functions of the Admin application.

Sending the log data off to a remote machine seems as though it would be a drain on server performance, but it really isn't. The reason is the way that the Macintosh OS handles this information exchange. WebSTAR isn't the one actually sending the data. In simple terms (the kind that I can understand), WebSTAR tells the operating system that it has a message for a remote machine and then goes back to processing; it is the operating system that takes care of sending the message (the log data or statistics update). The total effect is probably no worse than logging to disk and perhaps not even as much of a slowdown as that.

Performance Settings

Several settings affect the general performance of the server.

MaxUsers

This setting controls the maximum number of connections that the server will handle at any one time (concurrent connections). The lowest setting for this option is *four* connections (one for connections and three reserved for busy warnings). The maximum setting is theoretically 1000, but no CPU in existence can handle that load. In addition, WebSTAR 1.2 and earlier limit the server to 50 connections. MacTCP allows 64 total connections, so 14 of them are left for well-known services (FTP, Telnet, and Gopher). Later versions of Web-STAR should remove this limit for servers using OpenTransport.

WebSTAR always saves three of the connections in order to handle busy notices, so at least four connections are required to run. If your server has all of its connections tied up and another connection comes in, there will be no response, and the WWW client will tell the user that the server is either busy or not allowing connections. That's not very helpful. Therefore WebSTAR saves the three connections so it can hand back the new HTTP code **503 Service Unavailable**, which tells the client that the server is temporarily too busy and the client should try again in a few seconds. This is a much more graceful way of handling peak processing times, especially when clients like Netscape tend to overload a server by suddenly placing several simultaneous requests.

As the number of connections handled by a server increases, both the load on the CPU and the memory requirements increase. There are no hard figures on how many connections a specific CPU can handle, because of variations in network connections, system hardware, other applications running on the server, and the type and size of files being served. In general, though, a 68030 CPU can handle 15 connections without too much trouble, a fast 68040 or slow PowerPC can handle 25–30 connections before slowing down too much, and the faster PowerPC machines can handle the full load of 50 concurrent connections. In terms of memory requirements, 15 connections requires about 1.5MB, 25 connections needs 3MB, and 45 connections requires about 6MB of RAM. If you try to launch the server without enough memory allocation, it will warn you of the fact and then quit gracefully.

MaxListens

This setting controls how many free processes are available to listen for new connections. If you are running WebSTAR with the Thread Manager installed (it is required for version 1.2 and later), MaxListens should be set to the same value as MaxUsers, because WebSTAR creates every possible connection when it is first launched and has them all listening for connections. This is part of the way that WebSTAR handles the internal threading of connections.

If you are running an older version of WebSTAR without the Thread Manager or if you are running MacHTTP, you should set the MaxListens to somewhere between three and six. Three is sufficient for most sites, but a very busy site might need five or six, especially if there are many graphics in the page where Netscape clients could be sending new requests in rapid succession. When MacHTTP (or the unthreaded WebSTAR) is idle, it is listening for new connections on its port. When one arrives, the listening process is converted to process the new connection. If you had only one listening process, there would be a period between when the process was converted to handle the connection and when a new process was set to listening. During that period, the server might lose another connection. To avoid this, you want enough listening processes that you are unlikely to ever be without one handy when receiving connections and handing them off. Because of the speed with which new listening processes are allocated, it doesn't take very many to avoid this situation. If you have more than six processes listening, you are just wasting memory.

Use DNS

Each time a client connects to the server, WebSTAR receives a lot of information about the client in addition to the URL that is being requested. Part of the information it receives is the IP address of the client (**128.95.202.45**). Using either the WebSTAR or WebSTAR Admin menus, you can tell the server whether to log the IP address as it is or to first try to convert it to a DNS name (**www.tjp. washington.edu**). If you set **Use DNS** on, WebSTAR will convert this address to a machine name by sending a query to a DNS server. If the client machine has a DNS name assigned, the DNS server will return that name, and WebSTAR will use that name in the log entry. Not every computer has a DNS name assigned, though. Quite often lab machines and dial-up clients are not given DNS names, because they will likely be changing often, anyway. In these cases the DNS name lookup can be quite a limit on performance, because the DNS server has to wait until the search times out to figure out that no name was assigned.

If you want to be able to check who was visiting your site but don't want the overhead of leaving **Use DNS** turned on, check out some software called "ServerStat" (on the companion CD). ServerStat has the ability to take in a log file and write out a copy of it with DNS names replacing all known IP addresses.

Timeouts

This setting controls how long WebSTAR will wait before assuming that a connection has been dropped by the client. If WebSTAR does not receive a response from a client in the time specified as the *timeout period*, it will assume that the client has dropped the connection and will close the connection as well. There could be several reasons why the connection would appear to have been dropped. The client machine's connection to the Internet may be very slow or unreliable, so responses are being delayed. Another possibility is that the client software was unable to handle the speed of your zippy Mac server and has crashed or lost the connection. It is also possible that the user canceled the transfer. Whatever the reason, WebSTAR has no way to know what has happened, only that the connection was not working.

The default value for a timeout period is 60 seconds, meaning that WebSTAR will wait one minute before deciding that the connection has been dropped. You can set the value as high as 600 seconds (10 minutes), but higher timeout values can adversely affect server performance, because WebSTAR will be holding dead connections open longer. In general, the timeout period should not need to be set higher than 120 seconds. If you try to set it above 600, it will default back down to 60 instead.

Older versions of WebSTAR and MacHTTP used to try to gracefully handle a timeout by returning empty data, but that has turned out to cause problems with some clients. WebSTAR versions 1.2 and later simply abort the connection, which is the proper way of handling things as far as the protocols state. On the client side this usually results in a notice like `Socket not connected, please try again`, which at least lets the user know that something went wrong (unless it was the user who canceled the connection originally).

If you are experiencing a high percentage of timeouts, it may indicate a problem on your site. There is no set number for what would be considered a "high percentage," but I would consider anything above 3 percent to be a possible worry. You may have many large graphics on your site or too many graphics in a single page, so that users are often killing the connection before the graphics are completely transferred. It is also possible that some portion of the users visiting your site have a problem with the connection, although this is very difficult to determine and often not your fault. There are other possibilities as well. The fact is that nobody (including Chuck) knows exactly everything that could cause a timeout, so it is difficult to know exactly what they mean.

The timeout setting also controls how long WebSTAR will wait for a CGI application to return results to the server. If you are running CGI applications that do searching or other long tasks, you may want to set this value a little higher (two minutes or more). Since WebSTAR 1.2 and later supports server push, you could use this to return partial results from a search and keep the connection from timing out. This capability is discussed in later chapters and is demonstrated in the latest versions of the AppleSearch CGI, which returns the results from searching one database, then goes on to search the next one.

Buffer Size

This setting controls how much data is transferred in each block sent to the client. In general, the more information that you send in each block, the faster your server will be, because you save the overhead of sending more blocks. Problems with the various TCP/IP implementations and odd network interactions can cause problems with higher settings, though. Some Windows TCP/IP stacks cannot handle receiving more than 8K at a time and will crash if the buffer overflows. Clients on slower (modem) connections also may not be able to receive the data as quickly as WebSTAR can pump it out. In practical usage a setting of 4K is probably best and seems to make best use of the network connection.

Pig Delay

This setting controls how much CPU time each process will get. It is used only for MacHTTP servers or for older WebSTAR servers (before version 1.2) on computers that do not have the Thread Manager installed. If you are using WebSTAR and have the Thread Manager installed (added to System 7.1 or built into System 7.5 and later), the Pig Delay setting is ignored.

The Pig Delay is measured in ticks, which are equivalent to one sixtieth of a second. A setting of 30 (default for WebSTAR) means that each process gets one-half second of the CPU for processing before the next process gets to do anything. During this half second, not only do the other processes not get to do anything, but background applications also do not get any processing time. Therefore the higher you set this, the less time that will be available for background processing. This can be very important, because all of your CGIs are background processes if WebSTAR is in the foreground, so a setting of 60 would severely slow down CGI processing. On the other hand, a very small setting will make your WebSTAR server slower. This is something that has to be fine-tuned for each site separately.

Port

This setting doesn't really affect performance directly, but it can indirectly. The default port for HTTP services is port 80. This is the port used when a client sends a URL that does not specify a port number. Therefore it is not a good idea to run a public server on a port other than 80 except for these reasons:

- You don't want most of the public to find it.

- A more important server is already running on port 80.

- You enjoy making life hard on users.

If you do want to use a port other than 80, you can use any number higher than 1024 (lower numbers are reserved as defaults for existing services such as FTP, Telnet, and IRC). The most common choice for another number is 8001, but it really doesn't matter what you use, as long as no other server is already set to be listening to that port (unlikely on a Macintosh).

For a discussion of reasons to use alternate ports, see "Running Multiple Servers" in Chapter 8.

Suffix Mapping

WebSTAR uses suffix mappings to decide what MIME type to use for a file that it is returning to a client. The suffix mapping for a given file is determined by looking at the creator, type, and filename suffix for a file and matching that information against WebSTAR's internal database of suffix mappings, which are set using WebSTAR Admin's Options menu. When you first install WebSTAR, the default settings shown in Table 6.1 are configured (*not* in this order):

Action	Suffix	Type	Creator	MIME Type
TEXT	.html	TEXT	*	text/html
TEXT	.text	TEXT	*	text/plain
TEXT	.txt	TEXT	*	text/plain
SCRIPT	.script	TEXT	*	text/html
SCRIPT	*	TEXT	ToyS	text/html
CGI	.cgi	APPL	*	text/html
ACGI	.acgi	APPL	*	text/html
TEXT	.hqx	TEXT	*	application/mac-binhex40
BINARY	.sit	SITD	*	application/x-stuffit
BINARY	.pdf	PDF%20	*	application/pdf
BINARY	.au	*	*	audio/basic
BINARY	.gif	GIFf	*	image/gif
BINARY	.jpg	JPEG	*	image/jpeg
BINARY	.jpeg	JPEG	*	image/jpeg
BINARY	.pict	PICT	*	image/pict
BINARY	.xbm	*	*	image/x-xbm
BINARY	.aiff	*	*	audio/x-aiff
BINARY	.mov	MOOV	*	video/quicktime
BINARY	.mpeg	MPEG	*	video/mpeg
BINARY	.word	WDBN	MSWD	application/msword
BINARY	.xl	XLS3	*	application/excel

Table 6.1

Default Types for Suffix Mapping

These settings will handle the majority of files that you will be offering on your server, including QuickTime, AIFF audio, Adobe Acrobat (PDF), StuffIt, and BinHexed files. If you create additional settings, be careful where you place them in the listing. WebSTAR scans the list in order from top to bottom and uses the first setting it finds each time it handles a file. Therefore your server will perform more quickly if the most common settings are at the top. Also, more specific settings should go toward the top, with more general settings farther down; otherwise, the more general settings will always be encountered first and used.

MIME Type Matching

WebSTAR matches the MIME type first by looking at the filename extension and then by checking the Type and Creator fields. If a field is unimportant for matching (any value would be fine), you can use the star (*****) character in that field. Thus for Microsoft Word files, the file must be of type **WDBN**, creator **MSWD**, and extension **.word** to match. On the other hand, a file with the filename extension **.aiff** will be matched as a MIME type of **audio/x-aiff** regardless of its type or creator, because those fields are not defined (the star matches anything).

This process of matching is very important for CGI applications. As you can see, only two things are specified for determining whether a file is actually a CGI application: It must have a filename extension of **.cgi** or **.acgi** and must be an application. If you specify in a form that an application be used to process the form and the application name does not have the proper extension, WebSTAR will not treat it like a CGI application, and it will not receive all of the neat information that WebSTAR sends to CGIs. This is a good thing because it opens the door for using Actions, discussed later.

If the type or creator codes contain special characters, you will need to encode them by using the URL Encoding method. An example of this is the entry for PDF files, which is "**PDF**" (a space at the end). This had to be entered as **PDF%20** to encode the space character. All such codes are four characters long, so if you see a three-character code, suspect that either the first or last character is a space character. If you are uncertain about whether to encode a unique (nonalphabet) character, go ahead and do it. WebSTAR knows that the % sign means that there is something there to be decoded before matching.

The Default MIME Type

The last entry in the listing is treated as a default for WebSTAR. Even if it does not match the file type, creator, or filename extension, it will be used, because the file failed all other matches. WebSTAR comes with the default set to

```
TEXT *      *       *        text/html
```

This means that by default, all unknown files are treated as HTML text files. Let's look at an example of entering a new file type.

Adding New MIME Types

Suppose that you want to offer MacBinary files from your Web-STAR server. The new entry might look like this:

```
BINARY    .bin  *    *        application/x-macbinary
```

This means that the file should be transferred using binary methods and that all files with the filename extension **.bin** should be treated as being of this type, no matter what the type and creator codes are for the file. The MIME type that will be returned to the client software is **application/x-macbinary**, an experimental type.

It is not enough just to configure the server to handle MacBinary files, though. It is likely that the client software that people are using to connect to your site will not be configured by default to accept files of that MIME type. Therefore you should add instructions on your site that show users how to configure their client software to accept this new file type. It is also a good idea to offer a link to download some software for handling the new file type (in this case Peter Lewis's "MacBinaryII+" application).

RAW! Files

One exception to this MIME type–matching process is the RAW! file type. WebSTAR allows you to create files that are returned without any processing at all. These files must already contain a proper HTTP header and can be used to send back responses that WebSTAR does not yet support or to do really slick redirection. If WebSTAR is directed to a file of type **RAW!** and creator **wwwΩ**, it skips the MIME matching step and simply returns the contents of the file as the entire response to the client. It makes no difference what the name of the RAW! file is, whether it has a filename extension, because the filename-extension matching is never done in these cases.

Preprocessing

WebSTAR allows you to define a CGI application that can take over the processing of connections from WebSTAR. By default, no preprocessor is specified for WebSTAR. To define one, you must use the WebSTAR Admin application. Select the **Miscellaneous Settings...** item under the Options menu and fill in the appropriately labeled field with the full path and name for the application. The path is relative to WebSTAR and must begin with a colon to indicate the WebSTAR root folder. There is only one preprocessor for a single site.

When a preprocessor is defined, WebSTAR passes every connection to the preprocessor before doing any internal processing. If the preprocessor returns any data at all, WebSTAR assumes that it has completely processed the request, including building a proper HTTP response header and adding any required data. WebSTAR then returns that response to the client, just as it would with a regular CGI application. As with any other CGI application, WebSTAR will not check the returned data, so any errors made by the preprocessor will be passed directly to the client.

It is possible for the preprocessor to decide not to handle the request and pass processing back to WebSTAR. If the preprocessor returns an empty string to WebSTAR (no data returned), WebSTAR will resume processing the connection as if nothing happened (which it did). This means that WebSTAR can then pass the request off to a matching Action, a CGI, or whatever else would have happened had the preprocessor not been defined.

A preprocessor CGI application has several uses. The most obvious use is to implement your own security scheme. As will be mentioned later, WebSTAR is limited to storing about 500 user names and passwords before performance starts to slow down. This is because it uses the Resource Manager to handle the strings and, as you will read often in Macintosh programming documentation, the Resource Manager is not a database. If you want a scheme that will handle thousands of passwords, you will want a preprocessor that links to a database capable of handling that load with high speed.

Another common use might be to do a little creative redirection. You may want to screen requests based on the type of client making the request and redirect certain clients to another site or page, or you may look at the country of origin and redirect requests to pages in different languages for different countries. There are endless possibilities here for using a preprocessor to make a more user-sensitive site.

For the really tricky folks, the preprocessing function could be used to create entirely new services that just ride on top of the WebSTAR engine. A perfect example of this would be creating a caching proxy server by writing a preprocessor that handled the "outside" processing (finding the requested page in the cache or retrieving it and adding it to the cache) while using WebSTAR to handle the "inside" communications (handing back the page from cache to the client software).

There is one important caution to keep in mind when using a preprocessor CGI application: *It must be fast!* That preprocessor is going to become a bottleneck for your site, because every single connection will pass through it, whether it processes those connections or not. This is probably not a task for AppleScript. In fact, it really calls for an application that can do threaded processing of connections, or else it will turn WebSTAR back into a linear processing server.

WebSTAR will run the preprocessor CGI application as an ACGI Action type regardless of what its filename extension is. No checking is done to see what type of file it is or whether the name ends in **.acgi**. This is important, because it means that the burden is on you to make certain that the application you select (*not* a file, an application) can run as an asynchronous CGI application. The requirements are that it can handle multiple simultaneous requests without having them stomp all over one another or be refused.

Postprocessing

WebSTAR also allows you to define a CGI application that can do extra processing on each connection's data after WebSTAR is done with it. By default, a postprocessor is not specified for WebSTAR. To define one, you must use the WebSTAR Admin application. Select the **Miscellaneous Settings...** item under the Options menu and fill in the appropriately labeled field with the full path and name for the application. The path is relative to WebSTAR and must begin with a colon to indicate the WebSTAR root folder. There is only one postprocessor for a single site.

When a postprocessor is defined, WebSTAR processes each connection completely (returning the data first and closing the TCP/IP connection) and then passes all of the information about the results of the processing to the postprocessor, which should not return any data to WebSTAR. This allows it to work at its own pace without slowing down the server (except for the CPU cycles that it is stealing).

The postprocessor feature is very useful for implementing your own logging functions. It could be used to save information about each user's activity for generating a bill for services, or it could be used to set off an alert when an error occurs. It could also be used to keep separate log files for different entries (one for HTML file requests, another for errors, another for privilege violations, another for everything else) or to keep a log with even more information about every connection. If you write a postprocessor that interfaces with database software, you could have information about every connection dumped directly to the database to generate nearly real-time reports.

Very similar functions could be performed by writing an application that received the log data directly from WebSTAR, the way that the WebSTAR Admin application does. The difference between the two methods is that the postprocessor will get a different set of information about the connection than is included in the log file data that WebSTAR sends out, and the data will arrive in very different formats. An application that registers with WebSTAR to receive the log data stream will get bursts of data in the same format as it appears in the log window. This data must first be parsed into the individual pieces of information before any specific action can be taken (other than just writing it to disk). The postprocessor, on the other hand, will receive more data than that and will get it in a variety of parameters that can easily be worked with.

As with the preprocessor feature, the postprocessor CGI application will be run by WebSTAR as an ACGI Action type regardless of what its filename extension is. The file is not checked against the suffix mapping settings to see what type it is. This means that you have to be certain that you specify an application, not a file, and specify an application that can run like an asynchronous CGI application (handle multiple requests and protect global data).

Actions

WebSTAR uses Actions to determine how it should handle a GET request (which is about the only kind of request that it receives). Every GET request from a client specifies a file that the client wants to get for its user. WebSTAR uses the suffix mapping settings to determine what type of file is being requested. The same suffix mapping information also specifies an Action for handling the type of file found. Five types of Actions are built into WebSTAR:

- **Text**   WebSTAR returns the file to the client as text.

- **Binary**   WebSTAR returns the file to the client as binary data. Only the data fork of the file is returned.

- **Script**   The specified text file is loaded as an AppleScript script and executed. WebSTAR provides several global variables for the script (this is inserted at the start of the script before executing it). The results of the script processing are returned to the client as text with the appropriate MIME type.

- **CGI**   WebSTAR sends to the specified application a search doc event containing all of the information about the request. The CGI application is expected to completely process the request and return both a valid HTTP header and any required data to return to the client. WebSTAR then returns the response to the client. WebSTAR halts processing while the CGI application is processing the request.

- **ACGI**   This is just like a CGI application except that WebSTAR continues processing other requests while the ACGI application is processing.

MacHTTP also handled these five types of Actions, but now WebSTAR allows new Actions to be created. The new Actions are handled like ACGI Actions, with one key difference. With ACGI Actions, WebSTAR will parse the URL out, putting any data that was appended to the URL into the appropriate parameters in the search doc event. With a user-defined Action, though, WebSTAR passes the entire URL to the ACGI application without any parsing.

Defining New Actions

Defining a new Action and putting it into use is a two-step process. First, you define the Action; then you define what file types it will be used for.

To define the Action, you must use the WebSTAR Admin application. Select the **Actions...** item under the Configure menu; a window will appear . There are two fields for specifying a name for the Action (the name is case insensitive) and the application to use to process that Action. The path to the application must be provided, relative to WebSTAR and beginning with a colon to indicate the WebSTAR root folder. Both the Action name and Action path must not contain any spaces or special characters unless they are encoded using the URL encoding method. As an example, entering **CLOAK** as the Action name and **:cgi:netcloak.acgi** as the Action processor tells WebSTAR that all requests for a file that matches a type using CLOAK as its action are to be passed off to the application netcloak.acgi, located in the folder "cgi" in the root folder.

Assigning your new Action to one or more file types is also done via the WebSTAR Admin application. Select the item **Suffix Mapping...** under menu Configure to display the Suffix Mapping window. You can either edit an existing type to use the new Action or create a new type and assign it to that Action. To edit an existing type, click once in the list of types to highlight the one you want. Click once on the **Edit** button, and the data for that type will be put into the editable fields in the bottom of the window. Now use the pop-up menu of existing Actions to select your newly defined Action; then click on the **Replace** button to update the entry in the list. To create a new type, fill in all of the fields and select your new Action; then click on the **Add** button. When you have made all of the changes that you want, click on the **Update** button to send the new information to the WebSTAR server (or **Cancel** to forget the changes).

To extend our example, we will create a new type of file to use the "CLOAK" action. The new type has a filename extension of **.chml** (cloaked hypertext markup language) and is a "TEXT" file type (use

"*" for the creator). We have now told WebSTAR that any request for a text file having a name ending in ".chml" should be sent to the CGI application ":cgi:netcloak.acgi" for processing. As it happens, NetCloak is a real CGI application that will scan the HTML file, inserting information as specified, such as page counters or hiding protected information, and then will return the file to the client.

Converting CGIs to Actions

Any CGI application that is capable of being run asynchronously (ACGI) can be used as an Action processor. There are several reasons that this can be useful:

- *Hiding CGI processing.* If you want to use a CGI to process files before you hand them back to the client, you normally need to specify the CGI application in the HREF link, as in

  ```
  /cgi/netcloak.acgi$/net/www/directory.html
  ```

  This makes it obvious that everyone is getting a preprocessed file. Anyone who wants to bypass this can just enter the URL `/net/www/directory.html` to have the file (unless it was a virtual URL). By running NetCloak as an Action, you can specify a new filename extension, and the file will be preprocessed without any obvious sign of doing so and without the ability to bypass the processing.

- *Processing large numbers of files.* If you plan to use a CGI application to preprocess large numbers of files, it is easier to assign them all to an Action than to write all of those URLs as CGI links. This could be useful for tracking access to certain pages, for example, or running added security on sections of your site. In general, this works much like the preprocessor option except that it allows you to designate different preprocessors for different types of files, and it must always process the files, unlike the preprocessor, which can bail out if it wants to.

- *Using virtual URLs.* You can make virtual URLs (URLs to files that do not exist on disk) appear just like real files by passing them all to an Action. This can be a useful way of hiding files on your server. Your Action processor can read all of the files into memory and create virtual URLs for all of them in its memory.

Then the only way a user can get the file is from the Action processor. This could even work for reading files that didn't exist in the WebSTAR directory structure.

- *Simplifying your URLs.* Some CGI applications, such as map processors, require extra information to be appended to the URL to specify accessory files. As an example, with MapServe you might use a URL to indicate what map definition file should be used to process the imagemap:

  /cgi/MapServe.acgi$/maps/homepage.map

  However, if you create a type for all files ending in **.map** and make MapServe the Action processor for that type, you can write the URL like **/maps/homepage.map** and get the same processing done.

You can see that these are all minor variations on the same thing, but there is a lot of power available in using Actions. Once you get a feeling for how it works, I'm sure you will come up with many things that you can do with it that weren't available before.

As with pre- and postprocessors, you need to be careful that the application you designate as an Action processor is capable of acting as an asynchronous CGI application, meaning that it handles multiple simultaneous events without refusing or dropping them.

7

Security

Security is one of the big three topics that any Webmaster is interested in (the other two being Speed, and Cool Features). There are several types of security to worry about: the *physical security* of the machine from theft, tampering, and accidental interruption; the *security of the network and operating system* from those who would try to either make administrative changes in the server or site or try to use the site to launch an attack on another network; the *security of privileged information* offered by the site or copyrighted information; and the *security of communications* between clients and the server for transmission of privileged information. WebSTAR has features that address all four of these issues to provide one of the most secure servers on the market.

Physical Security

First, you need to consider the physical security of the server platform. Obviously you want to make use any of the theft-prevention measures with the server that you would with any other computer on your site, such as locking it to a secure base, engraving identification information prominently on the machine, and locating it in an area that would restrict casual access. The latter measure is often not very popular with Webmasters because there is a tendency to do all development and testing of new software right on the server. This is a no-no, and the next version of WebSTAR will ship with a ruler to rap your knuckles with when you feel the urge to do this. It is just too easy to make a mistake that instantly affects all of the users connecting to your site.

If you are developing a serious Web site, I highly recommend that you have a development server that is separate from the main (or "production") server. You use this development server to make all of your changes, test new software, install upgrades to see whether they work, and generally fiddle with things. Only when you know that the changes are working on the development server do you copy the changes to the production server. The added benefits of an arrangement like this is that the production server can be located wherever is most convenient for maximum network access (and security), and there will be mirror copies of the server contents on the development server in the event of a hardware crash. The development server does not always need to be a match for the production server in terms of speed and power. so this can often be done without a lot of extra expense.

If you are unable to isolate the server physically, you can still decrease the likelihood that anyone will mess with it by removing the monitor, keyboard, and mouse. WebSTAR Admin gives you complete control over WebSTAR from a remote computer once WebSTAR is running. You can also combine this with Timbuktu Pro, an excellent utility that lets you run a remote Macintosh from your own machine via TCP/IP or AppleTalk, so that there is no need for any input or display hardware on the server. If you are running several servers, this can also provide a substantial savings, since one monitor and keyboard can service all of the machines when all else fails.

If you are running WebSTAR on your own desktop computer or a community machine, both of which probably require that the monitor and keyboard remain attached to the server, you can still add a small measure of security by running WebSTAR as a faceless background application (FBA). FBAs do not have menus or windows and don't show up in the active application menu, so there is no way for someone else to change or even quit the application on the server once it has started. The only access would be via WebSTAR Admin, which is much easier to protect, since it does not need to be continuously running.

Network and OS Security

The Macintosh often takes an undeserved beating in this area (and UNIX avoids a deserved one). It is hard to beat the Macintosh for security from network "crackers," Internet viruses, and such. This protection extends to your whole network if you use AppleTalk instead of TCP/IP for network communications.

Macintosh OS

The first line of security in any Macintosh computer network is the Macintosh operating system. The UNIX operating system was designed with networking involved throughout, with dozens or even hundreds of processes all running independently and sharing data freely. Some point to this as if it makes UNIX the only choice for any network services, but what they forget is that it also makes UNIX a big security risk. There is just too much going on in any UNIX computer for all of the security problems to be reliably detected and corrected.

By comparison, the Macintosh OS is an operating system that completely controls all networking and limits applications to only very controlled access to the network and to one another. It requires some pretty good programming to create a network application that could mimic the security risks that are part and parcel of the basic installation of many UNIX operating systems. The resulting difference is that network software on a UNIX machine will likely have security holes unless the programmer is careful, whereas network software on a Macintosh requires extra programming if some crazy person wants to create a security hole. Have you ever wondered why there are so few security warnings for Macintosh users (beyond the occasional virus alert)? This is why.

AppleTalk Networking

The AppleTalk network support built into every modern Macintosh is another source of security. AppleTalk is a completely different protocol from TCP/IP, so information cannot pass from one to the other without the help of special software or hardware. If your server is providing Internet services and also sitting on your AppleTalk network (whether over LocalTalk or Ethernet connections), the two are completely separate. There is no way for someone to send data or commands over TCP/IP and affect anything on the AppleTalk side (again, unless you write special software to allow them to do so).

Program Linking

If you want to use WebSTAR Admin (and you will), you need to turn on Program Linking on the server so it can link to WebSTAR. Program Linking allows a Macintosh on the AppleTalk network to control software that is running on the server. This is different from regular File Sharing, which allows you to launch a copy of an application that is on the server so that it runs on your own computer. With File Sharing all you are really doing is running a copy of the application on your own computer; the server isn't really affected. With Program Linking you are affecting the application as it runs on the server.

WebSTAR ships with Program Linking turned on. As presented in Chapter 5, three factors control Program Linking on your server. First, there is the ability to allow or deny access to Program Linking on the entire server through the Sharing Setup control panel. Second, you can restrict this ability to specific applications by using the **Sharing...** command (in the File menu). I recommend that only WebSTAR have this ability, but you may be running other applications that would benefit as well. Third, Program Linking can be restricted so that it requires a user name and password for access. In addition, users having access to Program Linking do not necessarily need to be given access to any other capabilities on the server (such as file sharing privileges).

Remember that Program Linking is part of the Macintosh operating system, and as such it uses AppleTalk to communicate between computers. This means that it is not susceptible to those trying to gain access over TCP/IP networks. The only hazards are from your own AppleTalk network.

File Sharing

In many cases, it is very convenient to have File Sharing enabled on the server so that several groups on the local network can have direct access to the files on the server. You can restrict access to a folder on a per-group or per-user basis so each person can change only their own files. There are also software packages available that provide added monitoring and controlling of who can access the server, so you can trace who changed or read which files and lock out all access to files after business hours. As with Program Linking, the only real security danger with File Sharing is from the AppleTalk network, so it is important to be sure that you know who has access to that network. File Sharing does slow down a server, though, so if you don't need it, it should be turned off for optimal performance.

Information Security

WebSTAR has several features that provide several additional layers of security for your files.

Directory Restrictions

The first level of file security is provided in the way that WebSTAR manages access to files. Only files that are located in subfolders of the WebSTAR root folder can be accessed by WebSTAR (see Fig. 7.1). It doesn't matter where on your disk the WebSTAR root resides, because it is oblivious to the rest of the disk.

> Never, never, never put WebSTAR at the root level of your hard disk. This would give it access to your System Folder, which is obviously Not A Good Thing.

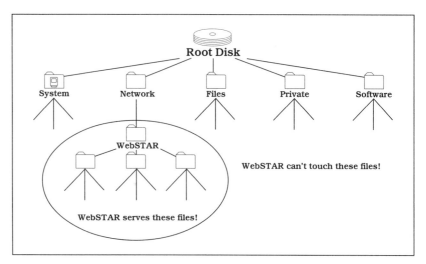

Figure 7.1

How WebSTAR Views
the Hard Disk

This directory restriction is built into the way that WebSTAR handles URLs. All paths in a URL received are treated as being relative to WebSTAR. In addition, WebSTAR never receives partial URLs, which instead are converted to full URLs by the client software before they are sent to WebSTAR. Finally, WebSTAR cannot be tricked by a URL with too many slashes at the beginning. If a user tries to send WebSTAR a URL like "///SystemFolder/System", WebSTAR first converts all slash marks to colons (:), meaning that the URL is now ":::SystemFolder:System". Then WebSTAR reduces all multiple colon characters to single colons.

For some sites, this security feature may become a limitation, especially if the files on the site are too large or too numerous for a single disk or if some of the files already exist on a remote volume. A Webmaster can get around this limitation, though, through the use of *file aliases*. WebSTAR allows you to make files in other folders or disks available by placing an alias to the folder or disk in WebSTAR's folder hierarchy.

URLs that address these files must use the path from WebSTAR to the alias and then from there to the files. Thus the files are addressed relative to the alias, not to their own disk or folder. This means that WebSTAR's directory restriction also protects files in those aliases. Only files in the aliased folder (or disk) or in folders inside the alias can be accessed. Any URL that attempts to access a higher folder is directed back into the WebSTAR directory structure and ultimately ends up in the WebSTAR root folder again.

Using the example shown in Fig. 7.2, the URL to the file "Listing.html" on Disk B would look like "/comp/network/Listing.html". If a user tried to get back to Disk B by using a partial URL, such as "../../FileA.txt", the client would use this to modify the previous URL and create the URL "/FileA.txt", which it would send to WebSTAR. WebSTAR would then look *in its own folder* for a file named "FileA.txt" (and presumably return an error when the file isn't found).

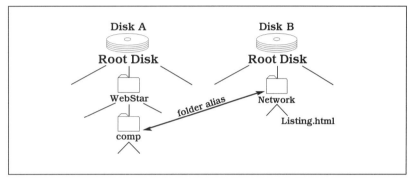

Figure 7.2
Referencing through
Folder Aliases

Folder Indexing

When a client sends a URL that indicates only a directory and not a specific file (one that ends in a slash, such as "/comp/net/"), there is no clear specification of how an HTTP server is supposed to respond. Many HTTP servers treat this as a request for a directory listing and return a list of all files in the folder specified. That can be a security problem, though, because it may be that the client does not have access to some or all of the files in the directory. Letting the client know that the files are there could be an invitation to attempts to circumvent the security. This kind of response also changes the way that people will use your site, perhaps allowing them to simply collect all of the graphics on a site and bypass the regular links.

WebSTAR lets the Webmaster control how the server will respond in those situations. The Index setting defines the name of a file that is considered the default for a folder. If a request is received for a folder and that folder has a file with that name in it, WebSTAR returns the file to the client. If no such file is present, an error is returned. The file could be used to return an index (or could be a CGI application created on the fly), or the file could return a nice-looking listing of only the files that you want a user to see with a nice header and some useful formatting.

ALLOW and DENY

WebSTAR provides a very simple mechanism for controlling access to your entire site, based on the IP address or DNS name of the client attempting to connect. You use a series of ALLOW and DENY statements to control who gets in and who stays out. ALLOW statements define addresses or names that are allowed to see your site; DENY statements, conversely, define those addresses or names that will be denied access.

Partial IP addresses can be defined to represent entire subnets. This can get a little confusing, even if you are used to working with IP addresses, so read this carefully. WebSTAR appends a period to the end of an IP address before it compares it to the list of allowed and denied addresses. If a number is followed by a period, only that number will match. However, if a number is not followed by a period, it will match itself or any other number that starts the same way. Here are some examples:

- **ALLOW 128.95.202.4**   This statement will match either 128.95.202.4 or anything from 128.95.202.40 to 128.95.202.49. It matches the first three numbers exactly and any fourth number that begins with 4.

- **DENY 128.131.24.12.**   This statement would refuse access to the single address 128.131.24.12. It does *not* deny access to 128.131.24.120 or any following numbers, because the 12 was specified exactly by using a trailing period.

- **ALLOW 128.95.**   This statement allows the entire network of computers with addresses of the form 128.95.*xxx.xxx*.

WebSTAR reads the statements from top to bottom, building a hierarchy of permissions. Later statements override earlier ones, so you can layer protections by specifying one action for a larger group and then the opposite action for a more specific group. Here is an example:

```
ALLOW 128.95.
DENY  128.95.202.
ALLOW 128.95.202.43.
```

This set of statements starts by allowing anyone in the 128.95.*xxx.xxx* subnets to access the site, then adds the exception that anyone from 128.95.202.*xxx* should still be denied, then adds another exception that the single address 128.95.202.43 should still be allowed. The general principle is that general restrictions should be put higher in the list, with restrictions getting more specific as you move down the list. If you accidentally put a very general statement far down the list (such as "ALLOW 1"), it will override many or all of the previous statements.

If no statements are defined, WebSTAR assumes "ALLOW *", meaning that everyone is allowed to access your site. On the other hand, if you define even one statement, WebSTAR assumes that the very first statement is "DENY *" (deny everyone). Unfortunately the statements "ALLOW *" and "DENY *" are not allowed in the actual list. Therefore if you want to deny only a few specific sites, you can get the equivalent of "ALLOW *" by using the following list of statements:

```
ALLOW 1
ALLOW 2
ALLOW 3
ALLOW 4
ALLOW 5
ALLOW 6
ALLOW 7
ALLOW 8
ALLOW 9
```

This series of statements allows any client with an address starting with any number from 1–9 to have access (which means everyone). Remember also that these statements need to be the first statements in your list, because processing runs from top to bottom.

If you have your server set to resolve DNS names, you can use DNS names instead of IP addresses in your ALLOW and DENY settings. The same general rules apply, with one important exception: *DNS names are evaluated from right to left.* This is because the more specific portion of a DNS name is on the left, whereas it is on the right in an IP address. Also, be sure to include a trailing period on the DNS name to force a match to an exact string, as with IP addresses. As an example, if you want to deny all access from Microsoft corporate computers, you would use an entry like

```
DENY .microsoft.com.
```

When a client is refused access to the site because of a DENY statement, WebSTAR returns a "403 Forbidden" error code to the user. There is no username or password request in this case, and it doesn't matter if there is a folder or file specified in the URL. The user is either in or out.

The ALLOW and DENY settings apply to the entire site. There is no way to have one set for part of the site and another set for another part. If you want to have this kind of protection on only a part of your site, you need to run multiple copies of WebSTAR, with different settings for each copy.

Assigning Realms

WebSTAR also allows you to control access on a page-by-page basis by using Realms. A Realm is nothing more than a string of text. If a URL is requested that contains the specified text string as part of the path or file name, an authorization request is passed back to the client. The client then presumably requests a user name and password from the user and sends another request back to WebSTAR, containing the user name and password provided by the user. If the results are correct, WebSTAR passes the file back to the client; otherwise, the client receives another error notice.

If you want to protect your log files, you could have them all stored in a folder named "logs" and then set the Realm string to "logs." Any URL that refers to a log file will have to have the string "logs" in it and so will be protected. As another example, you could create a Realm from the string "ZZ". Any file that you want to protect anywhere on your site can be protected by putting the string "ZZ" in the file name.

Because the string is tested as part of a URL, it is subject to the same rules as a URL string, meaning that it may not contain spaces or special characters ($, ?) and is treated as case insensitive (upper- and lowercase characters are treated as if identical). All special characters must be URL encoded when you use them in the Realm string.

You need to be careful when specifying a Realm with very short or very common strings. If you define a Realm with the string "html", you will be placing password protection on every HTML document on your site. Similarly, if you specify a Realm as something like "sh", you are likely to find files unexpectedly requiring a password for access.

Defining a Realm for use is a two-step process very similar to defining an Action. First, you define the Realm, giving it a name and the string to test for. Then you create a user name and password and link it to the Realm. You can have more than one user name/password combination assigned to a Realm if you want.

WebSTAR checks the list of Realms from top to bottom to match against a URL. The first match found is assumed to be the one and only Realm that applies to that URL. This means that it is very important to be certain that your Realms are unique or to know what the effects will be if they are not. Suppose that you define two Realms: "report" and "95" in that order. If the folder "1995" is inside the folder "report", only the "report" Realm will be noticed, and its password will be requested. A group that has the password for only the "95" Realm will be unable to access the files in the "1995" folder at all.

The **401 Unauthorized** code that WebSTAR passes back to the client specifies what authorization scheme is being used and requires that the client software be able to handle it correctly. Currently WebSTAR uses a basic authorization scheme that almost all clients support. A few older clients or old versions of current clients don't support this feature, but I doubt that any of them are in use in noticeable numbers. With the Security Kit (described in later chapters) or with security options that will be added in the future, though, the question of whether a client supports the authentication will likely become more of a problem.

Authorization is kind of a pain for the user. If a user is required to enter a user name and password for every secured page on a site, it can get very tiresome and will eventually chase the user away. To alleviate this, most Web clients have a mechanism for storing the authorization settings for reuse. There is a question of what the best way to handle this is, though. If the client stores the password too long, it becomes somewhat useless. In a shared environment, such as a student computer laboratory, "too long" could be a matter of minutes or less, since a new user could take over the client software at any time. It appears that most clients are settling on something like the following practice: As long as the user keeps requesting documents in the same Realm, the password is stored. If the user requests a file outside the Realm, then the password is dumped and must be reentered to reload the file. This doesn't usually apply to inline graphics, of course, since those are rarely directly requested by the user.

Secure HTTP Connections

We have covered a variety of methods for protecting data while it is on your site. The big question for the past year, though, has been how to protect data while it is being transmitted around the Internet. This is a new medium for most companies, and they are very uncomfortable with the idea that someone could possibly be sitting on the network with a packet sniffer, grabbing sensitive data that is being passed around. The original worry was credit card numbers, since online transactions are very desirable for most companies, but now other people are beginning to realize that it may be important to protect other data as well, such as research reports or patient data.

Two standards have been proposed and made mostly public for implementing secure communications between client and server software. The first, the Secure Sockets Layer (SSL) is being pushed by Netscape Communications Corporation and has wide corporate backing. The second, Secure HTTP (S-HTTP), is from Terisa Systems Inc. and is also gaining wide backing, including from Netscape.

Secure Sockets Layer (SSL)

SSL is a protocol designed by Netscape Communications Corporation to provide a layer of security for data communications between a client and a server. The security layer resides between the application protocols (such as HTTP, Telnet, or FTP) and TCP/IP. SSL provides several types of security, including encryption of data, integrity checks on the data, and authentication of both server and client. The specifications for the SSL protocol have been made publicly available by Netscape Communications, and a freeware implementation is already available, in addition to what Netscape offers. SSL has also been submitted to the W3 Consortium working group on security for consideration as a standard for server security on the Internet.

SSL is implemented as a new URL access method called "https" for connecting to HTTP servers. It is the full HTTP protocol with SSL support added. In theory, therefore, any server that handles "https" should also handle regular "http" requests. The Internet Assigned Numbers Authority has designated port 443 as the default port for "https" connections. This means that the same server can run both an unsecure HTTP server (on port 80) and a secure HTTPS server (on port 443).

There is some flexibility in how the various security features are implemented. Here is the way that the Netsite servers implement it.

- When a TCP/IP connection is first made to a secure server, SSL provides a security handshake that is used to agree on the level of security that will be used. The handshake is also used to fulfill any authentication requirements for the connection. This all occurs before the HTTP transmissions start between the client and server.

- Once the connection is negotiated, the only thing that SSL does is encrypt or decrypt the communications between client and server. All requests using "https" have the entire outgoing stream from the client encrypted, and responses to secure requests from an HTTPS server are also encrypted, including the response headers.

- Certificate Authority (CA) keys are used to verify the identity of a server to the client. CA keys prove that the server you are talking to is the one you think you are talking to and include the name of the CA that issued the CA key for the server. The Netscape Navigator client includes several embedded keys but does not have a mechanism for easily adding new keys (as of version 1.1). This means that Netscape clients will identify only any CA server that it has a key for, as well as any server that got its key from one of those servers.

- SSL brings together several existing standards related to security and authentication, providing a framework for their use. As examples, Netscape's implementation of SSL uses the RC4 stream encryption algorithm for bytestream encryption, the X.509 cryptographic certificate format for authentication, and RSA Public Key encryption for session keys.

- The current NetSite server software uses only a 40-bit key size for its RC4 stream encryption algorithm (which is used to encrypt the bytestream of all communications between the client and server). This key should take about 64 MIPS-years to break (a 64 MIPS computer would take on average a year to guess the 40-bit key). This is not the very best encryption that can be done, because of problems with exporting advanced encryption software and methods to foreign countries. However, it is definitely not a simple task to break this code quickly and little use in doing so slowly. Netscape Communications has announced its intention to distribute a version with 128-bit keys (practically unbreakable) for U.S. sale only.

Currently only one browser officially supports the SSL scheme: the Netscape Navigator browser, which has supported SSL since version 1.0 for all platforms. Based on the stated corporate support for SSL, it is likely that many other commercial browsers will add support for this type of communication soon.

WebSTAR will support SSL through the WebSTAR Security Kit or Commerce Kit. These kits include a version of WebSTAR that accepts "https" connections on port 443. The server cannot be assigned to a different port and will attempt to create a secure connection if the client will support it. Therefore you will probably want to also run another WebSTAR server for handling image files and other files that do not require secure communications. As an example, many business sites will run the majority of their pages off of a standard WebSTAR server, using the Secure server only for pages involving purchasing or secure data (filling out application forms, or viewing results from a proprietary database).

Secure HTTP (S-HTTP)

S-HTTP is an alternative security scheme originally proposed by Enterprise Integration Technologies (EIT). Actually, S-HTTP was proposed before SSL. Luckily the two can work together, since they attack the security problem from different angles. Unlike SSL, which works in a layer beneath HTTP or any other service, S-HTTP adds the message-based security directly to HTTP to form a new Secure HyperText Transfer Protocol. S-HTTP-capable clients and servers can still communicate with their unsecure counterparts as well through standard HTTP.

Except for that one difference, the two are mostly similar (except from an implementation standpoint). S-HTTP provides methods for encryption, authentication, and signature. These methods are very flexible, and the question of which methods and what implementation of the methods will be used in a transaction is negotiated at the start between the client and server.

Special Issues in Site Security

If you are using WebSTAR right out of the box (or CD-ROM), you don't have to worry too much about security, especially given all of the features for site and file protection. This changes, though, as you begin to add more powerful features to your site, such as CGI applications or user access. Here are a few of the added security issues that you will likely face.

Protecting Copyrighted Materials

One current shortcoming of the Web is that it is very difficult, if not impossible, to protect files from redistribution once you let a user have access to them. Most WWW clients allow the user to save the current document to disk, and some even allow specific graphics elements to be saved. Audio, video, and other special files are usually loaded directly to disk as well for external applications to display. This can cause serious problems for companies that don't consider it in their design plans, and there is nothing WebSTAR can do to stop it, since every request looks pretty much the same to the server.

There are other similar problems with file access. It is possible for another Web site to reference graphics or other files on your site directly; it doesn't actually have to copy the file, but with an IMG link it will appear inline in its pages anyway. In fact, it is a little worse because your site gets hit for the graphic but the other site's page gets the credit. The problem is even worse if the "file" being accessed is one of your CGI applications. If you have a database or some other particularly useful CGI, it is a good idea to put some protection on it. In most of these cases it is not practical to use a Realm for protection, because you would have to give the user name and password to everyone who came to your site. As you will find out later, though, it is possible to check in your CGI to see where the request for your CGI application came from and to reject requests that look suspicious.

Allowing Users to Upload Files

WebSTAR does not currently support the PUT method, so there is no way for users to upload files to your site with an out-of-the-box installation. However, there are many reasons for wanting to add this ability to your server. If you plan to do this, you need to know the risks.

Any method that you use to allow write access is likely to suffer from the same problem: There is no way to control what kinds of files are being uploaded. A user could as easily upload an application as a text file. Even text files aren't entirely safe, since they could be AppleScript or MacPerl scripts. None of these uploads are likely to hurt your site just sitting there. The problem comes when the application is launched.

As an example, if a user uploads to your site an application that ends in ".cgi" (whether it is actually a CGI application or not), that application can be launched simply by writing a URL to the application. WebSTAR will launch the application to make sure that it can receive the search doc Apple event. If that application suddenly takes off and starts erasing files from the disk, your site is in a bit of trouble.

In general, it is a bad idea to allow users to upload files directly into a directory on your server that is accessible from WebSTAR. Set up a folder outside of the WebSTAR directory tree and have the files initially placed there until they can be tested.

Controlling Your CGIs

CGI applications present the most likely source of a security breach on your site. CGIs have no limitations on what files they can access or what network services they use. It is possible for a CGI application to give a user access to files that are not in WebSTAR's directory tree, to allow users to change the server's settings, or even to make changes to the operating system of the server if you want (although I don't recommend it). This will be covered later, in the chapters on CGI applications. It ought to be a concern even when you buy commercial CGI applications, though. Before you install one on your computer, read the manual until you know exactly what it will do and allow on your server.

Interaction with Other Services

If you are running other Internet services on your server, you may be creating a security hole. Mail servers, listservers, FTP, and Telnet all present opportunities for users to upload files or to launch commands that can damage your server. Before you start one of these services, check to make certain that there are no unseen side effects and that they are secured against use by others who are not supposed to have access. An example of this would be a site that has a mail server set to automatically archive messages into a folder on the Web site. This is nice because the messages can be made accessible to users through the Web. However, if someone were to include a CGI application as an attachment, you could run into one of the problems listed.

8

Special Topics

Running Multiple Servers on One Macintosh

Sometimes it is useful to be able to run more than one copy of Web-STAR on a single machine. If you want to protect sections of your site by using the Allow/Deny settings (so connections are absolutely refused), you can run those sections under one server with restrictions in place and the rest of the site under another server that is open to the public. If you want to do some experimentation with your site or if you want to run a small site that you don't want other users to find by accident, you can run another copy of WebSTAR and use an odd port that won't be easily guessed. Although you could do any of these by using an additional computer, sometimes there isn't enough money for that, the benefits aren't worth the additional cost, or your current server just isn't doing all that much, anyway, and the CPU seems to have plenty of room left.

Whatever the reason, you can run more than one copy of WebSTAR on a single computer. WebSTAR has been designed to be very portable, so the multiple copies don't interfere with one another, except to compete for the CPU and disk. They can even share files and CGI applications if you set things up properly.

Two things are important when you are running multiple copies of WebSTAR:

- Each copy of WebSTAR must be in its own folder, because each copy of WebSTAR keeps its own Settings file in its folder. If you try to run two copies of WebSTAR out of the same folder, they will compete to open and use the Settings file. It won't be pretty.

- Each copy of WebSTAR must be assigned a unique port number. When a connection is received by MacTCP, the connection specifies the port it is arriving on. This determines which copy of WebSTAR the request will go to. If two copies of WebSTAR try to use the same port, whichever one is launched first will control the port, and the other will not be able to launch.

If you want to set up two or more copies of WebSTAR so that they can share files and CGI applications, you need to place one copy in a subfolder of the other. Any files or CGI applications that you want to share will need to be in a folder that is common to both WebSTAR servers. All files will work fine this way, but some CGI applications may not. The problems would arise when a CGI application sends messages back to WebSTAR (and doesn't know which one to talk to or completely ignores one) or when the CGI application makes assumptions during startup, based on one WebSTAR server, and those assumptions don't work with the other.

It is important to remember that each copy of WebSTAR will be competing with the others for system resources. CPU time will probably be the tightest competition. The Macintosh OS uses cooperative multitasking, which means that the application in the foreground has control of the CPU and shares it with others. Whichever copy of WebSTAR is in the foreground will be responsible for making sure that the others get some processing time. The hard disks can also become bottlenecks when serving very large files. Finally, each copy of WebSTAR will be grabbing connections from a common pool. Whichever copy starts first will get first chance at the connections, then the next copy. There are only 64 connections total (under MacTCP, unlimited under OpenTransport), so you cannot have two WebSTAR servers with each set to 40 connections. One will get its connections and the other will fail to launch.

Configuring Multiple Servers

WebSTAR Admin can connect to multiple WebSTAR servers simultaneously, but can only update one server at a time (whichever server is in the frontmost window). If you are running more than one WebSTAR server, whether on one computer or several, it can be difficult to keep your settings uniform across all of the servers. In many cases it is very important that every server have the same settings, especially when you are running a RAIC setup.

There is one useful trick for creating identical settings for multiple servers on startup. First, run one of the WebSTAR servers and set all of the settings using WebSTAR Admin. Now quit the server and copy its Settings file to all of the other servers. This will give each server exactly the same settings. Now launch each server in turn and change the registration key so that each server has a unique key. This isn't a very practical way to maintain servers with identical settings, but it does help at the start.

Running Multiple Domains on One Macintosh

People often ask, "Can I run multiple domains off one Macintosh?" The answer is yes. It is very easy to have a single Macintosh set to respond to several different domains, such as "www.companyA.com" and "www.companyB.com" and even "www.chipmunk.org" and as many other domains as you want. This is all done in the DNS server and isn't a function of WebSTAR at all.

The problem is that this isn't the question they really wanted to ask. What they really wanted to know was whether there is any way to have multiple, unique home pages on a single Macintosh, with each one accessible as the root page for its domain. This is a feature that has appeared recently in many UNIX and NT servers, and some service providers want to try to do the same thing on Macintosh computers. The answer to this question, for the time being, is no, you can't do that on a Macintosh. Of course, a lot of other computers also can't do that, but nobody goes around advertising that.

The Problem

The problem in this case is not WebSTAR but rather the HTTP standard, the way DNS works, and the Macintosh operating system. When the WWW client tries to connect to the URL "http://www.companyA.com/", the first thing it does is contact a DNS server to convert the DNS name "www.companyA.com" into an IP address. The IP address is the physical address of the server on the Internet, and this is what the client software uses to initiate the connection to the server. The way DNS works is that all three machine names (www.companyA.com, www.companyB.com, and www.chipmunk. org) return exactly the same IP number because they are three names for the same machine. This means that once the DNS name is converted to an IP address, all three of these URLs will appear exactly the same to the client software.

The WWW client does not send the server name portion of the URL to the server. The server portion is used to tell the client software how to connect to the server. Once the connection is made, the client sends only the path and file name portions of the URL. This probably made sense at first because, after all, the server surely knows what its own name is. The result, though, is that the server sees exactly the same request no matter what DNS name the user specified to reach it. Both "http://www.companyA.com/" and "http://www.chipmunk.org/" are reduced to a request for the root file (home page) from the same server.

There are ways around this, of course. One commonly used method is to create a different folder for each domain. Each domain's home page resides in that domain's folder, and the root URL for each domain becomes something like "http://www.companyA.com/companyA/" and "http://www.chipmunk.org/chipmunk/". This is not so bad and provides 100 percent of the capabilities of having the sites on separate computers. Another similar solution is to have the URLs directed to servers listening to different ports, such as "http://www.companyA.com:8001/" and "http://www.companyB.com:8002".

Both of these methods suffer from the same problem: user laziness. Many users do not pay attention to a URL. They see the domain name and make assumptions about the rest. So no matter how many times you emphasize that there is an extra folder name in your URL or that the server runs on a different port, the users will still enter something like "http://www.companyA.com/". To handle this, you need to have another home page at the root of the server (on port 80) that lists all of the domains that are serviced by that computer and allow users to jump from there to the site wanted.

For many companies this kind of setup is a blow to their corporate egos, since it implies that they either could not afford their own servers or didn't know how to get one. There is really no other explanation for the way some companies react to the suggestion that they share a server with one of the two arrangements cited. Of course, when they start saying that they will take their business elsewhere, it doesn't matter any longer what the reason was. All you want is a solution.

So how do some of those UNIX machines get around this problem? What these computers do is use more than one IP address for the server (have multiple Ethernet cards installed). Each domain is assigned to a different IP address, so requests for one domain come into one Ethernet card and requests for a different domain come in through a different card. The operating system is then patched so that it can send requests on one Ethernet card to one root directory and requests on another Ethernet card to another root directory. This is not something that is built into all UNIX systems, but most of them have found a way to make this work.

The Macintosh operating system does not yet support this kind of solution. MacTCP recognizes only one Ethernet interface per computer. OpenTransport will support something called *multihoming,* but that isn't quite the same thing. Multihoming will allow your Macintosh to have several network connections of all kinds and have all working at the same time. You could have an Ethernet card, a LocalTalk connection, and a dial-up connection on one machine, and the resources from all three would be available at one time. The current version of OpenTransport (1.07) still limits you to one IP address per machine, though, and will not allow any remapping of requests based on which Ethernet card they are received on. It has been reported that the feature will be supported in some future versions of OpenTransport, but it is hardly a feature that will make or break the Macintosh. The fact is that only a very small number of Macintoshes will make use of this feature, possibly even fewer than use the text-to-speech capabilities for real work.

The Solution

Two items offer some hope in this problem. First, changes to the coming HTTP/1.1 standard have been suggested that will require the client to include the original DNS name of the server in the

HTTP request. This would allow servers to implement the routing internally or through CGI applications or some kind of proxy service. Unfortunately even if it is included in the HTTP/1.1 specification, it will probably take a while for the client software to begin supporting it. Some companies are not going to be eager to implement it, because it doesn't help their servers at all, and others are just slow about catching up with the standards (and some are both).

Second, Macintosh computers are relatively inexpensive. In many cases service providers are using the "multiple unique roots" feature as if it is a benefit when really it is just a way to get more use out of their expensive servers. The majority of the Web sites installed have no need of the power of these servers, but there are no lower-cost options, either. On the Macintosh side it is very easy to find a computer at exactly the power level that you need so the client isn't paying for a bunch of wasted capabilities. A Quadra 630 has plenty of power for handling most Web sites, and you can find even cheaper models if you need.

There are several benefits to going with multiple Macintoshes:

• *Sites aren't forced to suffer common problems.* If one site does something stupid and comes under attack from users, the other sites are on independent servers and won't be bothered. Also, if one site has a security lapse, the other sites will still be protected.

• *Sites can easily be relocated.* If the company decides in the future to move the server in-house, it is ready to go at any time. If you want to isolate certain sites from others, that option is also easy to implement.

• *Many services can still be provided by shared servers.* Commonly used CGI applications, such as map processors, can be kept on one server only for that purpose. Database servers and text search engines can also be put on their own dedicated servers and shared by multiple sites. You could even have one server optimized for downloading graphics and other large inline files. In all of these cases users are very unlikely to be accessing the URLs directly, so it is less important that the server name will not match that of the server. And, since you can assign multiple domains to a single machine, you can give a name to each machine for each domain, such as "dbase.companyA.com" and "dbase.chipmunk.org" for the database server.

In short, there is little reason to need to put multiple domains on one Macintosh computer. Take advantage of the benefits that the Macintosh provides, and don't be tied down to the constraints introduced by other systems.

Running without an Internet Connection

Sometimes it is very useful to be able to run WebSTAR on a computer without being attached to a network. This could be the case when you're doing a presentation or doing some development when you don't have a network handy (like on your PowerBook 540c at 10,000 feet). Whatever the reason, it is possible to do this by pulling some trickery on MacTCP.

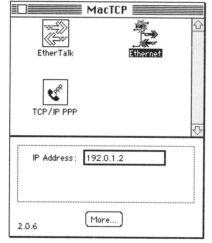

First, you must have MacTCP installed and AppleTalk turned on (this can be done from the Chooser. Now open your MacTCP control panel. The window will display all of your network drivers, one of which should be called LocalTalk (see Fig. 8.1). Click once on the LocalTalk icon to select that as your network driver. In the bottom portion of the window is a text field called IP Address where you can enter a fake IP address. The consensus seems to be that the address "192.0.1.2" is the best one to use for this.

Figure 8.1

The MacTCP Control Panel

Once that is done, click on the **More...** button in the bottom of the MacTCP window. This opens another window, where you can change the more advanced settings. Your settings should look exactly like the example shown in Fig. 8.2. The key is that you are going to remove the information on gateways and name servers, which MacTCP would try to use to get out to the Internet.

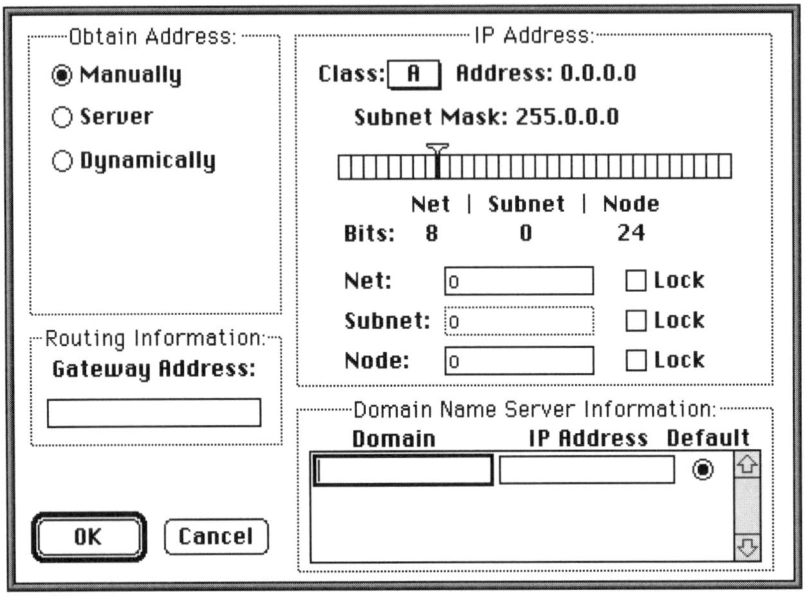

Figure 8.2
The MacTCP Additional
Settings Window

When you have the settings changed, click on the **OK** button to accept them and close the MacTCP window. You may get the notice `Your computer must be restarted to use these settings`. Go ahead and restart.

With these settings, you can refer to your server as "http://192.0.1.2/". If you want to use a DNS name for your computer, you need to modify the Hosts file in your system folder (or make a new one). This file is used by MacTCP to map DNS names to IP addresses (like a very simple DNS server). In your Hosts file make an entry that reads like this:

```
www.yourserver.domain   A     192.0.1.2
```

This tells your computer to map the name `www.yourserver.domain` to the address `192.0.1.2` (replace that computer name with your own, of course).

This setup may not be as stable as a real network connection. Several problems have been reported with clients, mostly Netscape Navigator, and with the configuration working one time and not the next. Of course, there are always more problems when you try to run client software on the server that it is connecting to.

Using File Aliases

File aliases, or representatives of other files, contain only the information that the operating system needs in order to locate the file represented. File aliases can be very useful to refer to files or folders on different disks or even entire disks. They can also be used to provide an alternative name for a file or to create a shorter path to a file that otherwise would be many directories deep in the site.

There are problems on some systems, though, with using file aliases. The problem occurs because the URL that the client uses specifies the file alias, which may not be in the same directory or even the same disk as the actual file. The client software stores this URL to use the next time it encounters a partial URL in the document. Thus any partial URLs in the document will be built-in reference to the alias, not to the document that was returned.

Another problem can occur due to some problems with the way the Macintosh OS handles aliases. When WebSTAR receives an "If-Modified-Since" request for a file alias, it tries to resolve that to the actual file so that the date modified reflects the file's last change and not the last time the alias was made. Sometimes, though, there can be an error if WebSTAR is checking the same alias twice at the same time for two different requests. There is nothing to do about this but wait for the system software to be fixed.

Improving Single-Server Performance

Whether you're planning a large site for a corporation or a small site to list the results of your kid's softball team, one thing is certain: You want the site to be fast. Internet users are getting spoiled by near-instantaneous access to sites around the world, so many of them won't hang around if it takes too long to download one of your pages. So far, though, there has been no agreement as to how to measure "fast." Some people look at the number of simultaneous connections that a server can handle, but that is an increasingly useless statistic, due to speed increases in both the server software and CPUs. Consider the fact that a server that processes every connection in at least three seconds (not unreasonable) can handle more than 200,000 connections every week and never process more than one connection at a time.

The only speed measurement that really matters is how fast your users *think* your site is, and the key to that is simply to get the data out fast. Toward that end you can do several things to improve the speed of your WebSTAR server. All of these suggestions are for a single CPU server.

Server Settings

The easiest way to improve server speed is to adjust the following settings:

- **Thread Manager**   The Thread Manager is a system extension that allows applications to run multiple simultaneous threads internally. WebSTAR uses this to provide each connection with its own thread, so all current connections are being processed somewhat simultaneously. Without Thread Manager, connections fight for attention in WebSTAR and slow connections eat up more time than fast ones, which slows your server down. With threading, each connection is somewhat isolated from the others, so fast connections are processed quickly without waiting for slower ones. The Thread Manager extension is distributed with WebSTAR and is also part of System 7.5. WebSTAR versions 1.2 and later will not run without the Thread Manager installed. There is no reason not to install it; the performance difference is incredible.

- **Use DNS**   WebSTAR logs the IP address of each connection. It also offers the option of logging the DNS name instead. This can be a lot of fun if you're the kind of person who would stare at the log for hours waiting for an "important" site to connect. ("Look, someone from Apple just looked at my bio page!") It can also be a significant performance hit, though, while WebSTAR waits for a DNS server to convert the IP address to a DNS name. In addition, for sites that don't have DNS names, the only way to find out is to wait for the DNS server to give up looking for a name, which takes much longer. For best performance, turn **Use DNS** off.

- **Buffer size**   This setting controls how large a block of data is sent to the client at once. The larger you make the blocks, the faster the data can be pumped out. The size option ranges from 512 bytes to 10K. Theoretically your best performance will come by using the 10K setting. In practice, though, this may slow your server down. There are two problems. The first is that slow connections, such as 14.4K PPP connections, cannot receive the data very quickly. For that modem connection, it would take at least five seconds to send a 10K block of data. Thousands of people access the Internet at these speeds and the numbers are increasing. Changing to a smaller block size may improve performance.

   The second problem is that some Windows TCP/IP stacks cannot handle that much data at once. Some are limited to 8K chunks and the extra data can cause them to crash. Some have trouble with anything more than 4K at a time. If your site is seeing a lot of timeouts, or if users report that their client often says `Socket not connected`, it is best to set the buffer size much lower, possibly as low as 2K.

- **Timeouts**   When a client fails to respond to the data from Web-STAR, there is no way to know whether the connection to the client was lost or is just slow, so WebSTAR just hangs on until the timeout period is reached. Keeping a dead connection open like this eats up processing time unprofitably and ties up a connection that some other client could be using. For best performance, keep your timeout setting as short as possible.

- **Foreground operation**   For best performance, keep WebSTAR running in the foreground. Because the Macintosh OS uses cooperative multitasking, the foreground application is in charge of deciding when other applications get to run. Keeping WebSTAR in the foreground (meaning that its menu bar is the one showing) gives it control of the CPU and the most processing cycles. If you need to temporarily move another application to the foreground, remember to move WebSTAR there again when the other application is done.

Hardware Improvements

This is where the largest performance improvements come from, but it's not cheap or even possible in some cases.

- **Network**   Probably the single biggest improvement you can make is in getting a better network connection. If your server is on a 56 Kbps connection (7K per second), adding a faster server will probably not improve the response, because the network cannot handle the traffic. Even a T1 line might not be sufficient for some sites, especially if the line is shared with other computers. Before you invest thousands of dollars in a powerful new server, make sure that you have (or will soon have) the network resources to let the server perform at its peak.

- **Computer platform**   Although CPU speed isn't the largest factor in performance, it does make a difference. WebSTAR spends a significant amount of time in the processor while it fixes bad URLs, checks security, creates log data, and so on. All of that work goes faster on a faster CPU. In addition, WebSTAR is PowerPC-native, so it will run even faster on the PowerMacintosh servers. If you have the network connection already, the next step is to move up to a faster server.

  There is some overlap between performance of 68040 and Power-Macintosh computers as WebSTAR servers. This is because the network driver (MacTCP) and the file system are both still running in emulation on the PowerMacintosh computers. I still recommend purchasing a PowerMacintosh, though, because of the future potential. The 68040 performance has hit its peak, whereas the PowerMacintosh gets better with every system revision.

  I especially recommend the new PCI machines, with the CPU mounted on a daughter card. This is a nice feature, since you can easily (and cheaply now) upgrade to faster CPUs as they are released. Also, the PCI slots should allow cheaper access to such add-ons as high-speed disk and network interface cards.

- **Disk drives**   Adding a faster disk drive can provide some performance improvement, especially if you are serving a lot of large files or are using an older Macintosh with the original 80MB disk.

The speed improvement is not going to be great, though, because most disks can pump out data much faster than the network can accept it. I recommend that more consideration be given to getting a disk with sufficient storage space or to getting a mirror disk than to getting a disk with the ability to pump out data at high speeds (more than 4 MB/s). Also be sure to put some money into getting a backup system for whatever disk you have, whether you go to tape or optical disk. Even the fastest site is useless if you suddenly lose all of your files.

* **Memory** Adding more memory will have almost no effect on performance. More memory is required to handle more connections, but you can handle the maximum number of connections for your Macintosh in 6MB of RAM, so 12MB is probably plenty of memory for most sites. If you are running a lot of CGI applications or linking to external applications, you may need more memory to handle those (about 32MB extra if you're linking to Microsoft Excel).

9

The HyperText Markup Language (HTML)

HTML documents make up the majority of the files served by WWW servers, and writing correct HTML is important. Since several good books on the subject are available, I am going to cover only the highlights and recommend that you find another source for the nitty-gritty details. By the highlights, I mean HTML 1.0 and 2.0, which are the current standards. HTML 3.0 is still subject to changes, and the Netscape extensions are even more so.

HTML Overview

Before you learn HTML, you need to understand how it works and the terminology.

HTML Terminology

HTML markup divides documents hierarchically into *elements*. Each element comprises text and one or more *tags*. *Opening tags* indicate the beginning of an element and take the form **`<TAGNAME>`**. *Closing tags* indicate the end of an element and take the form **`</TAGNAME>`**. The opening and closing tags typically delineate a block of text, with the tag indicating some way of modifying the display of the text, such as making it bold, increasing the font size, indenting the text block, or a combination. The result is an element that look like this:

```
<TAGNAME> text_block </TAGNAME>.
```

Some elements do not require closing tags, because the element does not affect a block of text, as in a tag that puts an image or dividing line in a document. In other cases the closing tag is optional, because the end of the text block can be assumed as soon as another opening tag is encountered. Also, some elements contain more than just opening and closing tags. Elements that provides lists of various kinds will have tags in the text block that indicate the beginning of each item in the list. These special elements will be more clear when we get into examples.

Within the opening tag of an element are often several settings, called *attributes*, that define certain characteristics of that particular element. As an example, an element that displays a graphic often has an attribute that specifies how the graphic will line up with the surrounding text (top, center, bottom). The result is that most opening tags look like this:

```
<TAGNAME ATTRIBUTE1="setting1" ATTRIBUTE2="setting2"
... ATTRIBUTEn="settingn">
```

The attributes are almost always optional, and an opening tag might have anywhere from zero to six or seven attributes. Closing tags never have attributes, since they affect presentation and therefore need to occur before the text or object they affect.

Many elements are already defined and cover most of what you need to mark up a document. Therefore many of the changes being proposed in the latest HTML are not for new tags, but rather for new attributes for existing tags to extend their functionality.

Interpreting HTML Text

So how do these elements work to display the document? And what does it mean that they're hierarchical? Imagine an HTML text document as a steady stream of text, starting at the first character in the document and continuing without break to the last character in the document, including carriage returns. An HTML viewer reads that text character by character. All of the text that it reads can be divided up into either an element or the text block of an element. When the viewer encounters a "<" character, it treats that as the start of an HTML element. The text between that "<" and the following ">" is considered the opening tag of an element. An opening tag contains instructions for the viewer on how all following text (all text downstream) should be displayed. The instructions might be *modifications*, meaning that they modify what was previously instructed, or they might be *directives*, meaning that they override what was previously instructed. These settings are applied to all text encountered between an opening tag and its closing tag (or its implied closing tag).

The hierarchical nature comes into play because elements can often be embedded within other elements. In fact, the HTML standard specifies what elements may be embedded inside other elements. By embedding elements in one another, you define in layers what the text will look like when the viewer displays it. Also, elements may not be overlapped, meaning that if you encounter opening tag A and then opening tag B, you must see closing tag B before you see closing tag A. In other words, the styles that elements apply to the text must be removed in the reverse order of the way they were applied.

White Space

A last important feature of HTML text display is that all white space is virtually ignored. *White space* includes spaces, tabs, and carriage returns. Whenever two or more of these are encountered, the viewer renders them as a single space (with a few exceptions). This means that you can use white space characters however you want to format the text file for easy reading without affecting how it will be displayed in the viewer. In addition, you can use white space within tags to format the space between attributes if you want to.

Special Characters

Because the "<" and ">" characters are used to delimit HTML element tags, you need to use special codes to represent these characters when they are to be displayed in the document. There are two different ways to write the special codes: a *character reference* and an *entity reference*. The character reference uses the format `&#xx;` where `xx` is the number of the character in the code table. The entity reference uses the format `&<code>;` where `<code>` is a special code that represents the character. In this case `&lt;` would be the "<" character (less than) and `&gt;` would be the ">" character (greater than). Dozens of characters should be encoded this way, including the ampersand (since it indicates the start of a special code) and most 8-bit characters. You can find the most common ones listed in the IETF HTML 2.0 specifications.

Writing Standard HTML

Here is your quick introduction to HTML. If you are still learning HTML, you will definitely want to get a book that deals specifically with HTML markup.

Document Elements

These elements affect the entire document and provide the client with information about how to interpret the document. In future HTML versions, these elements might contain information on what language was used, what standards the document follows, or how to override certain client features.

- **HTML**: `<HTML>Document Text</HTML>`   This element defines the beginning and end of a stretch of HTML text. In current use there is only one stretch of text per document, so this should be the first and last tag in the document. HTML 3.0 adds attributes to extend the functionality of this element. Both the opening and closing tags are optional.

- **Head**: `<HEAD>Head Text</HEAD>`   This element defines the head portion of your HTML document. Everything between `<HEAD>` and `</HEAD>` is considered the head portion. Any of the following head elements may be present in the head portion of a document. Both the opening and closing tags are optional, since the head portion may be considered to begin at the start of the document (or immediately following the HTML opening tag) and be done when the first body element is encountered.

- **Body**: `<BODY>Body Text</BODY>`   This element defines the body portion of your HTML document. Everything between `<BODY>` and `</BODY>` is considered the body portion. Any of the body elements listed later may be present in the body portion of a document. Both the opening and closing tags are optional, since the body portion may be considered to start when the first body element is encountered and end when the document is finished (or the HTML closing tag is encountered).

Head Elements

The head of a document contains information about the relationship of a document to other documents in a site and some special features, such as a title for the document. None of the information in the head section is displayed by clients. The following elements can be used only in the head of a document:

- **TITLE:** `<TITLE>`*`Title Text`*`</TITLE>`   This defines the title of a document. The document title is used by most browsers as the name of the link for use in making bookmarks. It is also used by graphical browsers as the title of the window displaying the document. This is the only element that is required in the head portion of an HTML document.

- **BASE:** `<BASE HREF="`*`URL`*`">`   This element specifies the fully qualified URL of the document. This information can be used by clients to resolve partial URLs even when the document is moved out of the directory (even to another machine). This is very useful if you use file aliases to refer to a document; if no base is defined in the header, the URL of the *alias* will be used as the base URL for the document. *Note: Base does not need to be the* true *URL, only the one you want used to resolve partials.*

Body Elements

The body of a document contains all of the information that will be displayed by the WWW client. This is where the real information you want to share with others should go.

- **Anchor:** `<A HREF="`*`URL`*`">`*`Anchor Text`*`</A>`   Anchors form the hypertext connections among documents, files, and servers. Anchor text is turned into a hypertext link that will take the user to the URL specified. Any valid URL may be used for the link.

Although it is legal to have the anchor text include any other body elements (except for another anchor element), it is a good idea to limit the elements used to character styling and image elements.

- **Name:** `<A NAME="Name">Name Text</A>`   Names are anchors to other locations within an HTML document. By appending `"#Name"` to a URL, a link can specify for the client software to jump to the position in the document where the name link is. The name given to the marker may contain any combination of letters and numbers. The name should be made only long enough to uniquely identify the marker in the document. The name text should be short and all on one line. Typically WWW browsers do not give any indication when a section of text is used as a marker, so there is no advantage to using large text selections as the name text. The name text can contain other elements, including anchor links.

- **Image (IMG):**
  `<IMG ALIGN={top|middle|bottom} SRC="URL"ALT="descriptive text" ISMAP>`

  The IMG element allows an image to be displayed along with the text in a document. The URL may specify any image file that can be displayed by WWW client software. Currently the browsers vary in what they are able to display. Almost all graphical browsers are able to display GIF images. Some of the new releases can display JPEG images as well, and some can display formats specific to the platform they run on, such as BMP (XWindows bitmapped graphic).

  SRC specifies the URL of the file to be embedded. The SRC attribute is required.

  ALIGN can take the values TOP, MIDDLE, or BOTTOM. TOP places the next text aligned with the top of the graphic; MIDDLE centers the image in the line of text; BOTTOM aligns the bottom of the image with the following text. The ALIGN attribute is optional. BOTTOM is the default if ALIGN is not specified.

  ALT defines text to be displayed if a graphic is not downloaded or if the browser doesn't support graphics. The ALT attribute is optional.

ISMAP tells servers that are capable to return mouse click coordinates from the graphic to be interpreted as a click on a region of the graphic. This is also known as a clickable map graphic. The ISMAP attribute is optional.

Netscape Navigator adds several more options for IMG as part of its proposed additions to HTML 3.0:

```
<IMG ALT={LEFT|RIGHT|TEXTTOP|ABSMIDDLE|BASELINE
|ABSBOTTOM}>
```

LEFT causes the graphic to align with the left side of the document in the browser. Text will flow around the right side of the graphic if room is available.

RIGHT causes the graphic to align with the right side of the document in the browser. Text will flow around the left side of the graphic if room is available.

TEXTTOP causes the top of the graphic to align with the top of the following and preceding lines of text.

ABSMIDDLE causes the middle of the graphic to align with the center of the following and preceding lines of text.

BASELINE causes the bottom of the graphic to align with the bottom of the following and preceding lines of text.

ABSBOTTOM causes the bottom of the graphic to align with the bottom of the following and preceding lines of text:

```
<IMG WIDTH=value HEIGHT=value>
```

WIDTH defines the width of the image file in pixels.

HEIGHT defines the height of the image file in pixels.

These attributes allow the size of the image to be defined. When that information is provided, Netscape is able to display all of the text as it arrives, using placeholders for the graphics until they are also downloaded. This allows the user to read the contents of a document while waiting for image transfers. If one of these attributes is used, both must be. These attributes are optional.

```
<IMG BORDER=value>
```

This attribute specifies the thickness of the border to display around the image if it is embedded in a hypertext link (as with a map graphic). If you use BORDER=0, no border will be displayed.

```
<IMG VSPACE=value HSPACE=value>
```

VSPACE controls the vertical space above and below the image. With larger values, more blank space will be left around the image.

HSPACE controls the horizontal space to the left and right of the image.

- **Comment: `<!-- comment text -->`**   This tag provides the ability to place a comment in a document. The comment is entirely ignored by the client software and is not part of the displayed document. The opening tag (`<--`) must not contain any white space, but white space may be in the closing tag (`-->`) between the last two characters. All text between the opening and closing portions of the tag should be ignored entirely, meaning that a comment section can include other HTML tags, which will not be displayed.

  There have been several interpretations of how commenting should be done in HTML prior to its inclusion in HTML 3.0. The result is that several clients do not implement comments in quite this way. The most common variant is to use a simple `>` as the closing tag, which means that the comment section is not able to contain other HTML tags. Otherwise, the first tag would be interpreted as the end of the comment section.

Format Elements

These elements have an implicit line break and appropriate amount of white space (line feed) before and after the element to set it off in the text. Paragraph elements are not needed around these elements.

- **Paragraph: `<P>`**   This element forces a carriage return and line feed. It should be used to start new sections of text. It is commonly put at the end of a paragraph, but that is not a proper use of it. It marks the *start* of a new paragraph and should be placed at the start of the paragraph. If you use it this way, you will have fewer `<P>` elements hanging around that aren't needed.

The closing tag for the paragraph element is optional and usually not used.

- **Line break:** `<BR>`   This element forces a line break and carriage return to a new line. The new line has the same indent as that of the line-wrapped text. Use this element to force the ending of a line of text. Use several of these in a row to force white space (blank lines) between sections.

  Netscape Navigator adds an attribute to the BR element:

  ```
  <BR CLEAR={left|right|all}>
  ```

  CLEAR causes the text to break and not begin again until the specified margin is clear (no floating images). ALL indicates that both the left and right margins must be clear.

  Break has no closing tag.

- **Horizontal rule:** `<HR>`   This element inserts a horizontal dividing line. This is much faster than downloading the line as a graphic element.

  Netscape Navigator adds three attributes to the rule element:

  ```
  <HR SIZE=value WIDTH={value/percent}
  ALIGN={left|right|center} NOSHADE>
  ```

  SIZE determines the thickness of the line that will be displayed (vertical size). WIDTH determines how wide the line will be. It can be either an absolute value (in pixels) or a percentage of the displayed page width. ALIGN determines how the line will be aligned on the page (since the line may not be the full page width). NOSHADE draws the line without any shading.

  Rule has no closing tag.

- **Heading:** `<Hn>Heading Text</Hn>` $n=\{1..6\}$ This element specifies a level of heading for the enclosed text, with H1 the most emphatic and H6 the least. Italic, underline, and some other character highlighting elements can be embedded in the heading text.

- **Address:** `<ADDRESS>Address Text</ADDRESS>`   This uses a particular style (depending on the client) to show the address. Line breaks should be used within long addresses for formatting lines.

- **Preformatted:**

  `<PRE [WIDTH={40|80|130}]>`*`Preformatted Text`*`</PRE>`

  This is used to present text with the spaces and tabs preserved. It should display the text in a fixed-width font. The preformatted text can contain anchors and character highlighting elements but not format elements.

List Elements

These elements present the information in various list formats. The common factor is that each item of the list is marked as a list item, with the presentation format determined by the opening tag. Lists elements have white space automatically included before and after the element.

- **Unordered list:** `<UL>(<LI>[list item text])*</UL>`   This list format is used to present a series of paragraphs of text, each preceded by a special mark or sequence (such as a bullet). Each paragraph is slightly separated from the next by white space. List item text can contain anchor and highlighting elements but no other format elements, except for other embedded lists.

- **Ordered list:** `<OL>(<LI>[list item text])*</OL>`   This list format is the same as the unordered list except that each item should be sequentially marked (numbered list).

- **Menu:** `<MENU>(<LI>[list item text])*</MENU>`   This list format is used primarily to present items that take only one line each. The list item text can contain the same elements as ordered and unordered list items.

- **Directory:** `<DIR>(<LI>[list item text])*</DIR>`   This list format is used to present very short text items, such as a file directory. The client software should be able to format the items into multiple columns to maximize use of screen space. List item text can contain the same items as the preceding lists.

- **Definition list (glossary):**

  `<DL>(<DT>[label text](<DD>[def inition text])*)*</DL>`

  This list format is used to present pairs of labels and definitions, as in a dictionary or glossary. The definition text is offset on the first line following the `<DD>` tag. A label can be followed by multiple definition lines. If the definition text is too long to fit on one line, it will wrap at the full width of the screen. Both the label text and the definition text are able to use the same elements as the list items previously discussed.

Character Styling Elements

These elements, extras to the HTML specification allow sections of text to be formatted in a particular way (emphasis, bold, underline, and so on). These elements do not cause a paragraph break and may be used on sections of text within paragraphs without disturbing the flow. These elements may be ignored by clients on systems lacking the graphics capabilities to display them.

- **Physical styles**   These elements attempt to specify a particular style or font for rendering. Not all clients will be able to support these styles and may choose to interpret them differently or to ignore them. All physical style elements should have cumulative effects, so that `<B><I>Hello</I></B>` results in both bold and italic text.

  Bold: `<B>[text]</B>`   Renders the text in boldface.

  Italic: `<I>[text]</I>`   Renders the text in italics.

  Typewriter: `<TT>[text]</TT>`   Renders the text in a fixed-width typewriter font.

- **Logical styles**   These styles do not specify a particular style but a relative one. There may be many variations in the interpretation by different clients.

  Emphasis: `<EM>[text]</EM>`   Emphasizes the text, typically italic.

  Strong emphasis: `<STRONG>[text]</STRONG>`   Stronger emphasis, typically bold.

  Source code: `<CODE>[text]</CODE>`   Used to display sections of code, usually in a monospaced font (not to be confused with preformatted text).

  Sample: `<SAMP>[text]</SAMP>`   A sequence of literal characters.

  Keyboard: `<KBD>[text]</KBD>`   Used to display text typed by a user, as in an instruction manual.

Variable: `<VAR>[text]</VAR>`   Used to display variable names.

Definition: `<DFN>[text]</DFN>`   The defining instance of a term. Typically bold or bold italic.

Citation: `<CITE>[text]</CITE>`   Used to display a citation, typically in italic.

Netscape Navigator adds two new character formatting elements to control font size:

> **`<BASEFONT SIZE=value>`**

This element sets the size of the standard font in a document. The default is 3 and the value can be from 1–7. This element has no closing tag and should occur only once in a document.

> **`<FONT SIZE=value>[text]</FONT>`**

This element sets the font size for all text between the opening and closing tags. The size can either be stated exactly (value of 1–7) or relative to the base font (by preceding the number with a + or – sign). The change continues until the closing tag `</FONT>` or until another font element begins.

Special Netscape Elements

Netscape Navigator has become so popular that these elements can't really be ignored, although these are not guaranteed to be supported by any other WWW client software and may be changed with the next version of Netscape.

- **Background color: `<BODY BGCOLOR="#RGB">`**   This attribute defines the background color for the page. The color is defined as three hexadecimal numbers representing the red, blue, and green components of the color (the RGB value). Thus red would run from 00 to FF, with 00 being the lightest shade; 000000 would be white; FFFFFF, black; and DDDD00, deep purple.

- **Background texture: `<BODY BACKGROUND="URL">`**   This attribute defines a pattern to be used for the page background. The graphic specified in the URL will be tiled to fill the background and should be either a GIF or a JPEG graphic.

- **Text color: `<BODY TEXT="#RGB">`**   This attribute defines what color will be used for text in the page. RGB is three hexadecimal values representing the red, blue, and green values for the color.

- **Link color: `<BODY LINK="#RGB">`**   This attribute defines what color will be used for page text representing a hypertext link. RGB is three hexadecimal values representing the red, blue, and green values for the color.

- **Visited color: `<BODY VLINK="#RGB">`**   This attribute defines what color will be used for page text representing links that have been visited. RGB is three hexadecimal values representing the red, blue, and green values for the color.

- **Active color: `<BODY ALINK="#RGB">`**   This attribute defines what color will be used for page text that the user is clicking the mouse on. RGB is three hexadecimal values representing the red, blue, and green values for the color.

The background color and texture attributes are exclusive with a background taking precedence. The text-coloring attributes can all be specified in one body element.

Obsolete Elements

These elements may still be encountered in some documents. Don't use them. They all have equivalents in HTTP 1.0, so there is no need to go on using them.

- **Plaintext: `<PLAINTEXT>`**   This element is used in old HTTP conventions to indicate that what follows is an ASCII body. This was an optimization indicating that the rest of the text could be transmitted clear and didn't require parsing. There is no closing tag.

- **Example: `<XMP>[text]</XMP>`**   This element allows text of fixed-width characters to be embedded absolutely as is into the document. The example text is displayed, so at least 80 characters are able to fit on a line.

- **Listing: `<LISTING>[text]</LISTING>`**   This is just like the example element, except that the lines can fit at least 132 characters.

- **Highlighted phrase: `<HPn>[text]</HPn>` n=1,2,...** This is used to highlight a phrase but has been replaced with more meaningful character-highlighting elements.

Forms

The World Wide Web is a great way of publishing information. That has been said before and is really the core of most sites. However, the real reason many of us run sites is not to publish information but to gather it. We want to run questionnaires, provide searchable databases, allow users to purchase items on line, or perhaps just want to provide a forum for user questions and comments. Whatever the reason, we want some method of interacting with users.

Currently there are only three ways to interact with users via the Web. You can use hot links in your pages and watch which links the users prefer. You can make maps that offer multiple choices and register which choice the users prefer (just like links only more visual). Or, you can use forms and get feedback from the users in a variety of formats.

What is a form? A form is the portion of an HTML document designated as containing elements that accept user input. In the browser these elements might display as text fields that a user can type into, radio buttons, checkboxes, pop-up lists, or scrolling lists. The result is the ability to put something in your WWW page that looks like a form that might be used for applying for a job, filling out a questionnaire, or ordering a product. The user can manipulate these elements (type in a field, select a button, check a box), and then the information entered can be sent to the WWW server for processing. Figure 9.1 displays a sample form page.

Before we get in any deeper, here are some terms pertaining to forms:

- **Form tag**   Any tag that can be used to present a field, button, menu, or other part of a form, including the tags that mark the beginning and end of a form area.

- **Form tag attribute (or attribute)**   A portion of a form tag, such as the row specification for a text field.

- **Form element**   The entire form area, including all tags.

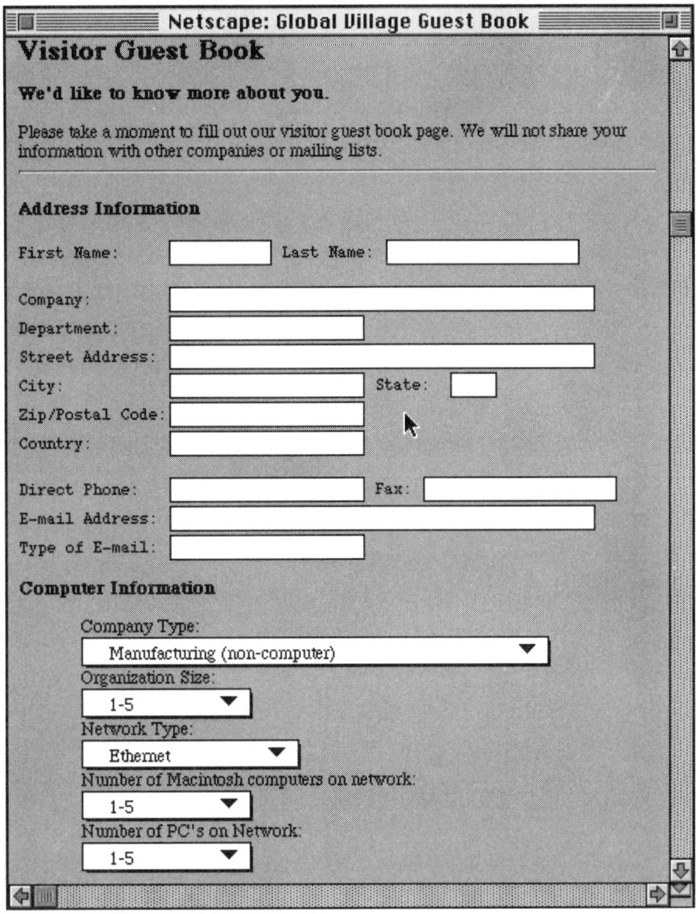

Figure 9.1

Sample of a Form as
Viewed in Netscape
Navigator 1.1N
(Macintosh)

- **Form field (or field)**   Any item in a form element, including text fields, buttons, pop-up menus, and the **Submit** button.

- **Form area**   A section of an HTML document delineated by a start and end tag for a form.

- **Form data**   The information sent from the form when the user submits the form to a WWW server. This includes the names of all form elements selected and all data entered by the user.

- **Form (on-line form, form page)**   Any page that has one or more form areas in it.

Form Elements

The tags used to make form elements are specified as part of HTML 2.0. Almost all WWW clients now support forms, and any that don't are not worth using. Here are the tags that are available for use in a form area.

- **Start**   This tag marks the beginning of a form area in an HTML document. The form area defines what information is returned when the user clicks on the **Submit** button. By using start and end tags, it is possible to have multiple form areas in a single HTML document; however, the forms are not allowed to be nested (one form within another).

  `<FORM ACTION="http://www.nowhere.com/cgi/ProcessForm.acgi" METHOD=POST>`

  `ACTION`   specifies the URL to which the form results will be sent. The URL must point to a CGI application capable of extracting the information from the form data and processing it. In this case an asynchronous CGI application is specified.

  `METHOD`   specifies the HTTP method to be used to submit the form information to the server. There are two options for use with WebSTAR (as defined in the IETF draft HTTP standard). `GET` (the default): The form contents are appended to the URL (after a question mark). This method severely limits how much information may be sent (WebSTAR limits it to 4K). `POST`: The form contents are sent to the server in the body of the message. This is the recommended usage, as it allows up to 24K of data to be sent.

  The default method is GET, and the client will use that if no method is specified or if there is any problem in determining the method. Some clients may treat POST and "post" as two different methods, so it is best to use the uppercase when specifying a method.

  The HTML 2.0 specification also allows the ENCTYPE attribute to be specified (that is, how the form data will be encoded before passing to WebSTAR). This is generally unnecessary with Web-STAR. With the POST method, the ENCTYPE attribute is a MIME type of "application/x-www-form-urlencoded", which means that the contents of the appended data are URL encoded.

- **End**   This tag simply marks the end of a form area.

  `</FORM>`

- **Text field**   The text field is used for the user to enter small amounts of information, such as a name, street, age, or favorite color. The text field displayed is only one line deep and can be as wide as the screen.

  `<INPUT TYPE="text" NAME="name" VALUE="" SIZE=20`
  `MAXLENGTH=40>`

  `INPUT`   specifies that this will be a place for the user to input information.

  `TYPE`   tells what type of input item will be used. The available types include text, hidden, radio, checkbox, password, image, submit, and reset. For a text field, the TYPE is "text."

  `NAME`   is the text string that will be sent by the client as the name of the element.

  `VALUE`   is the default value of the element. If the value attribute is not present, it is empty by default.

  `SIZE`   is the width of the text field, in characters. For a text field, the default size attribute is 20 characters.

  `MAXLENGTH`   is the maximum number of characters that may be entered in the text field.

- **Text block**   The text area is used for the user to enter large amounts of information, such as comments, e-mail messages, or essay-type answers. The text area can be several lines deep, as well as variable width. Text may be entered between the opening and closing tags to initialize the contents of the textarea field.

  `<TEXTAREA NAME="HomeAddress" ROWS=8 COLS=80>`

  `319 White Street`

  `Seattle, WA 98194`

  `USA`

  `</TEXTAREA>`

  `TEXTAREA`, the opening tag, contains the attributes that define the characteristics of the text area.

NAME   is the text string that will be sent by the client as the name of the element.

ROWS   is the number of rows (height) of the text area.

COLS   is the number of columns (width) of the text area. The WWW client should allow the user to type beyond the width of the window specified by scrolling to follow the input.

/TEXTAREA   is the closing tag and defines the end of any text that might be used to initialize the contents of the field.

• **Hidden text field**   This field provides a way of passing information that the user cannot see along with the information that the user enters. The name and value of this field are passed as part of the form data when the user submits the form. This is very useful for carrying state information in your forms.

```
<INPUT TYPE="hidden" NAME="UserID" VALUE="1099-4432">
```

NAME   is the text string that will be sent by the client as the name of the element.

VALUE   is the data that will be returned.

• **Password**   A password field is just like a text field, except that the text entered is shown as bullets. This is useful for requesting privileged information that shouldn't be entered in the clear. The actual text is sent as part of the form data.

```
<INPUT TYPE="password" NAME="creditnum" VALUE=""
SIZE=20 MAXLENGTH=20>
```

• **Checkbox**   The checkbox is used for the user to select any number of options, such as favorite foods from a menu.

```
<INPUT TYPE="checkbox" NAME="FavFood" VALUE=
"Hamburgers" CHECKED>
```

NAME   is the text string that will be sent by the client as the name of the element.

VALUE   is the data that will be returned if the button is selected.

CHECKED   is the attribute that determines whether the box is initially shown as being checked. If the checked attribute is not present, the box will be unchecked initially.

- **Radio button**   Radio buttons provide the user with many options from which one and only one may be chosen. Radio buttons are grouped so that selecting one button in the group will deselect all of the others in the group. You should always set one of the buttons to be the default for a group of buttons.

```
<INPUT  TYPE="radio" NAME="decades" VALUE="60s">
<INPUT  TYPE="radio" NAME="decades" VALUE="70s" CHECKED>
<INPUT  TYPE="radio" NAME="decades" VALUE="80s">
```

NAME   is the text string that will be sent by the client as the name of the element. Each group of radio buttons shares the same name. Only one button using that name can be selected at any one time.

VALUE   is the data that will be returned if that button is selected.

CHECKED   is the attribute that determines whether the button is initially shown as being selected. If the checked attribute is not present, the button will not be selected. Only one radio button in a group may have the checked attribute.

- **Pop-up menu**   A pop-up menu allows the user to select one option out of many. It is analogous to a group of radio buttons but takes up less space. Note that this is not a single tag but a group of tags, much like a LIST.

```
<SELECT NAME="Company">

    <OPTION>Ernst & Young

    <OPTION SELECTED>Pratt & Whitney

    <OPTION>Cheng & Tsui

    <OPTION VALUE="HBCM & F">Hartworth, Butterford,
Crestman, Meikin, & Fields
</SELECT>
```

SELECT   is the tag name and indicates that this tag will present the user with a number of options to select from.

NAME   is the text string that will be sent by the client as the name of the element.

OPTION   is a tag used to indicate one of the possible options in the pop-up menu. The menu will contain the text of each option as one line of the menu.

Within the OPTION tag, the SELECTED attribute is used to indicate the default selection to be shown when the menu is initially displayed. If the selected attribute is not used, the first option in the list will be displayed. Only one option may be selected within the pop-up menu options.

Also within the OPTION tag, a VALUE may be specified. This attribute contains the data that will be returned as the value of this option if it is selected. If no value attribute is set, the text of the option will be returned by default.

- **Scrolling list**   A scrolling list allows the user to select any number of options from a list of options in a scrolling text field. In this way it is analogous to a checkbox, but it takes less space on screen. Note that this is not a single tag but a group of tags, much like a LIST.

```
<SELECT NAME="KeeperCards" SIZE=6 MULTIPLE>

    <OPTION SELECTED>Jack of Spades

    <OPTION>Queen of Diamonds

    <OPTION>10 of Clubs

    <OPTION>King of Hearts

    <OPTION>2 of Diamonds

    <OPTION>5 of Clubs

    <OPTION SELECTED>Ace of Spades

    <OPTION>8 of Hearts

    <OPTION>4 of Clubs

</SELECT>
```

SELECT   is the tag name and indicates that this tag will present the user with a number of options to select from.

NAME   is the text string that will be sent by the client as the name of the element.

SIZE   defines how many lines will display in the scrolling field. The size attribute should always be less than the total number of options available.

MULTIPLE   is the attribute that defines this as a scrolling list instead of a pop-up menu.

OPTION is a tag used to indicate one of the possible options in the pop-up menu. The menu will contain the text of each option as one line of the menu. The text showing when the user makes a selection will be sent as the data for this menu.

Within the OPTION tag, the SELECTED attribute is used to indicate the default selection to be shown when the menu is initially displayed. If the selected attribute is not used, none of the options will be initially selected. Any number of options may be set to be initially selected in the scrolling list.

Also within the OPTION tag, a VALUE may be specified. This attribute contains the data that will be returned as the value of this option if it is selected. If no value attribute is set, the text of the option will be returned by default.

- **Image** The image type is used to present a graphic as a **Submit** button. When the graphic is clicked on, the x and y coordinates of the click (relative to the top left of the image) are sent as part of the form data. The x-coordinate is submitted under the name of the field with **.x** appended, and the y-coordinate is submitted under the name of the field with **.y** appended. Any VALUE attribute is ignored. This can be a useful way to provide multiple options when submitting form data or just a way to add a little flourish to your form.

```
<INPUT TYPE="image" NAME="Pict" SRC="buttons.gif"
ALIGN=middle>
```

NAME is the text string that will be sent by the client as the name of the element.

SRC specifies the location of the image to display. This attribute may be either a full or partial URL but must fully specify the file location.

ALIGN specifies the alignment of the image, just as it does for the IMG tag.

Note: this tag may be rolled into a changed version of the Submit button tag in future versions of HTML.

- **Submit button** This button is provided for the user to click on when ready to send off the data entered in the form. Every form must have at least one **Submit** button in order to work. If there are several such buttons, each one will do exactly the same thing, although the names and values may be different.

```
<INPUT TYPE="submit" NAME="S" VALUE="Submit this Form">
```

NAME is the text string that will be sent by the client as the name of the element.

VALUE is the text that will be displayed inside the button. The button will be automatically resized to fit whatever string of text you use as the **VALUE**, up to the width of the screen.

• **Reset button**   This button allows the user to clear all of the information entered so far and begin again. All buttons, menus, and lists are reset to their default values.

```
<INPUT TYPE="reset" NAME="R" VALUE="Clear this Form">
```

NAME   is somewhat irrelevant, since this button doesn't cause any data to be sent anywhere.

VALUE   is the text that will be displayed inside the button. The button will be automatically resized to fit whatever string of text you use as the **VALUE**, up to the width of the screen.

Making a Form Page

The tags listed previously are the keys to creating the tag elements, but you still need to use other text and HTML tags to make the form presentable and clear to the user. Paragraphs, line breaks, and even lists can be used to create the proper spacing for form elements. Additional text is needed to label each form element with instructions for the user, such as "Enter your name here:".

Here is an example of a form area from an HTML document (the rest of the document is not displayed). This example pulls together all of the samples given earlier. Notice that the hidden text field is not displayed in the following screen shot. You can also see in this example how a graphic might be used to replace a simple **Submit** button to give more flexibility to the form.

Figure 9.2 shows how that form would be displayed by the Netscape WWW client software.

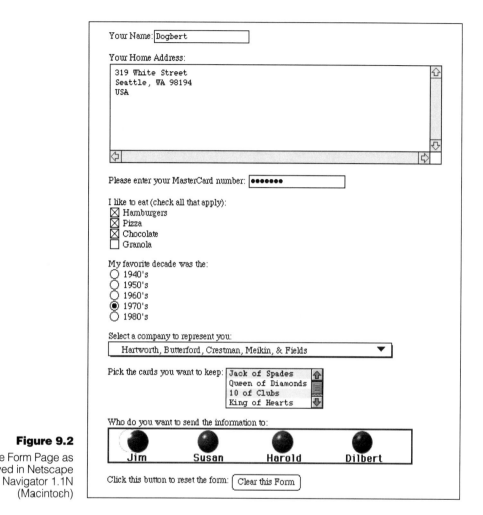

Figure 9.2

The Form Page as Displayed in Netscape Navigator 1.1N (Macintosh)

```
<FORM ACTION="none" METHOD=POST>

<BR>40 Character Field (text):<INPUT TYPE="text"
NAME="name" VALUE="" SIZE=20 MAXLENGTH=40>

<P>Your Home Address:

<TEXTAREA NAME="HomeAddress" ROWS=8 COLS=80>319 White
Street

Seattle, WA 98194

USA

</TEXTAREA>
```

```
<P><INPUT TYPE="hidden" NAME="UserID" VALUE="1099-
4432">

<P>Please enter your MasterCard number:

<INPUT TYPE="password" NAME="creditnum" VALUE=""
SIZE=20 MAXLENGTH=20>

<P>I like to eat (check all that apply):

<BR><INPUT TYPE="checkbox" NAME="FavFood" VALUE="Ham-
burgers" CHECKED>Hamburgers

<BR><INPUT TYPE="checkbox" NAME="FavFood"
VALUE="Pizza">Pizza

<BR><INPUT TYPE="checkbox" NAME="FavFood"
VALUE="Chocolate">Chocolate

<BR><INPUT TYPE="checkbox" NAME="FavFood" VALUE="Gra-
nola">Granola

<P>My favorite decade was the:

<BR><INPUT TYPE="radio" NAME="decades" VALUE="40s">
1940's

<BR><INPUT TYPE="radio" NAME="decades" VALUE="50s">
1950's

<BR><INPUT TYPE="radio" NAME="decades" VALUE="60s">
1960's

<BR><INPUT TYPE="radio" NAME="decades" VALUE="70s"
CHECKED> 1970's

<BR><INPUT TYPE="radio" NAME="decades" VALUE="80s">
1980's

<P>Select a company to represent you:

<SELECT NAME="Company">

    <OPTION>Ernst & Young

    <OPTION SELECTED>Pratt & Whitney

    <OPTION>Cheng & Tsui

    <OPTION VALUE="HBCM & F">Hartworth, Butterford,
Crestman, Meikin, & Fields

</SELECT>

<P>Pick the cards you want to keep:
```

```
<SELECT NAME="KeeperCards" SIZE=4 MULTIPLE>
    <OPTION SELECTED>Jack of Spades
    <OPTION>Queen of Diamonds
    <OPTION>10 of Clubs
    <OPTION>King of Hearts
    <OPTION>2 of Diamonds
    <OPTION>5 of Clubs
    <OPTION SELECTED>Ace of Spades
    <OPTION>8 of Hearts
    <OPTION>4 of Clubs
</SELECT>

<P>Who do you want to send the information to:
<BR><INPUT TYPE="image" NAME="Pict" SRC="buttons.gif"
ALIGN=middle>

<P>Click this button to reset the form:
<INPUT TYPE="reset" VALUE="Clear this Form">
</FORM>
```

Tips on Form Design

It is important to remember that there are differences between an on-line form and one that you might distribute in printed form. Limitations imposed by screen displays and variations among WWW clients affect what you can do with a form and what will be most effective. Here are some ideas to keep in mind:

- *Keep your forms short.*   If you want to gather a lot of information, present it in small pieces and reassemble the data behind the scenes. A form that scrolls on forever is very daunting to users, and few will take the time to finish the whole thing.

- *Use the right element for the job.*   If there is a small, fixed number of possible responses from a user, it is better to use a list or buttons than a text field. If there are fewer than six possible answers, it is probably better to use radio buttons instead of a pop-up menu so that the user can scan all of the answers at once without any interaction required. If there are many answers but they can be grouped into logical sets, it may be better to use checkboxes rather than a scrolling list, for the same reason.

- *Maintain a consistent style.*   Once you use a certain element for a certain task, stick with it. Using too many different elements can make the form more confusing for the user (which is an immediate turn-off).

- *Know the limitations of each element.*   Each form element has its own limitations and unique qualities. As an example, a scrolling list should not be set to a size of less than 4, or the scrollbar will not be drawn properly.

- *Use white space effectively.*   Each element in a form should be clearly delineated from others. Elements that belong to each other (such as options to a question) should be grouped more closely together than those that are unrelated.

- *Clearly locate the **Submit** button.*   Whether you use the **Submit** button or an image tag to submit the form, the purpose of the button or graphic should be made clear to the user. **Submit** buttons typically come at the end of a form. If you must relocate the button, you might want to add some information to the end of the form, telling the new location. If you have multiple **Submit** buttons in a form, make their purpose clear, as well as which button should be used for what purpose.

Ready, Set, Go!

That's it. You are all ready now to go forth and create HTML documents with impunity or whatever other software you find handy. Of course, by the time you read this book, HTML will be fading into memory because the next generation of HTML editors will build on the experience of word processing to remove the HTML tags from sight. Think about it—who would buy a word processor that required the user to type in PostScript or RTF text? Ridiculous! The same will soon hold true for HTML editors. The only thing that is needed is a word processor that has HTML as its underlying language, which means that it won't do two-column text but will have the ability to create hypertext links without directly typing in the URL.

Actually, I'm not being a psychic in predicting this, because I have seen it in action with the PageMill and SiteMill software from Ceneca Communications (`http://www.ceneca.com/`). This software brings all of the experience of several generations of word processing software to bear on the problem of HTML editing. With support for drag-and-drop links, error checking for hand-typed HTML tags, imagemap graphics editing, and much more, it is simply the only choice for creating Web pages.

10

CGI Applications

CGI applications are special applications that can provide added features to your WebSTAR server either by doing special processing or by acting as intermediaries between WebSTAR and other applications, such as databases or text search engines. CGI applications allow you to add site-specific services to your server. You can also use them to replace services that WebSTAR provides, such as site security, with more powerful alternatives. The possibilities are nearly endless, and new CGI solutions are announced every week. Even if you don't plan to write a CGI application yourself, this overview will help you understand how they work and how best to use them on your site.

The CGI Standard

The Common Gateway Interface (CGI) standard defines a common interface for applications to communicate with Internet servers. So far, only HTTP servers use the CGI standard, but theoretically it could be used with any information server. The CGI standard defines three things:

- The information an HTTP server will pass to a CGI application

- How the client should encode information being passed to a CGI application

- The responsibilities of the CGI application

The information sent to a CGI application includes more than just the data that the client sends. When communicating with a CGI application, the HTTP server also sends information about the

209

request, such as the client's IP address or DNS name, the user name and password entered (if a secure page was requested), which CGI application was requested in the URL, the referring page (the page that contained the link to the CGI application), and what method was used in the request. This information describes almost every aspect of the client-server communication, so the CGI application has access to the same sorts of information about the connection that the server does.

The responsibilities of the CGI application, as defined by the CGI standard, are basically to take over processing of the connection for the HTTP server. This means that the CGI application has to form a proper response that the server can return to the client software. The response consists of an HTTP header with a result code and possibly some data, depending on the code. This will be covered in much greater detail later. The thing to remember for now is that the CGI application is a stand-alone application that acts as an extension to your WebSTAR server.

CGI Applications and Apple Events

One thing the CGI standard does *not* define is how the HTTP server communicates with the CGI application. No standard for sharing information between applications works across all computing systems, although the better computer operating systems usually have some method for applications to exchange information to one degree or another. On the Macintosh the preferred method of inter-application communication is Apple events, and these are what WebSTAR uses to talk to CGI applications. Apple events are high-level events that can be sent to applications to control their actions. If you are using System 7.x, you have already used these several times. When you shut down your computer, the shutdown procedure sends a "quit" event to open applications to make sure that they have all properly closed before the power is shut off. If you double-click on an icon or drag one over an application, you again use an Apple event, this time to send an "open document" command to the application.

WebSTAR created a new Apple event to use for communicating with CGI applications. The event, called WWWΩsdoc, is sent to a CGI application whenever a user specifies one in a URL. The main qualification for being a CGI application on Macintosh, therefore, is being able to receive the WWWΩsdoc event, process it, and send a reply event to WebSTAR. The WWWΩsdoc event contains all of the data sent to WebSTAR by the client, as well as the additional information listed earlier. Exact specifications of this event are given in later chapters.

WebSTAR and CGI Application Interactions

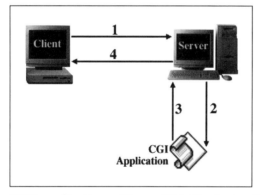

Figure 10.1

Basic Communication among the Client, WebSTAR, and a CGI Application

The interaction between WebSTAR and a CGI application is not very complex, but a few details may not be immediately evident. To save yourself many hours or even days of troubleshooting, make sure that you understand what is going on before you begin working with CGI applications. Figure 10.1 illustrates the process, which can be described as follows:

1. The user clicks on a link to a CGI application, submits a form, or takes some similar action that would be processed by a CGI application.

2. The client software creates the proper URL to address the CGI application, appends any data provided by a form or link, encodes it all for safe transmission, and sends it off to WebSTAR (step 1).

3. WebSTAR receives the request and determines that it is a request for a CGI application (using techniques discussed later). WebSTAR extracts the necessary information and data from the

request and repackages it as a WWWΩsdoc event, which it sends to the proper CGI application (step 2).

4. The CGI application receives the WWWΩsdoc event and extracts the information that it needs to process the event.

5. The CGI application processes the request from WebSTAR. This could be done entirely by the CGI application, or it could involve sending another request (via another Apple event) to a different application and waiting for the results. Either way, the processing results in the CGI application's forming a complete response for the client software, including HTTP headers and data.

6. The CGI application packages up the response and sends it in a reply event to WebSTAR (step 3).

7. WebSTAR receives the reply event, extracts the response information, and sends it back as a complete response to the client software (step 4).

8. The client software processes the response for the user.

There are a few key points to make about this entire process:

• WebSTAR does not make any changes to the data going to the CGI application or of pages being returned by the CGI application to the client. The only thing WebSTAR does is package the data in an Apple event (to go to the CGI) and remove it from the Apple event reply (to return to the client). Any errors in the data from the client or CGI are merely passed on as they are.

• The client software encodes the URL and any data being passed to the server, using the URL encoding scheme. As described previously, characters may be encoded or left clear, with the exception of the defined special characters. Therefore the CGI application needs to be ready for a variety of encoding sets that different clients may use. The fewer assumptions that the CGI application makes about what will be encoded, the better it will be able to handle new or rare clients.

• Just as WebSTAR sends the data to a CGI application for processing, the CGI application can send that data on to another application for further processing. In fact, this process can continue for several steps, or the CGI application can call several applications in sequence. The only restriction is that all of the data must be processed and returned to the server before the timeout period is exceeded.

- If a CGI passes data to another application, that application cannot respond directly back to WebSTAR without some real trickery. The application needs to return its data to the CGI and the CGI then responds to WebSTAR.

- A CGI application *must* reply to WebSTAR, unless there is an error in the processing (and good CGI applications will still attempt to return a useful error report). If WebSTAR does not receive a response, it will hang on until the timeout period is exceeded and then return an error to the user. That means that not returning a response to WebSTAR makes every connection to the CGI tie up a connection to the server for a minute or more (HTTP connections usually last only a few seconds) and will reduce the number of connections that your server can process. Therefore, some CGI applications return only a short page to say that they are done. This might seem like a waste of time for the user, but it closes the connection more quickly by indicating to WebSTAR that the CGI application is done, so it actually speeds things up for everyone.

Limits to CGI Application Use

The only limit to using CGI applications is that the CGI application must be running on a computer that is also running a copy of WebSTAR (or MacHTTP). When WebSTAR determines that a URL is specifying a CGI application, the first thing that WebSTAR does is look to see whether the CGI application is running and, if not, launch the application so it can receive the WWWΩsdoc event. If the CGI application is on another computer, WebSTAR will not be able to check whether it is running and also won't be able to link to the CGI application. Linking to applications on remote computers is done via Program Linking, which has no facility for an application to directly enter the user name and password for a remote machine in order to make the link. Therefore the CGI application has to be where WebSTAR can see it and connect to it.

A very similar problem arises when someone tries to preview a site by loading the pages directly into a Web client. In these cases the URL for the file looks something like

```
file:///Your%20Disk/WebSTAR%201.2%20Folder/YourHome
Page.html
```

The file:/// scheme indicates that the page was loaded directly off your hard disk and not from WebSTAR. When you load a file directly from disk, links that go to a CGI application will not work, because the client software cannot talk to CGI applications directly; it must go through WebSTAR or MacHTTP.

WebSTAR and MacHTTP CGI Differences

Although WebSTAR builds on the roots that MacHTTP provided for CGI applications, the two handle CGI applications somewhat differently. The primary difference is that WebSTAR provides more parameters for the CGI application than MacHTTP does. This mean that CGI applications running under WebSTAR will receive additional information for their processing. If a CGI application requires this additional information, it will not work under MacHTTP. Similarly, if a CGI application written for MacHTTP is not expecting the additional information, it may get confused and be unable to run under WebSTAR (this is not usually a problem with CGI applications written in C or AppleScript). If the CGI application does not specifically mention WebSTAR and MacHTTP compatibility in its documentation and if the CGI application is not a commercial product, it is a good idea to contact the programmer directly to find out whether there may be a problem.

The second difference is that CGI applications running under WebSTAR can do a special feature called "server push." This means that the CGI application returns data to the client directly and returns the data in several chunks over a long period of time. A common example of this is animation; after each frame of data is returned, a pause allows the client software to display the frame before the next one is sent. Another example is a search on several databases; the results for each database are returned as soon as they are available instead of waiting to return all of the data in one large chunk. The advantage to "server push" is that it allows feedback to be given to the user during very long periods of processing. It also allows the connection to be held open longer than the timeout period, as long as some data is occasionally returned. The disadvantage to "server push" is that it is not supported by MacHTTP, so any CGI application that uses "server push" will crash with MacHTTP.

A final difference between WebSTAR and MacHTTP, when working with CGI applications, is that WebSTAR does some minor processing of the incoming request string before handing it off to a CGI application. This ability was added to counteract a problem with the way that CERN proxy servers (which are widely used but not supported) encode URLs for requests from their clients. The solution is that Web-STAR now converts the first instance of an encoded dollar sign (**%47**) in a URL to a real dollar sign. That dollar sign usually means that the client was trying to append some data to the URL to be sent to a CGI application. By encoding the dollar sign character, the CERN proxy server interferes with this ability for WebSTAR and MacHTTP servers. A side effect of this workaround is that you are not allowed to use a dollar sign in the name of a folder or file on your WebSTAR server.

Synchronous versus Asynchronous CGI Applications

When CGI application support was first introduced in MacHTTP, the CGI applications were run *synchronously*: MacHTTP sent an event to a CGI application and then stopped processing connections while it waited for a response. This allowed the CGI application to control the CPU, which made it run faster, and it was also easier to code (which made Chuck work faster). However, it could also have the overall effect of slowing down a server that had one or more heavily accessed CGI applications. Essentially MacHTTP was turned into a single-connection processor whenever CGI applications were used, which isn't a good idea in general.

Later on, Chuck added support for CGI applications to be run *asynchronously*: MacHTTP would send an event to a CGI application and then go on processing connections until the CGI responded. This allowed several CGI applications to be run simultaneously or other types of connections to be processed while a CGI application chugged away in the background. A couple of new problems were introduced, however, by the asynchronous processing.

The first problem was that it is possible for MacHTTP to send another event, or even several more events, to a CGI application while it is already processing an event. The CGI applications therefore had to be modified so that they could either queue up events for later processing or process multiple events in different threads. This meant that not all CGI applications could be used asynchronously, although all that had been modified to specifically run asynchronously could also still be run synchronously. This problem has diminished greatly since the introduction of WebSTAR (which still offers both CGI formats) and several CGI application shells that show programmers how to write for asynchronous processing. Still, if you are using an older CGI application or a product that you are not sure of, it is worth the time to contact the programmer and make sure that the CGI application will support asynchronous processing.

There are still times when it is a good idea to run a CGI application synchronously. The main reason for this is that very slow CGI applications would not finish in time if they were run asynchronously (and competing with WebSTAR for CPU time). This might be the case with a very large database, proprietary software, or a CGI application that pulls together several other applications. If this case arises on your server and you are torn between slowing the server down and not being able to run the CGI application, try moving the CGI application to another server all by itself. The other server may not even need to be a very powerful machine, as long as the CGI is the only thing running (along with a copy of WebSTAR, of course, to communicate with it).

When Is a CGI a CGI?

If you look at the HREF element, you will notice that there is no attribute to specify whether the file specified is a CGI application. It is up to the HTTP server to make the decision whether a URL is pointing to a CGI application. Some servers have special directories for CGI applications, and all applications in those directories are assumed to be CGI applications. WebSTAR gives you a little more flexibility than that.

If you recall, WebSTAR keeps a table that maps filename extensions, file type codes, and file creator codes to specific Action types. Using WebSTAR's default settings, there are three ways that WebSTAR checks to see whether an application is a CGI application:

- The file is an application and its name ends in ".cgi"; this means that the application is a synchronous CGI and the Action type is "CGI."

- The file is an application and its name ends in ".acgi"; this means that the application is an asynchronous CGI and the Action type is "ACGI."

- The file is specified as a preprocessor or postprocessor for WebSTAR; all pre- and postprocessor applications are assumed to be asynchronous CGI applications and are assigned the Action type "ACGI."

If a URL specifies a file with the filename extension ".bob" or anything else other than ".cgi" or ".acgi," it will not be treated as a CGI application. Similarly, if you put the extension ".cgi" on an application, it will be treated like a CGI application whether or not it is suitable to be used as one. WebSTAR has no way to check the application itself to see whether it can really handle the WWWΩsdoc event and return data. It can only depend on the MIME mappings table to make its decision.

Using Actions

In WebSTAR (not in MacHTTP) there is another way to designate CGI applications for use, and that is by creating a new Action. An Action is a designated way of processing files. Every file type in the MIME mappings table has an assigned Action type that tells WebSTAR how that type of file is to be processed. The three built-in types—TEXT, BINARY, and SCRIPT—are handled by WebSTAR directly. The other two types—CGI and ACGI—tell WebSTAR to pass off data as a CGI application. New types can be defined through WebSTAR Admin.

When you define a new type, you also are asked to designate an application that will handle the processing for files of this new type.

WebSTAR assumes that the application is an asynchronous CGI application and will treat it as such no matter what the file name is. As an example, if you want to implement a new security scheme, you could create a new Action called SECURE and assign the application **SecureCGI.acgi** to be the Action processor. Then you could create a new file type called **.shtml** (type TEXT, creator *, MIME type text/html) and assign it the Action type SECURE. The result is that every URL requesting a text file with the name ending in **.shtml** will be handed off to **SecureCGI.acgi** instead for processing. If you had specified a file named **SecureCGI.not** instead of **SecureCGI.acgi** for processing the Action, it will still be treated as a CGI application. And if **SecureCGI.acgi** turns out to be a text file instead of an application, WebSTAR will still try to launch it and send it an event. The launch will fail, of course, so WebSTAR will return an error to the user.

As an interesting aside, it doesn't matter in this example whether the file specified in the URL actually exists. The entire URL is passed to the CGI application for processing, so WebSTAR assumes that the CGI application will take care of determining whether a file was specified. This is interesting because it allows the use of what are termed "virtual URLs." A virtual URL specifies a file that does not physically exist on disk. Instead, the file name is passed as data to the CGI application, which will return a document from memory. With virtual URLs, there is no guarantee that the same URL will return the same data each time or that it will even be accepted again by the CGI application. This can be extremely useful for an additional level of security (for the incredibly paranoid) or for providing an easy interface to services. An example of this is the AppleSearch CGI, which generates form pages on the fly for accessing designated AppleSearch indexes. These pages do not exist on disk and will change, depending on what databases are currently available.

Passing Data to a CGI Application

Although WebSTAR sends quite a bit of information to a CGI application on its own, the CGI application usually needs some data from the client (or the user) in order to do anything very interesting.

Additional data can be sent to a CGI application in three ways, and you can even use two or three of them at once.

Path Arguments

The data for the path argument is appended to a URL by adding a dollar sign (**$**) to the URL and then appending the data after that. The resulting URL looks like this:

> `http://www.comvista.com/cgi/MapServe.acgi$notamap.map`

The CGI application **MapServe.acgi** should get the data **notamap.map** sent to it as a path argument. If search argument data is also included in the URL, that data must come first and includes everything between the path and search delimiters.

There is a limit on how much data can be sent in the path arguments. The total length of a URL to WebSTAR must be less than 1024 characters (1K). Since the entire URL counts, you will not be able to pass as much data if you are using long path names.

If you are writing a URL that includes path argument data, all special characters must be encoded in the path argument, just as in the path for the URL.

The CERN Proxy Conflict

The use of a dollar sign as a path argument delimiter is not standard on HTTP servers; in fact, nothing is specified as being standard for this purpose. Most UNIX servers use a forward slash for the purpose, but that can lead to ambiguous interpretation of the URL and so was discarded in favor of the dollar sign in the design of MacHTTP. The change has resulted in a conflict with the proxy server that CERN produced. This proxy server is widely used because it is free, but for the same reason, CERN does not go to any lengths to make sure that it is compatible with existing servers or clients.

The problem arises because the CERN server does extra encoding of the URLs that it receives before it passes them on to the server. Since every WWW client has a slightly different set of characters that it chooses to encode (in addition to the required set of special characters, it can be very difficult matching URLs from different clients. To address this the CERN proxy server reencodes the URL, using a superset of characters that includes everything that any client encodes. This way every URL will match no matter which client it came from.

Unfortunately the dollar sign is one of the characters that the CERN proxy server chooses to encode (which is odd because there is not a client that encodes this character). There is nothing "wrong" about choosing to do that, because the standard specifies that a client or server can encode any additional characters that it wants to, as long as it also encodes the required set of special characters. It is undesirable and unnecessary, though, for the dollar sign to be encoded, and the server would work just as well if it didn't include that character in the encoded set.

WebSTAR version 1.2 introduced a fix for this problem. With version 1.2, WebSTAR interprets the first encoded dollar sign (%24) in a URL to be a *real* dollar sign. This means that you cannot use a dollar sign in any of the file names on your site or it will be interpreted as the start of path argument data.

Search Arguments

The data for the search argument is appended to the URL in the same way that the path argument data is. The only difference is that the search argument delimiter is a question mark (**?**). An example of a URL including search argument data is

`http://www.comvista.com/cgi/Guestbook.acgi?view`

This sends the text string "view" to the CGI application **Guest book.acgi** as the search argument.

The amount of data passed in this method is limited by the total size of the URL to something less than 1K, and the data must be URL encoded. If the search argument data is added by the Web client, the client will take care of encoding it; otherwise, the document author must do that when typing the hypertext reference.

A URL may include data for both the path argument and the search argument. The order is very important in this case, with the path argument occurring first, followed by the search argument. This is often the situation with a map-processing CGI, where the hypertext reference uses the path argument to specify a map definition file, then the client software uses the search argument to append the *x,y* coordinates of the point where the user clicked on the map. The resulting URL might look like

```
http://www.comvista.com/cgi/MapServe.acgi$notamap.map?
110,24
```

In this example the path argument gets everything from the dollar sign to the question mark (between the two delimiters), and the search argument gets everything after the question mark. In case you didn't notice it before, the delimiters are not part of the argument data and are discarded by WebSTAR when it creates the WWWΩsdoc event to send to the CGI application. The total size of the URL still cannot exceed 1K, counting both the path and search arguments.

The search argument is used by the client to pass data when the GET request is used. This is the default method for most clients, so it is used with image maps, with search fields on ISINDEX pages, and with form elements when no method is specified (or when GET is specified).

Post Arguments

The post argument data is treated differently from data for other arguments. Instead of appending the data to the URL, the data is appended to the HTTP request, like a file enclosure. This is covered in detail in the discussion on the HyperText Transaction Protocol. The enclosure can contain much more data than the URL can. For WebSTAR, since the post argument can contain up to 24K of information, the POST request is recommended for use with CGI applications whenever possible, especially with forms.

The post argument data is automatically appended to the HTTP request by the WWW client when the POST request method is specified, as when somebody clicks on the **Submit** button in a form. You can still use the search and path arguments to send additional data to a CGI application in addition to the post argument. This way the client can put information that a user entered into the post argument data, and additional commands can be sent at the same time in the search argument data.

Historical Notes

The Apple event type that WebSTAR sends to CGI applications is WWWΩsdoc. WebSTAR also supports another event, called the WWWΩsrch event. This is a remnant from the days before CGI support, and there is no guarantee that support for it will remain in future versions. Any application that communicates with WebSTAR through the WWWΩsrch event is likely to stop working in the future, and so use of that event is not recommended.

WebSTAR allows you to use AppleScript scripts directly in much the same way as CGI applications. This was originally added for people who did not have access to ScriptEditor or a similar application for compiling scripts into CGI applications. AppleScript is now included with the Macintosh operating system, and several third-party editors are also available, as well as many precompiled CGI applications. As a result, using scripts as text files is not recommended. If you have some incredible urge to do this, the instructions are in the WebSTAR and MacHTTP documentation.

Part III

Extending WebSTAR

This section deals with topics that require a bit more experience. A good understanding of how the Macintosh operating system works behind the scenes is needed, as well as some understanding of general computer theory. You still don't need to know any programming, though.

11

A CGI Example: Maps

If you have been using the World Wide Web for any length of time, you probably have already heard of maps. No, not those folding paper things that seem to breed wildly in the glove compartment of your car but rather a special kind of inline graphic that can be used in WWW pages. A map is a graphic with designated "hot" areas that act like buttons. Each button is linked to a specific URL. When users click on the map graphic, the clicks are translated, and the user is sent to whatever URL maps to the area clicked on (a default URL is used if no button is clicked on). These may also be called image maps, or "those kind of pictures that you can click on."

What Can Be Done with Maps

Functionally a map is just a flashy way of presenting a list of URLs. A map requires an extra graphic (which means more download time) and extra processing by the server to do the same thing as a short amount of text. Therefore maps should be used only when they present a distinct advantage to the user in deciding how to navigate the pages. Of course, no one follows that rule. The real rule is "use maps only when you want to," which is why so many sites have maps on their pages.

A map can enhance your site in several ways. The simplest use of a map is to present a "menu bar," which is a horizontal bar-shaped graphic that presents the user with menu options. A menu bar can present both graphics and text for the user to make the selection more clear, and it transmits much more quickly than using multiple icon graphics. Presenting the same menu bar on every page can help a user to navigate a large site, as well as contribute to creating a "look" for your site.

Another use of a map is to show relationships among choices, such as a hierarchical staff directory. You could use a map as a real map, of course, to provide information on a building or country, or you could use the map to enhance real images, such as a team photo (click on a player) or wildlife scene (click on the raccoon). The most common use, though, is probably as a "front page graphic." Many company or personal home pages have a large graphic that doubles as an advertisement and a map of services. This makes the page a little flashier and may attract people to dig into the site a little bit.

Here are some samples of maps at various sites to give you an idea of how they can best be used:

Good, basic map graphic	(`http://www-lib.iupui.edu/ erefs/erefs.html`)
Cute and easy map	(`http://www.info.apple.com/`)
A bookshelf	(`http://www.novell.com/`)
Starship console	(`http://generations.viacom. com/GenerationsMenu.html`)
Clickable group picture	(`http://funnelweb.utcc.utk. edu:80/ladyvols/`)
A world map	(`http://www.xerox.com/map/`)
Map of Washington, D.C.	(`http://sc94.ameslab.gov/ TOUR/tour.html`)
Old-fashioned map	(`http://www.gomedia.com/`)
Clickable fish tank	(`http://oberon.educ.sfu.ca/ splash/tank.htm`)
Cute map but hard to use	(`http://www.sbc.com/`)

How Maps Work

Several parts work together to form a map in a Web page. Here are the key terms relating to maps:

- **Map graphic**   The graphic file that is displayed in the document for the user to click on. This can be any type of graphic that the WWW client will display, which usually means a GIF file.

- **Map click**   The x,y coordinates of where the user clicked on the map graphic. The coordinates are relative to the top-left corner of the graphic.

- **Hotspot**   A region of the map that is sensitive to map clicks and redirects the user to a new file. Each hotspot region is set to redirect to one file.

- **Map definition file**   A file that describes where the hotspots are located on the image.

- **Map processing CGI**   A CGI application that processes the map click, using the map definition file to figure out what to return to the client.

- **Map link**   The HREF element in the HTML document that tells where to find the map-processing CGI.

- **Map**   Usually means the whole package: graphic, CGI, and definition file. It may also be used to refer to the graphic itself when the graphic is displayed in WWW client software.

The process by which a map works is not difficult, but because so many parts are working together, it can be confusing until you get the hang of it. Here is a quick overview of the process:

1. The client loads a page containing a graphic. The graphic has the ISMAP tag and is embedded in a map link.

2. The user clicks on a portion of the map.

3. The client translates the click to a pair of x,y coordinates, where 0,0 represents the top-left corner of the graphic.

4. The client builds a new URL by appending the coordinates to the end of the URL that was in the link. The new URL will look like:

   `http://www.machine.org/cgi/MapServe.acgi?x,y`

   The coordinates of the map click are x,y.

5. The client sends the URL to WebSTAR.

6. WebSTAR creates an "sdoc" Apple event containing the coordinates and sends that event to the map-processing CGI listed in the URL (**/cgi/MapServe.acgi**).

7. The map-processor CGI receives the event and extracts the coordinates.

8. Using one of various methods, the map-processor CGI matches the coordinates to a URL (most map-processor CGIs use a map definition file to do this).

9. The map-processor CGI returns the URL, along with a **302 FOUND** code for WebSTAR to return to the client.

10. The **302 FOUND** code tells the client software to redirect its connection and to try to retrieve the document specified by the returned URL instead.

11. The client tries to get the new URL and display it for the user.

One thing that you should notice in these steps is that the real work is done by the client and the map-processing CGI. WebSTAR (the server) has very little involvement, except to expedite communications between the two. This is not true on all servers. Some servers know how to handle map requests. This is not the best way, though, since the server must be updated every time a new map feature is developed, and the map processing cannot be offloaded to another CPU.

Creating a Map

Now let's look at the process involved in making a map for your site.

Create the HTML Document Containing the Map Graphic

There are two keys to doing this. First, the IMG element that specifies the map graphic must contain the ISMAP attribute. Second, an Anchor element must surround the IMG element to specify where the CGI application is that will process the map click information.

This can all be one line in the HTML file (but I'll use three). An example might look like this:

```
<A HREF="/cgi/MapServe.acgi$/map/test.map">
<IMG SRC="/grc/test.gif" ISMAP>
</A>
```

The HREF tag might vary, depending on what CGI you are using to process the map clicks. Quite often the name of the map definition file is included in the tag to be passed to the map-processing CGI.

Create the Map Graphic

There is nothing really special about a map graphic. Any graphic that can be displayed inline by a WWW client is eligible to be a map graphic. The GIF format is usually used because it is the most widely supported. JPEG has been appearing in more and more browsers, however, and most XWindows browsers support the XBitmap format. The choice is up to you.

One common mistake is a misunderstanding of how the hotspots are defined. Nothing in the graphic does anything to create the hotspots. The hotspots are defined in the map definition file, and the graphic is there only to provide visual clues to the user, such as "Hey, click here if you want anything to happen." In fact, if you don't want anything that looks like a button, you don't have to put it in. Just realize that without the visual feedback, users may not figure out exactly where to click.

If you choose to use a transparent graphic for your map graphic, remember that the transparent portion is still part of the map graphic and will respond to user clicks. In this case it is best to use a default Action that merely returns the current page, forcing the user to click in one of the hotspots instead.

Create the Map Definition File

The map definition file, the key to map processing, contains a single line for each hotspot; that line defines where on the graphic the hotspot will be (with 0,0 representing the top left of the graphic) and the URL to send the user who clicks on that hotspot. This information is used by the map-processing CGI to decide which hotspot the user clicked in. There are five possible shapes for a hotspot:

- **Rectangle**   This hotspot is defined by its upper-left and lower-right corners:

  ```
  rect 12,20 52,40 http://www.comvista.com/whoweare.html
  ```

- **Oval**   This hotspot is defined by the upper-left and lower-right corners of the rectangle that would exactly bound the oval:

  ```
  oval 40,10 80,20 http://www.comvista.com/whatwedo.html
  ```

- **Circle**   This is a type of oval:

  ```
  circ 300,100 30 http://www.comvista.com/circleme.html
  ```

  However, unlike the oval, a circle is defined as a center point and a radius. There is little need for this type, since the oval can define the same shape.

- **Polygon**   This is a multisided closed shape:

  ```
  poly 100,20 110,25 100,30 90,15 http://www.comvista.
  com/polyme.html
  ```

  The sides and interior angles are not necessarily uniform (like a hexagon). Despite a practical limit to how many sides the shape can have, based on the map processor you choose to use, the limit should be well over 100 sides, which is a pretty complex shape. The shape is described as a series of points representing the corners of the shape in sequence.

- **Point**   This is a unique feature recently added to maps:

  ```
  point 400,310 http://www.comvista.com/pointtome.html
  ```

  Points don't define hot spots. Instead, when a user clicks outside of a hotspot, the click maps to the closest point on the map. A point is defined by the x,y coordinates of the point on the graphic.

The hotspots on a map can be overlapped. When that happens, the order is determined by where the line defining the hotspot occurs in the file. Lines at the beginning (top) of the file have precedence over lines occurring later, because the map-processor CGI typically runs through the lines until it finds a line defining a hotspot containing the point. If a later line defines another hotspot containing the same point, that line will not be reached. Points, of course, are not processed until it is determined that the map click was not inside any of the hotspots.

The map definition file usually has a default mapping set to handle the situation when the map click is outside any hotspot. The default action is usually to return the same page with the map in it, forcing the user to click in one of the hotspots. The idea of a default mapping existed before points were implemented. If a map has a point defined, the default will never be used, because every click will map to either a hotspot or one of the points.

Maps became popular as a feature of the NCSA httpd server for UNIX, and on that system the map definition file is a text file. As a result, other servers have been sticking to using a text file format for map definition files. It could just as easily be a binary file, though, unless you plan to share map files across systems. In addition, the format listed here is what would be considered the NCSA standard format for a map definition file. There is no reason that you can't make up your own format, though, as long as you have a map-processor CGI that can handle it. On the Macintosh side some software that is coming out to create map definition files will take advantage of these possibilities to speed up processing and simplify the whole process.

It is also possible to have maps without having a map definition file at all. This is the case when the information about the map is coded into the map-processor CGI itself. Map definition files were created so that a single map-processor CGI could handle several maps. If the map information is coded directly into the map-processor CGI, that CGI will be able to handle only the one map, and you will have to recompile the code every time you change the map—not a good idea.

When you save your map definition file, it is common to use the filename extension **.map**. If you give the map definition file and the map graphic the same filenames, just using different filename extensions (such as **menubar.gif** and **menubar.map**), it will be easier to remember which map goes with which graphic. Many sites have taken to using an Action to process the map clicks. In these cases, the **.map** extension is set as a new file type and assigned to an Action (like "MAP") that passes the `.map` file to a map-processing CGI. This is handy if your server is having problems with the CERN proxy server. Using the Action, you specify only a map definition file in the HREF tag, and the CGI is launched automatically.

WebMap is software from Rowland Smith at City.Net (`http://www.city.net/cnx/software/`) that helps to simplify the process of making a map definition file. WebMap loads the map graphic and displays it for you, then gives you paintlike tools for defining the hotspots. If you want to define a rectangle, use the rectangle tool to drag from the top-left to the bottom-right corners. A rectangle is displayed overlayed on the graphic, and the coordinates are added to the definition list. In addition, a new entry is made in a list to the right and you type in the URL there. If you want to move the hotspot or resize it or both, all of its information follows it. If you delete the hotspot, its URL is also deleted from the list. There are tools for rectangles, ovals, irregular shapes, and points.

This is a tremendous improvement over the tedious and error-prone practice of creating map definition files by hand. By drawing directly onto the map graphic, you get a good feel for where the hotspots will be. You can test the hotspots directly from within WebMap by going to test mode. If you are using complex polygons, this software could save hours of work.

WebMap also allows you to output map definition text files in either NCSA or CERN format, but for its own use it does something very different. WebMap saves the hotspot information in the resource fork of the map graphic. This means that the proper map information is always stored along with its corresponding graphic, so there is no need to tell the map processor which map definition file to use. WebMap also allows the data to be stored in whatever format is easiest to process and to be read in and parsed more quickly than a text file can be. Finally, putting the information in the resource fork does not modify the map graphic itself, since only the data fork of a graphic file is used to display. If you transfer the map graphic to another type of computer (UNIX or DOS), only the data fork will be transferred, and the map information will be lost in the transferred copy.

Select a Map-Processor CGI

Several map-processor CGI applications are available, written in C, FORTRAN, MacPerl, and other languages. For speed and ease of use, though, I recommend MapServe by Kelly Campbell (`http://www.ksu.edu/~camk/`). MapServe is a standalone CGI written in CodeWarrior C, which is available as a fat binary. It is very fast and very stable, provides a log window of recent requests, and is usually the first to take advantage of new Web-STAR features, such as Actions. Running a close second is Mac-Imagemap from Lutz Weimann (`weimann@zib-berlin.de`). It is also pretty fast and easy to use, but it has been slower to be updated and doesn't provide the useful log information. WebMap 2.0 should also include a map-processor CGI that is a fat binary. The advantage to WebMap will be that the CGI can read the map definition information directly from a map graphic's resource fork, so there is no need to specify which map file to use and less possibility for error, especially for beginners. You probably won't go wrong using any of these.

Install the Map Parts

Proper installation of the various map parts depends somewhat on what map-processing CGI you choose to use. They all share some common features, though. First is installation of the map-processor CGI itself. I recommend that in the WebSTAR root folder you make a "cgi" folder and use it to hold all of your CGI applications, if possible. The CGI application needs to be in that folder, not in another folder in that folder. The advantage of this is that you will always use the same path when referring to a CGI application, which should decrease the possibility of making an error.

Second is installation of the map definition file, if you are using one. If it is possible, I recommend creating a "map" folder in the Web-STAR root folder and putting all of your map definition files in there. Again, this will help reduce errors, since every map definition file path will be the same. It will also help to organize your site for easier maintenance.

Third is installation of the map graphic and the HTML document that will contain the map. The HTML file should, of course, go wherever it belongs on the site. The graphic should be put in one of two places: either in the folder along with the HTML file or in a "grc" folder in the WebSTAR root folder, to contain all of the graphics for your site. The advantage to the former is that there won't be a need to specify a path to the graphic; it will be in the same folder. This also keeps each graphic closely associated with the page that refers to it. The advantage to the latter is that you can use the same path for all map graphics, and they are neatly grouped in one place.

If you go back to the start of this section, you will see that the HTML example shown there references the files as if they had been installed according to these guidelines.

Tips on Using Maps

A few points about design are important from a performance aspect.

Debugging Maps

One common mistake is trying to use a map when you don't have it installed on WebSTAR. Although you can load the HTML document containing the map directly into your Web client and have it display properly, the browser will report an error when you click on the map, because it is the server, not the client, that communicates with the map-processor CGI. You must be running WebSTAR to test your map installation.

The log information that MapServe shows is very useful for debugging installations. It will note whether the map definition file was not located or whether it is improperly formatted or whether MapServe was never called at all. WebSTAR's log file is useful also. If you set it to Verbose Mode, it will display the entire request from the client and WebSTAR's response, which will help you track down what went wrong. In my experience the majority of problems are due to incorrect paths for one or more of the files, which is another reason to use the structure that I suggested here.

Server Load

Yes, maps place an additional load on your WebSTAR server. This can happen in two ways. First, extra memory and CPU are needed for the map-processor CGI to run. Second, WebSTAR has to hand off the map click information and wait for the return information. The first one can be minimized by using as fast a map as you can. That means not only using fast image map processing software but also keeping your map no more complex than is necessary. The second factor can be minimized by using an asynchronous map-processor CGI so that WebSTAR can continue to process other connections while the map processing is going on.

No matter what you do, though, the map will place an extra load on your server. Therefore make sure that you really need (or really, really want) to use maps before you go throwing them all over a busy site.

Simplification

A map can be a good way to simplify your site and can actually speed up your site in some cases. If you have several small graphics (four or more) that you use as a menu of selections, you might benefit from converting these to a single map graphic. The benefit comes because each graphic requires the client to open another connection. On most clients opening a connection is almost as slow as downloading a small graphic. On Netscape, it does not appear quite as slow, because it can open multiple simultaneous connections. However, if you have six or seven graphics, Netscape can quickly overload your server by trying to open seven or eight connections at once. Thus using one map reduces the number of connections required by the client to get the entire page and transmits that data more quickly. In addition, with a map you control how the graphics are displayed in relation to one another instead of counting on proper line wrapping in the client.

Text Alternatives

Although you don't hear much about them anymore, there are still several text-only clients for the World Wide Web and people are still using them. Lynx is one that is very popular with those stuck on text-based systems (as is the case in many universities), and Emacs has a WWW browsing mode. In addition, many people with slower Internet connections (14.4K or less) eschew graphics to get better speed.

If you want to provide support for these people, you need to create a text menu to duplicate your map graphic. This menu can be offered on the same page with the map or on a separate page with a link like "Also try our *text-only page.*" I prefer the former because the text menu can enhance the map, providing an explanation of each option, in addition to the text link. It also means that the menu will be available immediately, whether or not the user is viewing graphics.

Of course, it's not your fault that these people don't view graphics. If you don't care about them as customers, feel free to have an entirely graphic site.

12

Recommended CGI Applications

The market for CGI applications is still very small but is growing rapidly. Users who first put up Web servers were, in many cases, programmers and so were not daunted by the task of writing their own CGI applications. Now, however, hundreds of new servers are going up every week, many by people who are willing to pay for good solutions that don't require programming. The CGI applications I discuss here are the best of those available at this time. Most of them are interfaces between WebSTAR and a commercial application, written mostly by the companies that produce the products as they see a new market opening up. Being commercial solutions, they generally include good documentation, technical support, and the assurance that they will still be there in the future.

Hundreds of shareware and freeware CGI applications are available on the Internet from various Webmasters who have solved a tricky problem on their own sites and then made the solution available to others. Such solutions will not be covered here, however, because there are far too many to list; the list changes daily, with new solutions appearing and old ones fading away or radically changing design; these solutions generally are poorly documented and require some knowledge of how CGI applications are written so the source code can be modified to meet a specific site's needs. There is nothing wrong with these solutions if you have the skills to use them and the time to weed through to find the best, but they are not drop-in solutions by any measure. My favorites among these can be found on the companion CD-ROM, along with links to many more.

Maxum CGI Applications

Maxum Development was the first company to release a commercial CGI application for the Macintosh. The company has the further distinction of selling what is probably the single most useful CGI application available for any HTTP server. The two main products, NetCloak and NetForms, have become a mainstay for serious Macintosh Web developers (and even some silly ones).

NetCloak is a CGI application that allows you to create dynamic HTML documents. NetCloak can show and hide portions of a document, based on the client's IP address (or DNS name) or the type of client software being used. This allows documents to be made sensitive to clients with special features (like Netscape) and those without (like Lynx). Sensitive information in a document can be hidden from certain addresses, or customized responses can be created for certain groups of users. NetCloak can also show or hide portions, based on the Referer (the page that the user was previously viewing), the time of day, day of the week, or username and password provided (for protected documents). In addition, NetCloak can be used to insert information in a page, such as the date, time, client type, client address, user name, a predefined macro, and more. Perhaps the most-used feature, though, is NetCloak's ability to insert page counters, with separate counters for each of any number of documents. Despite all of those capabilities, NetCloak is very fast and hardly seems to slow a server down at all, even under heavy load. One reason is the use of RAM to cache files for speedy access (or to protect the original files).

NetForms, as its name suggests, is a form-processor CGI application. NetForms takes in information from form pages and processes it for saving as files on disk. Each form has an associated form definition page that defines what NetForms should do with the form information in creating the disk file. In its simplest form, the disk files can contain the form data in a constant format that would be easily readable by some batch processor for adding to a database or purchasing system. More advanced commands allow disk files to be linked to previous files, have user information inserted, and HTML markup added. This is often used to create discussion areas on line with all of the features of a newsgroup, such as threaded topics and lists of new entries. A better application of the software is for internal use in a company, such as with job listings or sales group discussions or regional representatives sharing information.

Text Searching

If you have hundreds or thousands of documents that you want to make available on the World Wide Web, an index just won't work. Nobody is going to download the entire index, much less read it. The best solution is a text search engine that can help users find the document they want. Specifically the text search engine should rank the matching documents to suggest those that are most likely to match (relevance ranking). This is done by weighting such things as how often the word occurs in a file relative to the file size and how closely together the occurrences of the word are.

The text search engines generally do not require any special processing of the documents as long as they are in text format. A folder or set of folders can be specified and all documents within those folders will be indexed for later searching. This can be very useful on larger sites, where users may want to do such a search on the site pages themselves rather than wander around hoping to find what they are looking for.

AppleSearch CGI

The AppleSearch CGI is an extremely easy-to-use CGI application that provides a front-end to the AppleSearch search engine. AppleSearch is the text search engine that can not only index files on a server but also provide access to WAIS databases on the Internet. The CGI application builds a form page on the fly that lets the user enter search terms and select which databases they want to search from among those that the local AppleSearch server offers. It then returns the results of the search as another Web page. If you are using WebSTAR 1.2 or later (with the server-push feature), the data from each selected database is returned as it finishes instead of forcing the user to wait for all of the searches to finish.

The AppleSearch CGI really could not be easier to use. There are no forms to write and only two possible links to use to the CGI: one for a simple search interface and another for a more complex form interface. AppleSearch CGI is a product of Apple Computer. You can download it from **http://kamaaina.apple.com/**. The author is Robin Matherus, and he does a good job of adding new features as they are needed (and available).

TR-WWW

TR-WWW is both a CGI application and search engine in one package. It does relevance ranking of returned documents, just as Apple-Search does, but it is only intended for use on documents that are less than 15MB in size. It does not preindex the files that it searches, so you can add files as often as you want and they are immediately available for searching. This can be a very good option for busy search sites, such as mail or news archives.

TR-WWW was a shareware product by Dr. Adrian Vanzyl from Monash University in Australia (**http://www.monash.edu.au/ informatics/tr-www.html**). Dr. Vanzyl has announced, though, that he wants to sell the code to someone who could turn it into a commercial product. The latest version of TR-WWW remains available for purchase and will work with all current versions of WebSTAR and MacHTTP, but expect a new product to emerge soon to take its place.

Database Linking

These CGI applications provide very easy interfaces for making the information in your database available over the Web. In most cases there is no need to write anything more than a single link to the CGI application; everything after that point is automated.

ButlerLink/Web and Tango

Butler SQL, a standard SQL database from Everyware Corporation (**http://www.everyware.com/**), can either be a database or act as a front end to other SQL systems, such as Oracle. The ButlerLink/Web

CGI provides an interface for searching the database from Web pages. Version 2.0 of the ButlerLink/Web CGI, now called Tango, is written in C, which provides both more speed and more flexibility than version 1.0 which was written in AppleScript. For the beginning user, it completely removes the need to write any SQL or any but the most basic HTML tags by providing a graphical interface to designing search pages. For advanced users it has facilities to create customized solutions that can then be used on several sites. Tango also takes advantage of the new server-push feature for long searches and offers a "shopping basket" feature that allows the results of multiple selections to be carried over as the user does more searches. This is used with online purchasing systems to allow users to locate all of the products they want before filling out a purchase form.

Everware Corp. has also announced upcoming products that will provide user tracking, additional security for sites needing tens of thousands of passwords, and the ability to send WebSTAR log data directly to a Butler database for creating custom activity reports on the fly.

NetLink/4D

There are several solutions for connecting to 4D databases via the Internet. Many of them add direct TCP/IP support to the 4D database to turn it into an HTTP server. This sounds as though it would be the best solution, and it may be if all you want to do is access the 4D database. In most cases, though, the majority of the site does not belong in a database, and forcing it into that mold may result in a slower site and less flexibility. Also, support for other CGI applications or HTTP server features that you may want to use may be absent or unreliable.

The best solution for connecting to 4D from WebSTAR is with NetLink/4D from Foresight Technology, Inc. (**http://www. fsti.com/**). NetLink/4D installs directly into your 4D server to give it the ability to be a threaded CGI application that can communicate directly with WebSTAR. NetLink/4D uses PowerPC-native code, can handle multiple threaded databases searches, and supports the server-push feature for returning partial results from a search. Using NetLink/4D, a 4D server can also be used as a preprocessor or Action for implementing new security methods.

FileMaker CGIs

FileMaker is not the most powerful database available, but it is widely used and can be the best tool if you are in a hurry or don't have much database experience and need only a flat-file database. The searching can be fast (not blazing but fast) but it is heavily dependent on how the CGI application is constructed that interfaces with FileMaker. Many tricks and tweaks are needed to get the best speed out of FileMaker when communicating through Apple events, so don't be surprised to see some solutions running several times faster than others.

WEB FM

The best solution for FileMaker access via Web pages is WEB FM, a CGI application from Eric Bickford (**eric@macweb.com**). WEB-FM has the fastest interface with FileMaker of any solution that I have tried. It has an easy-to-understand interface so that you will have pages ready to search your database in only minutes (if you read the directions). Eric announced plans to improve the interface so that it actually helps you build the search forms and plans to offer a new interface written in C, which should speed access tremendously. More information is available at **http://www.macweb.com/webfm/**

ROFM

ROFM CGI (Russell Owen's FileMaker CGI) is available freely on his site at (**http://rowen.astro.washington.edu/**). This may be a great starting point for the do-it-yourselfer. Russell will answer most questions sent to him and maintains a mailing list for the product, but the support is not guaranteed and the documentation is sufficient (as HTML pages) but doesn't go into any great depths on the topics. This CGI is also generally a bit (or a lot) slower than WEB FM.

Others

Several other databases are on the market, of course, and CGI solutions for them are also starting to appear, although this is not always easy. dtF, a relational database system from dtF Americas, Inc. (**dtF@thetagroup.sub.org**), has a CGI interface available by writing to the company. Some of the other systems can be accessed via HyperCard, which can be easily altered to act as a CGI application. The biggest problem is with accessing FoxPro databases. I haven't seen any canned solutions for this, and I read of several problems; the only way to transfer data is through the clipboard, which can be very unreliable. This might change with the next release of FoxPro, though.

WebSTAR Commerce Kit

WebSTAR now has a Commerce Kit that consists of several CGI applications for interfacing with various banking and financial services. The kit is available from StarNine Technologies, Inc., as an add-on to the WebSTAR package. There are currently three interfaces in the package: FirstVirtual, MacAuthorize, and an Apple-Script interface (which I won't get into here).

First Virtual

First Virtual Holdings Inc. (`http://www.fv.com/`) is a financial services company that operates entirely through electronic communications. Louis Slothouber of BIAP Systems (and now of StarNine) has written a CGI application that allows automated purchasing through the First Virtual system. Online purchasing systems have been slow to appear on the Macintosh, due to problems implementing SSL ("open standard" is a relative term). First Virtual gets around the need for secure communications by removing the sensitive information from the transaction. With First Virtual both the buyer and the seller open accounts by filling out an online form and then making a toll-free phone call to provide the sensitive information. After that, a buyer purchases from First Virtual sellers by submitting a request to First Virtual. First Virtual sends e-mail to the buyer for verification of the purchase and then takes care of the transaction, charging the buyer's account and crediting the seller's. Sensitive information, such as a credit card account number, is never transmitted over the Internet and is not even stored on a computer connected to the Internet.

The First Virtual CGI application runs on a Web server and takes care of collecting purchase requests and sending them off to the First Virtual server. The CGI application is threaded for multiple request processing and will send transactions via e-mail if the First Virtual server is not available. It includes a FORM Creator for making the forms that people use to make purchases online and is very easy to install.

MacAuthorize

MacAuthorize is a software package that allows credit cards to be authorized automatically. The Commerce Kit CGI application provides an interface to MacAuthorize that will take credit card account numbers from a form page and feed them to MacAuthorize to verify that the account is good and has enough in it to cover the purchase. This solution is preferable to First Virtual because it removes several intermediate steps, verifies the purchase almost immediately, and gets those impulse purchases. It assumes that you have a secure method for communicating with the Web client to get the credit card numbers, though, and right now the only client that can do that is Netscape Navigator. Other clients are jumping on the security bandwagon as quickly as they can, though, and it shouldn't be long before all of the major players have support for secure communications.

Part IV

Writing CGI
Applications

Most of the topics in these chapters, excepting the AppleScript
lessons, require prior programming experience. If you lack that
experience, go ahead and read the chapters and just turn the page
when it stops making sense. There is still a lot of useful material
here before you hit the code.

13

Technical Overview of CGI Applications

If you haven't read Chapter 12, be sure to do so before continuing here. I will be building on the concepts and terminology introduced there to dig into the information needed to write your own CGI application.

The CGI 1.1 Standard

The Common Gateway Interface standard is a loose definition of how an application can communicate with an information server. Since HTTP servers are the only information servers using the CGI standard, the specifications lean heavily toward support for HTTP servers. Although many people have contributed to the standard, it was started by several authors of UNIX-based servers, and the standard also has some portions that are not meaningful except on UNIX systems.

The CGI standard defines only three things: what information will be passed to a CGI application, how to pass data to the CGI as part of a URL, and what the CGI application will return to the server. There are several recommendations about how a server and CGI application should respond to certain situations, but many of these make sense only on a UNIX system. In most cases the specifics of what is passed and how the server and CGI application react are left up to the individual servers to decide.

This is important to keep in mind when you read that a particular server supports the "CGI/1.1 Standard," or whatever version is the most current. It is possible for every server to support the standard and still be using CGI applications that are incompatible with all other servers. Although it is questionable whether it is possible or even desirable to have an implementation designed to work on every single operating system, it is definitely a Good Thing for server authors to get together and agree on one implementation for each operating system. This way, CGI authors will be able to write for multiple servers, which means a larger user base and justification for putting more work into the products.

Since WebSTAR was the first HTTP server on the Macintosh (back when it was MacHTTP), the question of how to implement CGI support was wide open. The information provided here is based on the WebSTAR (and MacHTTP) implementation. If you see other HTTP servers for the Macintosh operating system claiming to be able to use the same CGI applications as WebSTAR, they have chosen to use the same implementation, so most of what I write here should apply to those servers as well.

How WebSTAR Implements CGI Support

WebSTAR defines four areas regarding CGI applications: what information will be passed to the application, how to pass data to the CGI as part of the URL, what the CGI application will return to the server, and how the server and CGI application will communicate. The first three follow as closely as is possible to the CGI standard (where it makes sense for a Macintosh), and the fourth is not covered by the standard.

Environment Variables

These variables contain information about the request that is being processed. The CGI application is taking over responsibility from the server for processing the request, so it needs access to the same information that the server has about the connection and what request the client made. It is the responsibility of the server to add this information to the message that it sends to the CGI application. Some of it is contained in the request headers from the client, and some of it is added by WebSTAR when the message is sent to the

CGI application. Because it is being provided by the server, it is not URL encoded and can be used directly.

In fact, there are no environment variables for the Macintosh CGI implementation. What you have instead are Apple event parameters, which amount to the same thing. The names used here are the variable names often used in AppleScript scripts to refer to the parameters being sent by WebSTAR. You can change the names in your own applications if you want, and they will probably be different if you are using a different language. If you use these names, though, most people will know what data you are referring to. Each of these parameters is filled by WebSTAR with data it has about the connection. Therefore none of them should be URL encoded (only the client software does that).

Here are the parameters that WebSTAR sends with the WWWΩsdoc event:

- **method (meth)**   The method used to call the CGI application (GET or POST).

- **client_address (addr)**   The IP address of the client making the request. If **Use DNS** is on, the DNS name is provided instead.

- **username (user)**   The user name given by the client. This is empty unless the request is in response to a request for authorization.

- **password (pass)**   The password given by the client. This is empty unless the request is in response to a request for authorization.

- **from_user (frmu)**   More information about the user. Usually this is the e-mail, although it is often left empty.

- **server_name (svnm)**   The name of the server that sent the message to the CGI application.

- **server_port (svpt)**   The port number that the server is running on.

- **script_name (scnm)**   The URL (path and file name) that was sent to the server to request the CGI application. The path is relative to the WebSTAR root folder. If the CGI is running as an Action processor, this will contain the path and file name portion of the URL.

- **referer (refr)**   The URL of the page that contained the link to the CGI application; may also be simply the page that the client software was displaying when the user typed in a link to the CGI application. Not all client software provides this information.

- **user_agent (Agnt)** The name of the client software. This is a string that the client keeps internally and has nothing to do with what the software is called on the user's hard disk.

- **content_type (ctyp)** The MIME content type of the data sent in a post argument.

- **action (Kact)** Tells how the CGI application was called. It can be one of PREPROCESSOR, POSTPROCESSOR, CGI, or ACGI. If a CGI application is called as an Action, this field will contain the name of the Action.

- **action_path (Kapt)** If the CGI application was called as an Action, this will contain the path to the Action processing CGI application. Otherwise, it contains the same information as `script_name`.

- **client_ip (Kcip)** Always contains the IP address of the client, even if **Use DNS** is on.

- **full_request (Kfrq)** The complete, unmodified text of the request received from the client. Anything that isn't in one of the other variables can be found here. This is the one parameter in this group that may contain URL-encoded text, since it includes the data variables (see the following).

- **connection_id (Kcid)** This is a unique identifier used internally by WebSTAR to track each connection. It is unique for each and every connection for as long as WebSTAR is running. The data type is a long integer.

Here is an example of what might be returned for each field in a typical transaction:

```
path_args: /cgi/MapServe.acgi
http_search_args: 112,34
method: Get/post_args:
client_address: jon.comvista.com.
username:
password:
from_user:
```

server_name: www.comvista.com.

server_port: 80

script_name: /cgi/MapServe.acgi

content_type: text/html

referer: http://www.comvista.com/us/whoweare.html

user_agent: MacWeb/1.00ALPHA3.2 libwww/2.17

action: ACGI

action_path: /Computing/WWW/Lessons/Script1.acgi

client_ip: 205.142.19.4

full_request:

GET /cgi/MapServe.acgi HTTP/1.0

Accept: video/quicktime

Accept: video/mpeg

Accept: image/x-xbitmap

Accept: image/pict

Accept: image/jpeg

Accept: image/gif

Accept: audio/x-wav

Accept: audio/x-aiff

Accept: audio/basic

Accept: application/x-stuffit

Accept: application/x-powerpoint

Accept: application/postscript

Accept: application/pdf

Accept: application/mac-binhex40

Accept: application/html

Accept: */*; q=0.300

Accept: application/octet-stream; q=0.100

Accept: text/plain

Accept: text/html

User-Agent: MacWeb/1.00ALPHA3.2 libwww/2.17

Data Variables

These variables contain data that the client is sending to the CGI application either as part of the URL or as an attachment to the HTTP request headers. This data must be URL encoded by the client before it is sent to WebSTAR.

- **path_args (----)**   This variable is specified by the CGI standard as a method for appending data to a URL. On the UNIX and Windows side, where filename extensions are heavily used, this is defined as the data following a forward slash when the slash is right after the name of a CGI application. On the Macintosh side, this can lead to an ambiguous interpretation of a URL, so Macintosh servers use a dollar sign (**$**) instead to delimit the path args. This data is limited to 1024 characters (1K), including the entire URL.

- **http_search_args (kfor)**   This variable contains the data from a GET request (everything after the question mark in a URL). This data is limited to 1024 characters (1K), including the entire URL.

- **post_args (post)**   This variable contains the data from a POST request. This is the data that is appended to an HTTP request and can be much larger than the data in a GET request or in the path_args. This data is currently limited to 24K.

CGI Responsibilities

The CGI standard also defines how the CGI application and the server split responsibilities for processing a request. When a request comes in that specifies a CGI application in the URL, the server's responsibility is to package up the environment variables and data variables and send it all off to the CGI application. The CGI application's responsibility is to fully process the connection. This means that the CGI application has to build an HTTP header for the server to send back to the client, as well as to generate the data to return from the CGI processing. If the CGI application makes an error in building the header or the data, the server still passes it back to the client and makes no attempt to correct the error.

Server-CGI
Communications

WebSTAR uses Apple events to communicate with CGI applications. Thus you can write your CGI application in any language that
allows new Apple events to be received, processed, and responded
to. The list of eligible languages includes not only all of the major
languages (such as C, Pascal, LISP, SmallTalk, FORTRAN, and Prograph) but also scripting languages, such as AppleScript and Frontier, and even applications with scripting languages that qualify,
such as HyperCard, 4D, and MacPerl.

Using Apple events for communication with a CGI application has a
couple of limitations, though. The most important one is that the
event must be sent to an application that is already running so that
there is a mechanism in place to receive the event. WebSTAR takes
care of this by checking to see whether the application is running
before sending the event. If the application is not running, Web-
STAR sends a "launch" event to get the application running first.

Another limitation is on the amount of data that can be returned by a
CGI application to WebSTAR. The upper limit for data transferred by
an Apple event is 64K. A CGI application should set the limit a bit
lower, perhaps 60K, to be safe, but even that may not be enough. In
practice, problems may appear even when only 40–50K of data is
transferred. In general, the safest practice is to return no more than
32K of data at any one time from a CGI application. If you need to
return more than that, it is likely to cause other problems for the user,
since that much data may take a long time to fetch (as in a database
search) and to transfer to users on slow lines. When large amounts of
data absolutely must be returned, the best practice is either to write
the data to disk and return a URL redirection to the file or to use
server push to send the data in several acceptable chunks.

The "sdoc" Apple Event

Unique Apple events are specified by a four-character event suite
and another four-character event code. For WebSTAR, the event
suite is WWWΩ (use option-z to type the omega character). Every

event that WebSTAR supports begins with this event suite designation. For the Search Doc event sent to CGI applications, the event code is "sdoc." When you create a new event handler in a CGI application to receive the events from WebSTAR, the resulting event designation is WWWΩsdoc.

The event that WebSTAR sends to a CGI application has 1 direct parameter (----) and 18 indirect parameters. The direct parameter is used to contain the path arguments in the URL. The other parameters are assigned as shown previously. The four-character codes listed in parentheses for each of those variables are the Apple event keyword codes for each of the parameters.

When a CGI application responds to the "sdoc" event, WebSTAR expects the reply's direct parameter to contain the entire response for the client, meaning both the HTTP header and any expected data. The type of the reply data will be text no matter what you are returning, because of the headers. If you want to append binary data, as in a GIF image, that is fine, but the type is still text.

Processing Form Data

One of the more difficult tasks you will encounter in writing a CGI application is processing the information that a WWW client sends when it submits a form page. The data received needs to be decoded several different ways before it is in a usable format. Once it is decoded, processing the data often requires an intimate knowledge of how the form was written, since the data is identified by the names of the fields in the form element. Since users are able to type free text into some of the form fields, there may also be a need to format that text or filter certain characters (such as carriage returns) out of it. It is all worth the effort, though, because forms provide the best interface for creating a site that interacts with your users.

How Forms Are Submitted

Unlike a map or ISINDEX search field, where only one item of information is being sent to the server, a form contains possibly many items of information, all of which must be sent to the server. On top of that, the number of items is variable from form to form, and the amount of information in each item is variable. The method that was devised to handle this is what I will call *form encoding*. It has a MIME type of "application/x-www-form-urlencoded".

Before we get into the specifics of form encoding, we need to get a feel for what is happening in general when a form is submitted. The first step, of course, is for the user to submit the form, either by clicking on the **Submit** button (in a graphical browser) or using the submit command (for text-mode browsers). When this happens, the client software kicks into action. The client begins by assembling a target URL specifying where the information is to be sent (usually a CGI application) based on a URL provided in the ACTION attribute of the opening tag of the form element. An example of this (using the Guestbook CGI) would be:

```
<FORM ACTION="/cgi/guestbook.acgi" METHOD=POST>
```

Once the method and target URL are determined, the client combines all of the information from the form into one large block of information to be sent to the location specified in the target URL (this is a somewhat complicated process, so I will return to it later). If the target URL specifies a CGI application on the server, the data is sent to the WebSTAR as part of a request for the CGI application. WebSTAR then makes a special Apple event that contains the form data and sends the event to the target application. Some clients can do other things with the form data, such as sending it off in an e-mail message (we won't worry about those possibilities, since they don't involve WebSTAR at all). When the CGI application receives the Apple event, it extracts the form data and whatever other information it needs, processes the information, and returns a response to WebSTAR.

That is all very straightforward, since it is pretty much the same process used with any link to a CGI application. The only part that is really different is the way that the client software packages the data in a form to send it to the server. Since every form will have a different number of fields, of different sizes and kinds, it is not possible to send data from every field as a different part of the HTTP request. Instead, all of the data from the fields needs to be pooled into a single piece of data (a *form data block*) that can be sent. In addition, since some way of identifying the data to the CGI application is needed, the name of each field must also be sent and used in some way to identify the field data that it represents.

The following method for encoding form field data is used by all WWW clients that support forms:

1. *Encode the data in each field.*   This is done by using URL encoding, which was discussed earlier. Remember that a "field" may also be a checkbox, pop-up menu, radio button, or some other input type that the user does not specifically type in. The values of these fields are still encoded, though. Thus if you have a checkbox with a value of "Chip & Dale," the ampersand will be encoded before it is sent to the server.

2. *Create name=data pairs.*   Each field in a form has a NAME attribute associated with it. This name is used as the identifier for the data from that field. The name is paired with the data contained in the element by putting an equal sign (=) between the two to form one text block. Thus for a field named "Name" containing the text "Jim", the result would be "Name=Jim". Because the equal sign is used to concatenate the name and value of a field, all occurrences of equal signs in the actual data of a field must be URL encoded (see step 1).

3. *Concatenate all pairs into one data block using an ampersand.*   Each of the name=value pairs for each field are now concatenated using an ampersand, which results in something like this:

   ```
   name1=value1&name2=value2&...&namen=valuen
   ```

   This forms one single block of data, with all of the information from all of the fields in a format that is safe for transmission over the network. As with the equal sign, any occurences of an ampersand in the data from a field must be URL encoded (see step 1).

This is not complicated, but it is also not something that is easy to figure out just from looking at the data sent from a form. If you want to see some examples of this, use one of the basic CGI applications included on the companion CD-ROM. These applications don't do much processing of the data they receive. All they do is break the parameters up and create a page that lists the name of each parameter and what was sent in it. If you look at the

http_search_args parameter (for the GET method) or **post_args** (for the POST method in one of these CGI applications, you should be able to see the formatting clearly.

The method for sending the field data block in an HTTP request is specified in the METHOD attribute of the opening tag for a form element. The options at this time for WebSTAR are GET or POST. If no method is specified, GET is assumed. With the GET method, the field data block is appended to the URL, using a question mark (**?**) to separate the two. The limit on how much data can be sent using the GET method is 1K, including the entire URL. If the POST method is used, the field data block is appended to the request, and the limit on how much data can be sent rises to 24K. I highly recommend using the POST method whenever possible. It not only allows you to send more data but also leaves the GET data variable free for sending other information, such as a command for the CGI application to quit. If you use the GET method, you can still include additional data in the path arguments, but they will count against the 1K limit for the total length of the URL.

Decoding Form Data Blocks

Decoding the form data blocks means simply reversing the process of encoding. Thus you have to:

1. Parse the block into separate name=field pairs by separating the data wherever an ampersand is encountered (toss out the ampersand characters; they have no use anymore).

2. Parse each name=value pair into the separate field name and field value (the data that was in the field). Use the first equal sign that you encounter to split the data. If there is more than one, something went wrong on the client end. Again, toss out the equals characters when you are parsing.

3. Undo the URL encoding of each field's data.

This should all be very easy to do, but there are a couple of possible problems that you need to prepare for.

The first problem occurs because nothing dictates what order the fields will be concatenated in. Although it seems logical that the fields should be concatenated in the order in which they occur in the form, it is entirely acceptable for a WWW client to process them in the reverse order or to group them according to type or anything else it wants to do. This means that you need to check the name of a field before you know which one it is. Of course, most of the clients do go ahead and add the fields in order. If you have a very large form, it may be worth the time to put the fields in order first, planning that most of the time they already will be so.

The next problem is that not every field is sent by the client. If a text field is left empty, it is sent anyway with an empty data field. With a scrolling list, though, if nothing is selected, neither the field name nor the data will be sent. The same is true of checkboxes; if a checkbox is not checked, it is not included in the form data block. In these cases it is important to prepare for the possibility that a field may not be present.

The final problem is just the opposite. It is possible that more than one piece of data will be sent for the same field name. There are two ways that this can happen. It could be that a mistake was made when designing the form and more than one field was given the same name. This might not even be a mistake if there was some reason for wanting to group fields by name (such as with checkboxes). The more likely possibility is that a scrolling list was used. Scrolling lists allow several options (lines) to be selected, and each will be sent as a separate piece of data with the name of the field. The result, for a scrolling list of ice cream toppings, might look like this:

```
...&toppings=sprinkles&toppings=nuts&toppings=fudge&...
```

To handle this situation, you need to be certain that you check the entire list and use a variable type that can hold more than one piece of data if necessary.

Form-Processing Tips

The URL decoding has to be done separately for each field's data, since the decoding comes after the parsing steps. Since you have to step through each field anyway, that is also a good time to force the fields into a specific format. One useful thing to do is to watch for duplicate fields and either group the data together for duplicate field names or create a new piece of data containing the data from all of the duplicate fields.

If you write software routines to look up specific data from the form data block by searching for a field name, it is a good idea to return a default value for a field that does not exist in the block. That will prevent errors in the event that a checkbox field is not returned (or that there is a misspelling in the field name).

Be sure that your URL decoding routine can handle 8-bit characters. All 8-bit characters will be URL encoded by the client, along with the special characters. If your code is not careful to decode them properly, any foreign text will be ruined. If you format the text or delete special characters, you must also be careful to check for double-byte characters (such as Japanese and Chinese), which are destroyed if one byte of a character is deleted.

If you have TEXTAREA fields where a user can type in lots of text, you may need to do some special processing of that text. Most WWW clients do not wrap the text in a TEXTAREA field, so users are likely to insert carriage returns. It is probable that you will want to strip these out or convert them to an HTML equivalent, such as **
**. Also, Web users are learning that many times they can enter HTML tags in these text fields and the HTML will be displayed in the processed document. If this is not desirable (for instance, you do not want people adding IMG tags to load large images), it is easy enough to strip them out. A larger problem is that quite often these tags are typed incorrectly, for whatever reason. In those cases both stripping them out and correcting them can be a problem.

CGI Design Issues

Every CGI writer faces several issues, regardless of the language being used. Even if you do not plan to write a CGI application, understanding these issues will help you to understand why some features are so difficult to implement or why your favorite CGI application has suddenly stopped working.

The Pitfalls of Asynchronous Design

Asynchronous CGI application handling is a big bonus in terms of speed on your server, but it also introduces some new problems for the CGI writer. The main problem that a CGI author will face is how to handle a new event that arrives while another event is being processed. When an event is being processed by a CGI application, new events that arrive are queued up by the system until the CGI application checks for them. When a CGI application finishes processing one event, it must check to see whether another is queued up. If it does not do so, as happens in an application that quits immediately after processing, the queued events will be lost, and the connections that sent them will receive an error from WebSTAR. In most languages all this requires is a simple call to WaitNextEvent when processing is finished. Most scripting languages make that call automatically if the application does not quit immediately.

Threading Your CGI Application

Another problem that arises with asynchronous CGI applications is the need to add threaded processing capabilities to your CGI application. If your CGI application is not too busy, you can process connections using first-in-first-out processing, and things will work fine. My definition of "not too busy" is that on average, no more than one new event arrives while the current event is processing. If, however, several new events usually arrive before the current event can finish processing, you are going to have an ever-increasing backlog of events waiting in the queue to be processed. The result will be that the CGI will eventually get so far behind in processing events that every event will be timing out before the CGI application even starts processing it.

The solution is to use the Thread Manager to add multithreaded processing to your CGI application, just the way that WebSTAR does. Processing multiple events at once is more efficient than processing one at a time, so several events can be processed simultaneously in only slightly more than the time it would take to process one event. A side benefit is that multiprocessing tends to even out the processing peaks. Connections do not always arrive in a nice, even distribution. If several events arrive at the same time, the last to arrive may time out before the previous events are processed. With threaded processing, every event gets to start processing as soon as it arrives and has a better chance of finishing before the timeout period is reached.

The companion CD-ROM has example shells in C that demonstrate how to write a threaded CGI application. Not all languages have support for the Thread Manager, especially such high-level languages as AppleScript and HyperTalk, so your choices for creating high-use, threaded CGI applications is somewhat limited.

Quitting a CGI Application

When it is time to quit your CGI application, you may encounter another problem. During the short period it takes an application to quit, it may receive an event, but it is too late for it to recognize that the event arrived and process it. Any event arriving during that period will be lost and result in a timeout error for the user. If the CGI application is written in C, Pascal, or a similar language, the period is so short that the likelihood of losing an event is very small. In a language like AppleScript, though, this period can be several seconds long or longer, so the likelihood of losing an event increases. In addition, if the CGI application does any processing while quitting, such as saving information to disk, the period will also be longer and the likelihood again increases.

The only solution for this is to avoid quitting unless absolutely necessary. Even if you try to set a global variable to tell whether the CGI application is busy processing an event (which is a good idea), there will still be that period during quitting when a new event coming in could be lost. There are two ways to reduce the odds of this happening, though. The first is to wait until the CGI application has been idle for a while before quitting. In general, the longer a CGI application has been idle, the longer it is likely to go on being idle. The second is to quit only CGI applications that you are sure are not in use, either because you are the only one who uses them or because you have somehow stopped people from reaching them, perhaps by setting WebSTAR to temporarily refuse connections.

At one time I recommended writing CGI applications that would quit whenever they weren't in use, to save on RAM usage. This seemed like a good idea at the time, since I was trying to run a Web site and dozens of CGI applications on an 8MB Macintosh SE/30. I have since received several e-mail messages explaining why this might not be as useful as I thought (you can all stop writing now). Because of the way that the Macintosh allocates memory, it is possible that quitting idle CGI applications will not only not save memory but also actually use up more memory. Since there is also the possibility that events will be lost while quitting, I have to say that it no longer seems like a good idea.

Remote Control for CGI Applications

As discussed before, there are two ways to send data as part of the URL to a CGI application. If one of these ways is not in use, you can use that to send remote control commands to your CGI application and control it over the Internet. As an example, if your CGI application is using only the post argument data, you can add a command via the search argument to tell the CGI application to quit itself:

```
http://www.comvista.com/cgi/register.acgi?quit
```

Since the data is not touched by WebSTAR, except to transfer it to the Apple event for the CGI application, you can put anything you want in that data. The only limits are that the total URL length must be less than 1024 characters and that any special characters you add in the data must be URL encoded. This is useful for interacting with search engines where you can put search terms, control information, and return format information all in the search data.

These commands can be very useful for maintaining control of CGI applications when you are away from the server. If the CGI application stores data in memory that is written to disk during quitting, you can add a command that allows you to force a write out to disk. If you are developing a CGI application, this can be used to quit the CGI when you want to replace it with a new version. If you're really ambitious, commands could be used to alter the functioning of the CGI application, such as turning on a debugging mode. Be careful what keywords that you choose, of course, or you may find that someone else is controlling your software.

Using Virtual Pages

The same trick can be used to send requests for virtual pages from a CGI application (which is the only place they can come from). If your CGI application uses a form page to receive information from users, it may be a good idea to have the CGI application build the HTML page and return it from memory. In this case you could use a URL to tell the CGI application to return a standard form to the client so a user can fill it in and submit the data to the CGI application:

```
http://www.comvista.com/cgi/MailerCGI.acgi?FORM:
standard
```

This increases the ease of use of your CGI application manyfold, even for experienced Web developers. A form-processing CGI application usually needs to know exactly what names the fields in the form page will have, so combining the two into one CGI application takes care of that problem.

Speed Tips

Here's the part you really wanted. Fancy features are nice, but in the end you will want only one thing: faster CGI processing. When you are working to speed up your CGI application, it is important to keep in mind exactly what the goal is. The only speed measurement that really matters is how quickly the user gets a response from the server. Your CGI application could spend days doing the actual processing as long as it took only two seconds to respond to the user before doing the rest of the processing. This is the key to some of those CGI applications that seem to respond almost instantly on other systems. For all you know, they might still be chugging away on your request for days after they sent you that nice notice that "Your request has been processed."

Here are some tricks that can be used to improve the apparent speed of your CGI application.

Idle-Time Processing

The best way to respond more quickly to users is to put off as much of the processing as possible until the CGI is idle. In many cases there is no real need to do any processing in order to respond to the user. You are responding only because WebSTAR expects a response to the event it sent (and to reassure the user that something happened). If your CGI application can return to the client a small page that says "All is well. Your request will be processed," the user can move on to more interesting things, and your CGI application can process in peace.

This is easier said than done, however. In AppleScript, for example, responding to the event terminates all processing for the event. There are ways around this, but they all involve the same basic solution, which is to get the user data out to external storage before sending the reply. An easy way to do this is to write the data to a global variable. There are two problems with this, though. First, if you are processing multiple events, you need to have some structure to the global variable that makes sure that the data for one event doesn't get mixed up with data from other events. Second, if the data is going to be at all large, you may run into memory problems trying to keep it in temporary storage. Once you have the data in a temporary storage, you can then add a routine that is launched when the CGI is idle to process the data.

If you are doing some tricky things with pages in memory or storing databases in RAM, you probably need to write data to disk to prevent losing everything in the event that the system crashes. Additionally, you may want to print out hard copies of the CGI activity or to send e-mail messages. This sort of activity does nothing to speed up response to the user, so it should also be left for idle-time processing, if possible. An idle-time routine can be created to save the latest information to disk, print new connection information, or do whatever is needed. In these cases it is a good idea to use a global variable to keep track of whether the information in memory has changed since the last idle time, which can save unnecessary activity during the slower times of the day. It is also useful to add the ability to send to the CGI application a command that will force the activity to take place as needed, or at least to make sure that the activity takes place one last time just before the CGI application quits.

This system will work well for CGI applications that might have short bursts of high activity but on average spend much more time idle than in use. If there is not enough idle time, the data just keeps piling up and eventually you hit some kind of limit. This system also works only for those situations when the user does not need to immediately see the results of any processing. If you have a guest-book, chat page, or some other system where the user expects to see the data processed quickly, you are stuck processing the entire data while the user waits.

Operating in Memory

Many times a CGI application is used to modify a document before returning it to the user. Caching the document in memory can improve response speed quite a bit. First, the page can generally be returned from memory more quickly than from a disk (you avoid a file system call, a disk seek, and the data retrieval). Second, it may be possible to keep the page in some preprocessed form in memory that makes modifying it go more quickly as compared to reading it from disk and then modifying it. As an example, if a page is to have variable information inserted in the middle of it, you can save time by storing the page as two cached documents: the prefix (everything before the insertion point) and the suffix (everything after the insertion point). When it is time to return the document, the data can easily be "inserted" by concatenating the prefix, data, and suffix back into one temporary piece of data to return to the user.

For best results, any pages served from memory should be read into memory when the CGI application launches. Presumably there is not much activity at that time, so it will be ready and waiting when the first event arrives.

Back-End Processing

Similarly, a CGI can act as a front end to another processing system. The CGI application accepts data from a user, then sends the data off to another application for processing. This can be done by saving the data to disk, sending it in an e-mail message, or using some other method, but the method needs to be relatively fast or the benefits are miminal. The CGI application can then respond quickly to the user while another application takes its time in the background to process the data. This is especially well suited to batch-processing situations, such as purchase requests, suggestion boxes, conference registrations, and other situations when confirmation would not be expected immediately.

MacHTTP versus WebSTAR CGI Design

There are only two difference between the way that WebSTAR and MacHTTP interact with CGI applications. The first difference is in the **Server:** header that is sent in an HTTP response. MacHTTP sends the simple line **Server: MacHTTP**. WebSTAR sends a much more complicated header that uses the form **Server: WebSTAR/ <version> ID/<id_num>**, where **<version>** is the version of Web-STAR being used and **<id_num>** is a special ID number for the server. When you write a CGI application, the **<id_num>** is simply "**ACGI**". Of course, there is no reason that you can't just return the old MacHTTP server line if you want. The information is being sent back to the client software, and most clients just ignore that line.

The second difference is in the variables that are sent to CGI applications by the servers. WebSTAR includes several new parameters as part of the WWWΩsdoc event to support new features such as Actions. The only parameters sent by MacHTTP in the **WWWΩsdoc** event are **meth**, **addr**, **frmu**, **user**, **pass**, **svnm**, **svpt**, **scnm**, **refr**, **Agnt**, **ctyp**. If you make use of any of the other parameters in a CGI application, it will not work with MacHTTP.

Writing CGI Applications to Support Actions

It takes very little to convert a CGI application for use as an Action processor. The main difference is that the CGI application must now check to see how it was called, whether it was called as a CGI application or an Action processor. This is done by looking at the action parameter (**Kact**). If the CGI application is called as a CGI, the action parameter will contain **CGI** or **ACGI**, depending on what kind it is. If the CGI application is called as an Action, the action parameter will contain the name of the Action. The path and file name used to call the CGI application as an Action processor will be in the action_path (**Kact**), and the path and file name specified in the URL will be in script_name (**scnm**), as usual.

Using Server-Push Features

WebSTAR 1.2 and later support *server-push*, a feature that was originally introduced by the Netscape servers. Server-push is a trick that the server does to keep an HTTP connection open longer than it normally should be. This has three uses: to return extremely large amounts of data that couldn't be done in one block, to return data in pieces for a process that will take a long time (such as searching multiple databases), or to return data at fixed intervals.

WebSTAR 1.2 provides a new Apple event parameter, the **connection_id (Kcid)**, which gives a unique indentifier to every connection that WebSTAR is handling. This ID is used to keep track of which connection is having data returned, since it is now possible for a connection to have data sent back more than once.

The general process for a CGI application that is going to use server push is the same no matter what language you plan to use. First, the CGI application sends a reply to WebSTAR that contains the string **<SEND_PARTIAL>**. There must not be any extra characters, and the text is case sensitive. This tells WebSTAR to hold the connection open because the CGI application plans to return data in several pieces. Next, the CGI application starts sending data to WebSTAR, using a new "send partial" event. The event to use is **WWWΩSPar** and has two associated variables, the **connection_id (Kcid)**, which is a long integer, and **more (Kmor)**, which is a Boolean that tells whether more data is expected in the future (whether to continue holding the connection open). When the last piece of data has been returned, the CGI application returns an event with more set to false, and WebSTAR will close the connection after returning the last data.

WebSTAR offers a shortcut in responding with partial data. If WebSTAR receives a "send partial" event for a connection, it will assume that the CGI application is going to use server-push (good guess). This means that it isn't strictly necessary to reply to the original WWWΩsdoc event unless the language you are using requires it (as AppleScript does).

If a CGI application is going to do server-push, it must run as an asynchronous CGI application, because it will be sending events back to WebSTAR. If the CGI is run synchronously, WebSTAR will be halted, waiting for return data. When the CGI application tries to send an event back, WebSTAR won't be able to receive it, and both of them will be locked up until the connection times out.

Since the CGI application has to run asynchronously and since server-push takes much longer than normal CGI processing, it is extremely important that any CGI application that will be doing server-push also be able to process requests in multiple threads. This is a little trickier than writing a normal threaded CGI application, because there is more information to track about each connection. It is also important that the load on a server running a server-push CGI application be reevaluated. Since these CGI applications hold the connection open much longer than usual, the server will have more connections open at any one time, and the 50-connection limit in MacTCP could become a problem.

14

Developing CGIs in AppleScript

Let's get this clear right at the start: AppleScript is not the best language for writing powerful CGI applications. AppleScript applets are slow compared to their equivalents in C or any other compiled language. Several limitations are imposed in order to keep the language fairly simple to learn, and quality AppleScript development tools are only now becoming really useful. If you want to write a powerful CGI application that will be responsible for most of what happens on your site, find another language.

There are still plenty of good reasons to use AppleScript, though. It is a very easy language to get started in, especially if you do not have prior programming experience, since it somewhat resembles the English language, unlike C, which most closely resembles a bowl of alphabet soup. AppleScript relieves you from almost all of the tedium of making an interface, initializing various things, and registering Apple events. It has plenty of speed for smaller tasks and can even be used for complex tasks, as long as multiple connections are unlikely to be waiting to be processed by the same CGI application. Finally, it is the easiest solution for sending information or commands to other applications.

I will use AppleScript to provide some specific examples of CGI programming and demonstrate some of the problems that may be encountered. If you plan to use a different language for writing CGI applications, you might still want to read this over. Think of the AppleScript scripts as pseudocode examples, if it helps.

Not the Gas Station

AppleScript CGI scripts use some special characters that you may not have seen, especially if you have never used Apple-Script before:

- «   This is not two left brackets but rather a special character called a "left chevron." It is typed as "option-\" and is used, along with the right chevron, to denote an Apple event or class.

- »   This is a "right chevron" and marks the end of the Apple event or class. It is typed as "option-shift-\".

- ¬   This "continuation" marker indicates that the next line is to be considered part of the current line. You can use this to break up very long lines for easier reading. This is made in AppleScript by typing "option-return". In regular text you can also type it as "option-l".

- Ω   The capital omega character, this is part of the name of the event passed from WebSTAR to CGI applications. It is typed as "option-z".

Creating a CGI Application in AppleScript

Before we get into any code, you need to know how to turn an AppleScript script into a CGI application. In order to use your script as a CGI application, it first needs to be compiled, and for that you need a script editor that is able to compile scripts. All of the examples I will be showing will use Script Editor, which comes free as part of the AppleScript package. You can do the same thing with Scripter, Script Debugger, or any other script editor available, but the process will be slightly different.

To save your script as a compiled application, do the following:

1. Open the script in Script Editor by using the **Open...** command from the File menu inside Script Editor or by double-clicking on the script in the Finder.

2. Click on the **Check Syntax** button at the top right of the Script Editor window. This will check your script for syntax errors and ask you to locate any applications or files that are specifically mentioned. For this step to work, you must also have all of the OSAXes properly installed that your script will use. If Script Editor complains that it doesn't understand a command or was expecting another word, this is often the problem. *If you saved the script as a compiled script, it will be automatically checked whenever you save, so this step will not be necessary.*

3. Select the **Save As...** item in the File menu. This brings up a standard dialog box asking for a file name and a location to save the file. *This will save the script as an application that can be edited. If you don't want to include the script text in the final CGI application, use the* **Save as Run Only...** *menu item.*

4. Select a name for the CGI application. Give it the extension **.acgi** or **.cgi**, depending on whether you want it to be used as an asynchronous CGI application.

5. Select **Application** from the pop-up menu above the file name (see Figure 14.1).

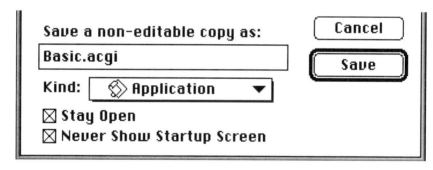

Figure 14.1
The Save as Run-Only…
Dialog

6. Check the two boxes for **Stay Open** and **Never Show Startup Screen** located below the file name. *These are very important!* Without these two options checked, the CGI application will not be able to launch properly or process the Apple events. The **Stay Open** option makes the application keep running and wait for events to be sent to it. Without this checked, the application would launch, run whatever code is present outside of a handler, then quit. The **Never Show Startup Screen** option prevents the

application from putting up a notice when it launches. If this is not checked, the application launches and then hangs there, waiting for someone to click on the startup screen before it continues. This is not good.

7. Select the folder you want to save the CGI application into and click on the **Save** button. You should now have a CGI application ready to use.

Most of the problems that people report to me are solved by properly following these steps.

Notes about AppleScript

There isn't room here to provide an introduction to AppleScript. Several books cover that topic, and I highly recommend purchasing one if you plan to use AppleScript for any serious work. Most people will ignore that advice, though, so here are the most common problems that beginners run into (and how to avoid them).

AppleScript is designed so that new commands can be easily added. This is done by installing OSAXes (Open Scripting Architecture eXtension) that contain both information about new commands and code to execute them. Installing an OSAX consists of moving it into the Scripting Additions folder inside the Extensions folder inside your System Folder. A common mistake is to copy the entire folder

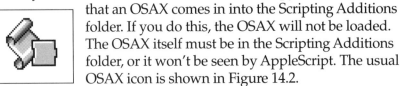

Figure 14.2
The OSAX Icon

that an OSAX comes in into the Scripting Additions folder. If you do this, the OSAX will not be loaded. The OSAX itself must be in the Scripting Additions folder, or it won't be seen by AppleScript. The usual OSAX icon is shown in Figure 14.2.

AppleScript is designed so that OSAXes can be added whenever you want. If you have a script open and then decide to add a new OSAX to your system, it should be recognized by AppleScript the next time that you check or compile a script. Unfortunately this doesn't always work. Sometimes the OSAX will not be recognized even though it is properly installed. This usually results in an error when AppleScript checks the script, such as "expecting end but found 'parse'." On these occasions the best solution is to reboot the computer and force AppleScript to start over.

When you open a script, you may see a line like

```
set formData to «event PCGIPCGI» post_args
```

The problem is that you are missing an OSAX that was present when the script was previously saved. The text between the chevron characters represents the Apple event that the OSAX was handling. If you install the OSAX (in this case, it is Parse CGI OSAX) and recheck the script, the commands from the OSAX will replace the event code. This happens only with scripts that are saved as compiled scripts or applications. If you were to check a script saved as text with an OSAX missing, you would simply get an error.

If you have two or more OSAXes that have similar commands, they can confuse AppleScript and cause problems with your scripts. This may happen if you install a newer version of an OSAX and forget to remove the older version or if you are trying out several OSAXes that all perform very similar functions. In these cases it might help to view your Scripting Additions folder by name to make sure that the troublesome OSAX isn't hiding somewhere in that folder.

AppleScript has several reserved words, and they cannot be used as variables. The most common example I see is people who try to use a variable named "name." But since "name" is a reserved word, when you try to use it as a variable, AppleScript is unable to understand what the command means, and an error results. Of course, if you bought an AppleScript book, you would have a list of those reserved words. It's just a suggestion.

A Basic CGI Application

First, we'll walk through the construction of a CGI application shell that can be used as the basis of almost anything you write. This basic CGI script, and all of the scripts I disuss here, are included on the companion CD-ROM in the folder Sample Code:AppleScript:CGI Scripts. I use the word "script" to refer to both the AppleScript script and the compiled CGI applications that the script creates. I think that it is more useful to think of what is happening in the CGI application in terms of the lines is the script.

Hello, World!

Every programming course begins with the simplest possible example for a language, which is an application that simply replies "Hello, world." In order to do this for a CGI application, I will have to admit that I have not been completely honest with you.

It *is* possible to return data from a CGI application without returning a proper HTTP header. In fact, what you can do is not return any header at all. If a CGI application doesn't return an HTTP header, the WWW client will make some assumptions about what happened. In all of the clients I have seen, the assumption is that the response was **200 OK** and that whatever was returned should be treated as plain text. This is something useful to know when you are hacking out a quick CGI application and don't want to mess with making sure that a header is created for every response.

Here is the code for a minimal CGI application written in AppleScript.

```
on «event WWWΩsdoc»
    return "Hello, world!"
end «event WWWΩsdoc»
```

These three lines replace quite a bit of C code. The first line declares that this handler (everything between **on** and **end**) will be run when the Apple event WWWΩsdoc is received by the CGI application. What you don't see behind the scenes is that AppleScript is taking care of registering that fact with the system and setting everything up to accept an Apple event. The second line takes the short text string and automatically inserts it into a reply event that is sent back to WebSTAR. The third line simply marks the end of processing for that event. Processing for an event is considered to be finished when it reaches the **end** statement, reaches a return statement, or crashes.

Actually, this CGI application has some usefulness. Since it is so incredibly simple, it is unlikely that anything will go wrong while it is processing. When you first start with CGI applications, it is useful to have one like this to practice with. If you can't make this one work, you either made an error when you were saving it as an application or used an incorrect link. You can use this to test how to write links to CGI applications in other folders or to see whether you have set up an Action processor declaration correctly or anywhere else that you want to test a CGI application.

Using HTML Text and Headers

That was nice, but when you have a finished CGI application, it really should be returning proper HTTP headers and HTML text (or whatever data you want to return). Here is the code for a more complete example:

```
property crlf : (ASCII character 13) & (ASCII character 10)
property http_10_header : "HTTP/1.0 200 OK" & crlf ¬
    & "Server: WebSTAR/1.0 ID/ACGI" & crlf ¬
    & "MIME-Version: 1.0" & crlf ¬
    & "Content-type: text/html" & crlf & crlf

on «event WWWΩsdoc»
    return http_10_header & "<HTML><HEAD>" ¬
        & "<TITLE>Hello World</TITLE></HEAD>" ¬
        & "<BODY><H1>Hello,
World!</H1></BODY></HTML>"
end «event WWWΩsdoc»
```

The first two lines (only two lines, remember the continuation character?) define two properties that will be used in the script. Properties are much like global variables but have two key features: Their value is saved in between launches of the script (globals are reset each time), and they are accessible from anywhere in the script (globals have to be specifically enabled in handlers). These two properties will be extremely useful in any script you write.

The first property creates a new variable that is a carriage return followed by a line feed. This is the marker for the end of a line of text in the UNIX world, and so you will use it a lot when building text to return from a CGI application. The second property is a complete HTTP header for the most common situation; returning a **200 OK** code and some HTML text. If you read the section on HTTP, you will see that this has a MIME type header that tells the WWW client to treat the text like an HTML document (the type is **text/html**).

The rest of this example is very like our first one, with the exception of the reply statement. This script returns the HTTP header and some HTML text (the ampersand indicates that the text is to be concatenated into one block of text). Because the properties have been added to the start of the script and outside of the event handler, they will be created when the CGI application launches. In fact, any code that you place before the first "on" statement in a script will be executed at launch time. We'll make use of this more later.

URL Redirection

Most of the time, your CGI applications will be returning the results shown earlier. When they aren't, the next most likely option is to send back a URL redirection code, which tells the client to retrieve a different URL and display it for the user. Here is a simple example that will do redirection instead of returning HTML text directly.

```
property crlf : (ASCII character 13) & (ASCII charac-
ter 10)
property http_10_redir : "HTTP/1.0 302 FOUND" & crlf ¬
    & "Server: WebSTAR/1.0 ID/ACGI" & crlf ¬
    & "Location: http://www.comvista.com/" & crlf ¬
    & "URI: http://www.comvista.com/" & crlf & crlf

on «event WWWΩsdoc»
    return http_10_redir
end «event WWWΩsdoc»
```

Did you notice how the **http_10_redir** is different from the **http_10_header** used in the previous example? The code being returned is now **302 FOUND**, which tells the client that the document is not being returned directly but that it can be found at the URI enclosed and the client should go there to get it. In addition, the **Content-type** header is no longer needed, since no content is being returned. The biggest change, though, is the addition of two headers for doing redirection. The **Location** header, originally defined in the HTTP/0.9 version, is used to tell the location of the found document. In version 1.0, though, the name of that header has been changed to

`URI`, which makes use of other standards. Many older clients will recognize only the `Location` header, whereas newer clients will recognize only the `URI` header. Luckily HTTP specifies that the client should ignore any unrecognized headers, so it doesn't hurt to specify both in the HTTP header. It's a bit inconvenient, but that should clear up as more of the clients get up to speed on the standards.

Using the Apple Event Parameters

A CGI application can't do much of interest until it starts using the data that is sent in the Apple event parameters. This data describes the client that sent the request to the URL and any data that the client sent along with the request. The exact parameters were listed and described in Chapter 13. In AppleScript each of these parameters can be assigned to a variable when the event is received. This is done by changing the line that defines the start of the event handler:

```
on «event WWWΩsdoc» path_args ¬

    given «class kfor»:http_search_args, «class
    post»:post_args, ¬

    «class meth»:method, «class addr»:client_address, ¬

    «class user»:username, «class pass»:password, ¬

    «class frmu»:from_user, «class svnm»:server_name, ¬

    «class svpt»:server_port, «class scnm»:script_name, ¬

    «class ctyp»:content_type, «class refr»:referer, ¬

    «class Agnt»:user_agent, «class Kact»:action, ¬

    «class Kapt»:action_path, «class Kcip»:client_ip, ¬

    «class Kfrq»:full_request
```

This is really only one line, with continuation characters used to make the line more readable. The **path_args** variable receives whatever was in the direct parameter for the event. The keyword **given** starts a listing of the indirect parameters. For each indirect parameter, the assignment is made by listing the class that is being received and the variable its data should be assigned to. All of the variables that you declare in this way are immediately available for use throughout the script.

This example lists every single parameter that the Apple event contains. It doesn't hurt anything to use this header in all of your scripts, whether or not you are using the variables. The data is sent either way. However, if it bothers you to have all of those extra variables floating around, feel free to remove any that you don't plan to use. AppleScript doesn't care whether you use the data, so the following would also be fine:

```
on «event WWWΩsdoc» path_args ¬

    given «class kfor»:http_search_args, «class
refr»:referer, ¬

        «class Kcip»:client_ip
```

Error-Handling Code

Before we go any further, it is time to introduce the most useful thing you will learn in this entire chapter: how to get your script to provide useful error codes instead of crashing. The key is the **try...on error** construct that you place around your code. When an error occurs inside this construct, processing jumps to the **on error** handler instead of simply quitting. The **on error** handler receives the error message and error number that AppleScript or the system provides and can continue processing or post a customized error alert.

The classic use of the **on error** handler is to return the message and code to the user so that the error can be reported to the Webmaster.

```
try
    [all of your code goes here]
on error errMsg number errNum
    return "Error: " & errNum & " - " & errMsg
end try
```

This example would return text to the WWW client, showing the error code and error description for the problem the script ran into. Of course it is much better to return a complete HTTP header (as any good CGI application does) and HTML text that not only informs the user that an error occurred but also provides an e-mail address that can be used to report the error. An example of this will be shown in a later script.

Avoid doing anything very fancy in your error handler, especially avoid using OSAXes or using a lot of memory. If you do anything in your error handler that causes an error, the CGI application will crash, and you will be back where you started. Returning a small HTML document should be fine, though.

Shutdown Processing

If your script is storing any information that needs to be written to disk or printed out, it is a good idea to include a **quit** handler in your script. The handler will tell the script to save the final information to disk or close any open files or even check to make sure that the current events finish processing before the CGI application quits. I include a **quit** handler in all of my scripts, even if I don't plan to use it in the final product. It can be very useful for checking things while the script is being developed. A basic **quit** handler would look like this:

```
on quit
    — put all of your shutdown code here
    continue quit
end quit
```

The **on quit** statement means that whenever your script is quit, either by a menu command or by telling itself to quit, it will run this handler as the last thing before it quits. This handler is *not* run when a script crashes, though. The statement **continue quit** must be the last line in your **quit** handler. Your **quit** handler has intercepted a command that tells the script to quit. If you do not tell it to go on quitting, it will stop right there, and you will have to crash it to make it quit (not a good design decision).

Basic Wrap-Up

That covers everything you need to know to create the CGI script shell that will be the basis of all of the other scripts that I discuss here. This first script, BasicCGI.script (you can find it on the companion CD-ROM), is a fully functional CGI application that receives the Apple event and returns an HTML page that lists all of the parameters that were received. Use this script to see what the data looks like that different clients send and to see how the parameters are used differently when a CGI application is run as an Action or preprocessor rather than directly as a CGI application.

Real-World Example: LinkTracker CGI

The WebSTAR log file keeps track of every page on your site that a user requests. When the user clicks on a link to another site, though, the log file has no way to track that, because the server isn't involved in the connection. The client software gets the URL from the page it downloaded and uses that to connect to the new server directly. The script provided here will create a CGI application that you can use to track these links after all. The trick is to rewrite all links to external sites so that they go through this CGI application. As an example, suppose that you had a link to the StarNine Web site:

```
<A HREF="http://www.starnine.com/">
```

You would change that to instead read

```
<A HREF="/cgi/LinkTracker.cgi?http://www.starnine.
com/">
```

The CGI application will receive the request with a complete URL in the **http_search_args** variable. It will log which link is being requested, then send a redirect command to the WWW client to go to the new URL. To speed things up a bit, the log data will be stored up and written out to disk only at idle time and only if there is significant data to write (more than 20 entries). Since the data is not critical (at least not on my site), we won't worry about whether the CGI applicaton could crash and lose all current entries.

This version could use several improvements. For example, this script has the file name hard-coded, and it assumes that the file already exists. It would be better to have a configuration command to set the file name and create the new file if it doesn't exist. Also, I have no idea whether there is any limit on the file size. If there is not room to write more data, the script will crash (and nasty things could happen to the disk, I suppose).

The entire script is shown in Listing 14.1.

Listing 14.1 LinkTracker CGI Script

```
property crlf : (ASCII character 13) & (ASCII character 10)
```

— This header is used when an error occurs to return an HTML page describing the error.

```
property http_10_header : "HTTP/1.0 200 OK" & crlf &
"Server: WebSTAR/1.0 ID/ACGI" & crlf & ¬
  "MIME-Version: 1.0" & crlf & "Content-type:
  text/html" & crlf & crlf
```

— This header is used to redirect the client to the external URL.

```
property REDIR_header : "HTTP/1.0 302 FOUND" & crlf &
"Server: WebSTAR/1.0 ID/ACGI" & crlf
```

— Save_entries is a counter that tells how many entries are waiting to be saved to disk.

— I use a global variable instead of a property so the value is reset to zero each relaunch.

```
set save_entries to 0
```

— New_entry stores the entries waiting to be saved to disk.

```
set new_entries to ""
```

— This is where you set the name of the log file to use.

— The file must exist before the CGI application is run, or bad things happen.

```
set log_file to "Hard Disk:WebSTAR Root:LinkTracker.log"

on «event WWWΩsdoc» path_args ¬
  given «class kfor»:http_search_args, «class
post»:post_args, «class meth»:method, «class
addr»:client_address, «class user»:username, «class
pass»:password, «class frmu»:from_user, «class
svnm»:server_name, «class svpt»:server_port, «class
scnm»:script_name, «class ctyp»:content_type, «class
refr»:referer, «class Agnt»:user_agent, «class
Kact»:action, «class Kapt»:action_path, «class
Kcip»:client_ip, «class Kfrq»:full_request
    try
```

— Announce the global variables this handler will access.

```
    global save_entries
    global new_entries
```

— Log the time, IP address of the client, and the URL being linked to.

— http_search_args should contain a complete URL.

```
    set new_entry to new_entry & (current date) & tab
& client_address & tab & http_search_args & return
    set save_entries to save_entries + 1
```

— Now build the redirect header to return to the client.

— Use both the Location and URI headers to be compatible with old and new clients.

```
    set return_data to REDIR_header & "Location:" &
http_search_args ¬
        & crlf & "URI:<" & http_search_args & ">" & crlf
& crlf
```

— Now reply to the CGI event. This ends the processing for the client.

```
    return return_data
```

— This handler is run if an error occurs.

```
  on error errMsg number errNum
    set return_page to http_10_header ¬
        & "<HTML><HEAD><TITLE>Error Page</TITLE></HEAD>" ¬
        & "<BODY><H1>Error Encountered!</H1>" & return ¬
        & "An error was encountered with this CGI." & return
    set return_page to return_page ¬
        & "<H3>Error Message</H3>" & return & errMsg &
          return ¬
        & "<H3>Error Number</H3>" & return & errNum &
          return ¬
        & "<H3>Date</H3>" & return & (current date) & return
    set return_page to return_page ¬
        & "<HR>Please notify the webmaster at " ¬
        & "<A
HREF=\"mailto:webmaster@this.site.com\">webmaster@
this.site.com</A>" ¬
        & " of this error." & "</BODY></HTML>"
    return return_page
  end try
end «event WWWΩsdoc»
on idle
```

```
      global log_file
      global save_entries
      global new_entries

   try
      if save_entries > 20 then
```

— This uses the File I/O OSAX commands from ScriptTools 1.3.1.

— Read the documentation for a description of the commands.

```
         set fileRefNum to open file (log_file as alias)
         position file fileRefNum at (get file length
         fileRefNum)
         write file fileRefNum text new_entries
         close file fileRefNum

         set save_entries to 0
         set new_entries to ""
      else
```

— Wait 5 minutes to save information.

```
         return 900
      end if

   on error
      close file fileRefNum
   end try
end idle

on quit
   global log_file
   global save_entries
   global new_entries

   try
      if save_entries > 20 then
         set fileRefNum to open file (log_file as alias)
```

```
        position file fileRefNum at (get file length
        fileRefNum)
        write file fileRefNum text new_entries
        close file fileRefNum
```

— No need to reset the variables, because we're quitting right away.

```
      end if
      continue quit


    on error
      close file fileRefNum
      continue quit
    end try
  end quit
```

Form-Processing CGI Script

If you plan to get information from a user, you probably will be using a form page. Getting useful information out of a form page can be a complicated process, as was shown earlier. Luckily several new OSAXes have appeared on the market to both simplify and speed up the process. These OSAXes take care of decoding the URL-encoded characters and parsing out the data for each field into a list, usually all in one step. For these example scripts, I am using the Parse CGI OSAX from Document Directions, Inc. (**ddi@document.com**). Another OSAX that does the same thing comes as part of the ACME Script Widgets from Wayne Walrath (**wkw@mail.futuris.net**), which is also included on the companion CD-ROM.

Using the Parse CGI OSAX is an easy two-step process. First, you pass it the data that you want to have decoded and parsed. If you used the POST method to send the form (the recommended method), the data will be in **post_args**. Otherwise, it will be in **http_search_args**. The line to decode the data looks like this:

```
set formData to parse CGI arguments post_args
```

The command to the OSAX is **parse CGI arguments <data>**, where **<data>** is the variable that contains the data from the form (**post_args**). The variable **formData** will receive the results of decoding and parsing the **post_args** data. When the command is finished, **formData** will contain a list of field names and variables.

The next step is to get the data for the fields that you are interested in. If you weren't interested in any particular field—for example, if you only wanted to include all of the information in an e-mail message to be sent off for later processing—you could use the following code to grab every field and list them each on a separate line.

```
set postargtext to ""

repeat with currField in formData

   set postargtext to postargtext & value of currField
   & return

end repeat
```

If you have some AppleScript experience, you will recognize this repeat structure as one that loops by taking each element of a list in turn and assigning it to the variable provided (in this case, **curr-Field**). The command to the OSAX to get the field data is **value of <list item>**, with the list item being **currField**. You can also send the command **field of <list item>** to get the name of the field, if you want.

In most cases you will want to get data from specific fields for some kind of processing. The command to do that requires that you know the exact name of the field that you want to get data from.

```
set firstName to CGI field "first_name" from formData
default value "No_Name"
```

This requests the data that is stored in the variable **formData** for the field named "**first_name**" and stores that data in the variable **firstName**. The default value option uses the string provided ("No-Name" in this case) as the value for the field if the field is not present.

I thought briefly of providing a sample here of what the code would look like to do entirely in "regular" AppleScript what Parse CGI OSAX does in one line, but that would take several pages. Even using the three OSAXes that I used to recommend (DecodeURL,

DePlus, and Tokenize) requires about 20 lines to get all of the fields into variables where Parse CGI OSAX uses 4. And if that isn't simple enough for you, check out a new product from Wayne Walrath called "Mama's Little Helper," which provides a completely new and simpler interface for CGI events in AppleScript.

A Real-World Example: E-mail Using Eudora

The best way to understand how this form processing works is to see it in action. A common need on a Web site is a page that allows users to send electronic mail to the Webmaster. Many browsers support the "mailto:" URL scheme now, but that isn't very flexible, and there are still plenty of browsers that don't support it or do so in some unusual way on the client side. We will design a form for users to fill in with their e-mail message and then put that form data into a new Eudora message and mail it off.

Since we will be requesting data on specific fields, it is best to design the form page first so we will know the exact names of the fields. Here is an example of a simple form page for this purpose:

```
<HTML>

<HEAD><TITLE>Send Jon Some E-Mail</TITLE></HEAD>

<BODY>

<H1>Send Jon Some E-Mail</H1>

Jon just loves to get electronic mail. He never
answers it, but it looks impressive when he prints it
out for his boss. Help contribute to the cause.

<HR>

<FORM ACTION="Email.acgi" METHOD=POST>

Enter your name:<INPUT TYPE="text" NAME="name"
VALUE="" MAXLENGTH=40>

<BR>Enter your e-mail address:<INPUT TYPE="text"
NAME="address" VALUE="" MAXLENGTH=50>
```

```
<BR>Enter a message subject:<INPUT TYPE="text"
NAME="subject" VALUE="" MAXLENGTH="40">

<BR>Enter the message:<TEXTAREA NAME="message" ROWS=8
COLS=80></TEXTAREA>

<P><INPUT TYPE="submit" NAME="S" VALUE="Submit">

<INPUT TYPE="reset" NAME="S" VALUE="Clear the form">

</FORM>

<HR>

<I>jw</I></BODY></HTML>
```

This form has four fields: name, address, subject, and message. (A fifth field will be sent, because the **Submit** button is treated as a field as well.) We will ignore it here, though. What we want to do in the CGI script is get the data from each of these fields and assign it to a specific variable that we can work with. Since the OSAX does all of the tough work, there really isn't anything here that difficult to understand.

Listing 14.2 provides an example to demonstrate how the data will be used when it is extracted from the form page. This script takes the data and does two things. First, it sends the data to Eudora and fills in the proper parts to create an e-mail message and then mail it off. Then it builds an HTML page to return to the user to verify that the message was sent. The order is very important here, since the **return** command sends a reply to the WWWΩsdoc event, which ends all processing of the event. It doesn't matter whether there are more lines waiting to be processed; AppleScript just stops right there.

Listing 14.2 Auto-E-mail Using Eudora 1.5.1

```
property crlf : (ASCII character 13) & (ASCII charac-
ter 10)
property http_10_header : "HTTP/1.0 200 OK" & crlf ¬
  & "Server: WebSTAR/1.0 ID/ACGI" & crlf & "MIME-Ver-
sion: 1.0" ¬
  & crlf & "Content-type: text/html" & crlf & crlf
```

```
on «event WWWΩsdoc» path_args ¬
   given «class kfor»:http_search_args, «class
post»:post_args, «class meth»:method, «class
addr»:client_address, «class user»:username, «class
pass»:password, «class frmu»:from_user, «class
svnm»:server_name, «class svpt»:server_port, «class
scnm»:script_name, «class ctyp»:content_type, «class
refr»:referer, «class Agnt»:user_agent, «class
Kact»:action, «class Kapt»:action_path, «class
Kcip»:client_ip, «class Kfrq»:full_request, «class
Kcid»:connection_id
   try
```

— *This parses and decodes the post_args data and assigns*
— *list of fields and values to the variable formData.*

```
      set formData to parse CGI arguments post_args
```

— *Get specific fields and assign their values to variables.*
— *The "default value" command assigns a default if the field is not found.*

```
      set username to CGI field "name" from formData ¬
        default value "nobody"
      set from_address to CGI field "address" from
      formData ¬
        default value "nowhere"
      set email_subject to CGI field "subject" from
      formData ¬
        default value "nothing special"
      set email_body to CGI field "message" from
      form Data ¬
        default value "nothing to say"
```

— *NOTE: Set the "to_address" to be the address to which you want all of the mail sent.*

```
      set to_address to "webmaster@this.site.com"
```

— *Create new message in Eudora 1.5.1 (it probably won't work for other versions).*
— *To compile this, you have to do "Check Syntax" and locate Eudora.*
— *Don't forget to configure Eudora correctly first!!*

```
      tell application "Eudora1.5.1Fat"
```

— Mail folder "" is the name for the folder that contain In and Out.

```
set newmessage to (make message at ¬

  end of mailbox "out" of mail folder "")

set field "To" of newmessage to to_address

set field "From" of newmessage to from_address

set field "Subject" of newmessage to
email_subject
```

— Field "" is the body of the message.

```
set field "" of newmessage to "From: " ¬

  & username & return & return & email_body
```

— Queue up the message for sending.

```
queue newmessage
```

— Connect to the mail server and send when connected.

```
connect with sending
end tell
```

—Build an HTML page to return to the client.

```
set return_page to http_10_header ¬

  & "<HTML><HEAD><TITLE>Email Form
Results</TITLE></HEAD>" ¬

  & "<BODY><H1>Email Form Results</H1>" & return

set return_page to return_page ¬

  & "E-mail has been sent to " & to_address &
return ¬

  & "The message you sent was:" & return &
"<PRE>" ¬

  & email_body & "</PRE>" & return ¬

  & "<P><I>Message generated at: " & (current
date) ¬

  & "</I>" & "</BODY></HTML>"
```

— This statement ends all processing for this CGI application by replying to the Apple event.

```
          return return_page

    on error errMsg number errNum
      set return_page to http_10_header ¬
        & "<HTML><HEAD><TITLE>Error
        Page</TITLE></HEAD>" ¬
        & "<BODY><H1>Error Encountered!</H1>"
        & return ¬
        & "An error was encountered with this CGI." &
        return
      set return_page to return_page ¬
        & "<H3>Error Message</H3>" & return & errMsg &
        return ¬
        & "<H3>Error Number</H3>" & return & errNum &
        return ¬
        & "<H3>Date</H3>" & return & (current date) &
        return
      set return_page to return_page ¬
        & "<HR>Please notify the webmaster at " ¬
        & "<A
HREF=\"mailto:webmaster@this.site.com\">webmaster@
this.site.com</A>" ¬
        & " of this error." & "</BODY></HTML>"
      return return_page
    end try
  end «event WWWΩsdoc»
```

This script demonstrates another important capability of CGI applications: the ability to link WebSTAR to external applications. In this case data from a form page is being sent to Eudora to go out as e-mail. It could also be sent to a database to update a record or sent to a word processor to create a new document or even sent to another AppleScript script for some custom processing.

The first thing to do in every case is to extract the data from the form and put it into variables that can then be sent to the external application. The next step is to tell AppleScript which application to send the information to. This is done with the **tell** command:

```
tell application "Eudora1.5.1Fat"
```

This command tells AppleScript that all following lines should be sent to the external application as commands until an **end tell** command is seen. In this case the commands tell Eudora to create a new message and put it in the "out" mailbox, then fill the various message fields with data from the proper variables, then queue the message for mailing. Finally, the **connect with sending** command tells Eudora to connect to the SMTP server and send all queued messages, which sends off the message just created. Then the **end tell** statement redirects all commands back to the script itself.

Once all of that is done, an HTML page is built to tell the user that the mail was successfully sent. This also serves as a reply to the Apple event, which ends processing for that event. This is the same general pattern that you will use with any CGI application that communicates with an external application:

1. Parse the form data and assign field data to variables.

2. Tell AppleScript to communicate with the external application and send variables for processing.

3. Wait for the external application to finish processing and possibly return data.

4. Return some data to the user. If any data was returned from the external application, that is what should be returned. Otherwise, just send back a short confirmation statement such, as "Your request was processed."

Problems with CGI Applications in AppleScript

In addition to the general problems listed earlier, you will encounter other problems with AppleScript if you are not careful in your script design. These are the things that have caused me headaches in the past; there may be more that I haven't run into yet. Again, though, this isn't to say that you shouldn't use AppleScript, only that you need to be aware of its limitations.

Problems with Asynchronous Processing in AppleScript

AppleScript is a very good language to use for writing small tasks to be done while other applications are running, because it lets other applications have lots of processor time. If you write automated tasks in AppleScript, they will run without making everything else too slow to be usable. In most cases this is a very good thing, but with asynchronous CGI applications, this is a big problem.

The problem arises because of the way AppleScript handles checking for new events. The proper way to check for new events is to wait until your current event is done processing and then check the event queue to see whether another one is waiting. Any events sent while you are processing will be waiting there. In AppleScript, though, the application checks for new events even while the current event is being processed. If a new event is received, it interrupts the current event being processed, so the new event starts processing and the current one sits idle, waiting for the new one to finish.

This is not a good thing. When processing events, a CGI application is required to finish the processing in a certain time period (the timeout period), or WebSTAR will return an error to the user. If an event that takes a while to run is interrupted by a new event, the older event is unlikely to get to finish processing before it times out. Worse yet, for a busy CGI application, the new events would keep arriving and interrupting older events. The result could be that every connection would time out waiting for new events (which were also interrupted) to finish processing.

Unfortunately there is no nice solution for this. If this problem happens to you, you have only three choices: use a different language for writing your CGI application, run the CGI application synchronously, or find a way to reduce the load that the CGI application is handling.

Problems with Quitting

As mentioned earlier, there is a period while your CGI application is quitting when events can be lost. This is the point at which the CGI application is committed to quitting (meaning that it won't check for new events that may arrive) but still has some more processing to do before it completely quits. Since it has not yet completely quit, WebSTAR will think that it is OK to send new events. This can be a significant problem in AppleScript, for several reasons.

If you have a `quit` handler (and I did recommend that you have one), the time that it takes that handler to run is the period when events might be lost. If you have a significant amount of processing going on there, it is a good idea to avoid quitting, as much as possible. The same problem occurs if you use several script properties (or have a lot of data stored in them). These properties are written out to disk when the application quits, so the more there are, the longer it will take your application to quit.

There is one more problem with quitting your AppleScript CGI application, and that goes back to the way it handles events. If you tell the application to quit, either from the menu bar or by sending a command for it to quit, you are sending an event to it, and that event will interrupt whatever is currently processing. If the application was processing an event, the event will be suspended while the application quits. Luckily this is one problem that can be solved. If you are worried about this possibility, use a global variable to keep track of whether the CGI application is currently processing an event and wait for the event to finish before quitting (and find a way to lock out new events).

Debugging AppleScript

Before I list any debugging methods, I want to remind you that none of these techniques will work as well as a good AppleScript editor with debugging capabilities, such as Scripter or ScriptDebugger. If you are using AppleScript on a regular basis, these Script Editor replacements will soon pay for themselves in time saved tracking bugs.

Also, I am assuming here that you are using the `try...on error` construction and that the feedback from that hasn't been helpful (you probably need an AppleScript book to make much sense of the error descriptions).

Error -1701

This error code is returned by WebSTAR when a CGI application fails to return any information to WebSTAR. There are three common causes of this:

1. The CGI application was saved improperly. Be certain that it is saved as an application, not as a compiled script. Also be certain to check the two checkboxes. If they are not checked, the application will not be able to receive the "sdoc" Apple event.

2. The "sdoc" Apple event handler is not written properly. This could be because you have a parameter listed that isn't being sent (MacHTTP doesn't receive as many parameters as WebSTAR does, so this could be a problem there) or because one of the parameters is spelled incorrectly (the four-character codes are case sensitive) or some other problem that makes the parameters unreadable. The scripts contained on the companion CD-ROM list all of the events that are acceptable for either WebSTAR or MacHTTP (use the appropriate script for your server and version number), so the best solution is to open one of those and copy the entire event handler from there into your own script. Since there is no performance or memory penalty for listing all of the parameters instead of just the ones you will be using, I suggest that you always use the full handler as listed in the provided scripts.

3. The CGI application crashed, so it couldn't return any data. This should not occur if you are using the **try...on error** construction.

Note that this is not the same as error code **-1701** that AppleScript returns when a parameter is missing for a command. Again, for a discussion of AppleScript error codes, refer to the AppleScript book that you purchased. If you are using the **try...on error** construct, you should not see this code most of the time, because an AppleScript error code will be returned instead, along with some information about the error. If you see the WebSTAR error (it is returned as one line of plain text—very distinctive), your error handler crashed as well.

Debugging Tricks

Here are a few tricks that might help isolate a bug (and show why a commercial editor is so valuable).

First, use the "beep" command judiciously to try and isolate how far the CGI application is running. This can be time consuming because you can't use too many beeps at once or they will all blur together. First, use a few to divide your code into chunks. Put one at the beginning to make certain that the script is at least launching and one at the beginning of the "sdoc" handler to make certain that is being initiated as well. Then put one at the end to see whether the problem is perhaps after execution ends. With each run, you can move the three closer together to isolate smaller sections of code. Try using them to test subroutines: one before, one inside the routine, and one after it returns. Also try using two beeps to bracket calls to OSAXes that you have not previously used. Finally, remember to test your error routines as well. It is possible that the error routine is being launched and then *it* is crashing.

Next, try removing the "sdoc" event handler lines (**on...** and **end...**) and running the CGI as an AppleScript. Preload data into the parameters you are using, such as **set http_search_args to "city=Seattle"** so you can test the routines. Many errors will not be caught here, because a script does not work identically as a script and as an application, but it will be easier to see what is going on and to make changes.

Finally, look for errors external to your application. Try replacing all of the OSAXes used by the CGI application. Double check that you don't have two OSAXes that use the same language conflicting with each other (such as two OSAXes that offer a "replace" command). You may even need to do a fresh install of AppleScript or your operating system. Check with the Apple technical databases for reported errors with the version of AppleScript you are using and with the MacScripting mailing list to see whether anyone else has problems with the combination of OSAXes your script uses. These are all last-ditch steps, of course, but if they don't work, at least you know that you really have a problem.

Close It All Up

I've had my AppleScript lessons on my Web site for about half a year now. From that experience I can say with confidence that everyone will find something in this chapter that they wish I had discussed in more detail. Even if I had included a dozen examples, someone would still be wanting one that I didn't include. Luckily there are many examples on the companion CD-ROM, from many different authors. This chapter should get you up and running with AppleScript so that you can make sense of these examples and use them to provide the custom solutions that you need. Happy Scripting!

15

Developing CGIs in C

CGI applications are a powerful mechanism for extending the capabilities of a WWW server. However, the ease of CGI implementation when using a high-level scripting language, such as AppleScript or HyperCard, is balanced by the cost paid in performance. Interpreted or even precompiled script languages cannot perform at the same level as a native application written in a traditional programming language, such as C or Pascal. Further, the need to be many things to many people restricts the flexibility and power of these scripting languages for the advanced user. If you want to get the most from a CGI, it should be developed in a traditional compiled programming language. Although the up-front effort required to develop the CGI may be higher than with a script language, the performance payoffs are enormous.

This chapter discusses some of the key concepts involved in creating a CGI in a language like C. It assumes that you have a basic understanding of the C language and a passing familiarity with the internals of the Mac operating system and Toolbox. It will cover some of the spookier parts of the Mac Toolbox, such as the Apple Event Manager, and will discuss such architecture issues as multithreading and asynchronous processing of Apple events.

Most CGI development in C will start with a CGI framework that already handles the Apple event that WebSTAR sends to CGIs. In many cases developing a CGI is simply a matter of plugging a few standard C statements into one of these frameworks. However, you can do much more with external programs that communicate with WebSTAR than just simple CGI processing. The second half of this chapter addresses some of these functions, including remote logging and remote administration functions.

Taming the Apple Event Manager

Apple events are weird things. Apple gave birth to them with the release of System 7, but it took nearly five years before Apple events were widely supported across many Mac applications. Arguably they were waiting for tough problems like CGIs to come along, and it took many developers a long time to figure out just what CGIs were good for. As it turns out, Apple made a brilliant decision to put a standard interprocess communications mechanism in the Mac O/S. It is a feature that no other operating system has or at least no other operating system's third-party developers have embraced so thoroughly. It definitely makes life easier for the CGI developer on the Mac.

The basic method of getting data passed between two programs running on a Mac requires the construction of an Apple event. In a C program this requires several steps before an event is assembled and ready to be sent. Likewise it takes a similar number of steps to disassemble the event when it is received and then assemble and send the appropriate response. Luckily it is WebSTAR's job to build the event, so most of the hard work is done. You simply have to pull out the parameters and use them. The default reply event is already constructed for the CGI, and the programmer only has to stuff the return data into the reply and the data is sent automatically back to the server.

Here is the basic sequence of events that a Mac program wanting to run as a CGI application for WebSTAR must do, both to configure itself at startup and then to handle the incoming event:

1. Initialize all of the Mac Toolbox managers, and so on.

2. Set up an Apple event handler for the WWWΩsdoc event sent by WebSTAR.

3. Run its main event loop until a high-level event is received.

4. Once an event is received from WebSTAR, the CGI needs to extract the Apple event parameters, placing them in variables that can be used for additional processing.

5. Perform any CGI-specific processing, using the data received from the server.

6. Generate an appropriate HTTP header and return it, along with any data generated by the CGI as the direct parameter to the reply Apple event.

Most CGI shells, including the examples on the companion CD, handle steps 1, 2, 3, and 4 for you. Step 5 is where you get to be creative. Step 6 is usually just a matter of a few string manipulations; then you're done. For the sake of completeness, we'll briefly discuss steps 1 through 4 and step 6. What goes on in step 5 is up to you!

Initializing a CGI Application

Step 1 is a no-brainer. Most Mac programs start with a standard preamble of initialization calls to get the program up and running. If the required calls aren't familiar to you, take a minute to look at the examples on the companion CD-ROM or dig out your favorite beginning C book.

Installing an Apple Event Handler

Step 2 involves identifying your program subroutine that will handle the incoming Apple event from WebSTAR by passing the address of this subroutine to the Apple Event Manager. With the addition of PowerPC Macintosh CPUs to the mix, you should make sure that you always pass a Universal ProcPtr (UPP) instead of a simple address of the subroutine if you want to be able to build a PowerPC-native version of your CGI. Here is an example of how you might define your Apple event handler in the startup routine:

/* *define the event class and code for the "WWWΩsdoc" event* */

```
#define kWebSTAREventClass 'WWWΩ'
#define kSDOCEvent 'sdoc'
```

/**a simple handler declaration*/

```
pascal OSErr HandleSDOC( AppleEvent *theAppleEvent,
    AppleEvent *reply, long handlerRefcon)
{
```

/ put your handler code in here!*/*

```
}
```

*/*somewhere in your initialization routines...*/*

```
err = AEInstallEventHandler( kWebSTAREventClass,
kSDOCEvent,NewAEEventHandlerProc( HandleSDOC ), 0,
false ) ;
```

This code fragment defines the class and code of the event, presents a skeleton event handler for the event, and shows how to register the event handler with the Apple Event Manager. As mentioned, the introduction of PowerPC-based Macs has made it necessary to use "universal procedure pointers" (UPP) to pass the address of callback routines in your code to the Mac Toolbox. In this example the **NewAEEventHandlerProc** call is actually a C macro definition. On 68K Macs it is simply a type cast. On Power Macs, this is actually a call to a subroutine that builds a UPP that describes to the Power PC. The gory details of this mechanism aren't as important as realizing that coding a CGI to be native on a Power Mac and a 68K Mac requires a little extra attention. Many older Macintosh programming texts may not address the issue of UPPs. In general, any time you pass the address of a subroutine in your code to the Mac O/S, you need to pass it as a UPP.

Receiving and Dispatching an Incoming Apple Event

Once you've registered an Apple event handler, most of the hard work gets handled by the Mac O/S. However, you have to do a little work in the portion of your program that handles incoming events to implement step 3. In your main event loop, you have to watch for "high-level events" and tell the O/S what to do with them. Here's what the code in your main event loop might look like:

```
while (!done) {
    doit = WaitNextEvent(everyEvent, &theEvent, sleep,
    NULL);
    if (doit) {
        switch (theEvent.what) {
```

```
case kHighLevelEvent:
  err = AEProcessAppleEvent( &theEvent ) ;
  break;
```

/*handle more events like mouseDown, etc. here*/

```
      }
    }
  }
```

Obviously the key to all of this is the call to **AEProcessAppleEvent**. This just tells the Mac O/S to pass the Apple event to the handler that we registered in step 2.

Important: A common mistake that CGI programmers make is forgetting to set the **Accept High Level Events** bit in your SIZE resource. If this flag isn't set, the O/S won't send you any Apple events. Most programming environments such as Think C or Code-Warrior, allow you to set this bit in the preferences for your project.

Processing the Apple Event

Step 4 is the hard part. Pulling all of the parameters out of the Apple event and getting them into local variables that you can use in your program requires a little understanding about the structure of an Apple event. You can think of an Apple event as a container with lots of data parts inside. Each part has a unique name, a specific data type, and a data value associated with it. These data parts can be Apple event attributes or keyword parameters.

For the most part, an Apple event attribute is event information that the Apple Event Manager assigns to the event when it is sent. Things like the address of the sender, the event class and code, and the Apple event transaction ID are passed as attributes. Values passed from WebSTAR to your CGI are passed as keyword parameters. Path arguments, search arguments, client IP address, and user name are passed in these parameters.

Keyword parameters are identified by a four-character keyword code. Once your Apple event handler is called by the Apple Event Manager, you can extract the data sent from the Web server by requesting these parameters by name, using the four-character keyword. There are two ways to obtain the parameters. You can request a pointer to the data in a parameter, or you can request a *descriptor.*

A descriptor is essentially a copy of the data contained in an Apple event. The Apple Event Manager takes a descriptor record that you pass to it, allocates the necessary amount of memory, and copies the parameter data to the descriptor. It is up to you to dispose of the descriptor when you are done, but you're free to do whatever you'd like with the data it contains, because you aren't affecting the event data at all. On the other hand, working with pointers to Apple event data can be a little misleading. You have to pass a pointer to your own data storage area to the Apple Event Manager. Typically you can use local variables of the appropriate type and pass a pointer to the specific local variable as the storage area. The advantage to using pointers instead of descriptors is that you don't have to remember to dispose of them once you're done, since the local variables go away when your event handler completes. For the remainder of this section, we will be dealing with parameter pointers instead of descriptors.

Once your event handler has been activated, it's up to you to pull the parameters you need out of the Apple event and use them in your code. The basic call to extract a parameter into a local variable looks like:

```
#define kForKeyword 'kfor'

pascal OSErr HandleSDOC( AppleEvent *theAppleEvent,
    AppleEvent *reply, long handlerRefcon)
{
char localString [256]; //local data storage
Size actualSizeOfData; //size of the data parameter
DescType typeCode; //type of the data

err = AEGetParamPtr( theAppleEvent, kForKeyword,
typeChar,
    &typeCode, (Ptr) localString, sizeof( localString
),
    &actualSizeOfData );
```

```
if (actualSizeOfData < sizeof (localString))
  localString [actualSizeOfData] = '\0';
else {
```

/* This is not good. More data was received than we have space for. Do something. */

```
}
```

/* more parameter extraction and processing from here on...*/

```
}
```

The parameters to the **AEGetParamPtr** call are as follows. The first argument is the Apple event as passed into your handler; the second parameter is the four-letter keyword that specifies which parameter you are interested in. The third parameter describes the format you'd like to extract the data in; **typeChar** indicates that you'd like the data returned as a normal C-style string containing character data. All of the parameters sent by WebSTAR are of type **typeChar** with the exception of the connection ID parameter, which is a long integer (type **typeLongInteger**). The **typeCode** variable receives the type of the data as sent from the calling application (WebSTAR). For CGI applications, you can generally ignore this parameter. The **localString** parameter is a buffer to receive the event data. You pass in the size of your buffer but receive the size of the data in the final parameter. You should always check that the size returned isn't larger than the size of the buffer you passed in. If it is, you need to handle the error condition, because more data was sent than you were able to process. For some parameters, such as post arguments, it may become necessary to allocate memory for the storage area by using **NewPtr** instead of relying on local variable storage.

This example shows how to extract a single parameter. CGI applications receive much more than one parameter, though. Table 15.1 lists all of the parameters that WebSTAR sends with the descriptive name of the parameter, the four character Apple event parameter keyword, the maximum size, and a brief description of the parameter. The parameters are listed in the exact order (top to bottom) that they will be received, which is useful information for some languages that need to match an exact order of variables to the parameters.

Name	Keyword	Max Size	Description
Path args	——	1024	Arguments following the **$** in a URL. This keyword is also the direct parameter of the Apple event (keyDirect Object).
Search args	kfor	1024	Arguments following a **?** in a URL.
User name	user	32	User name if authentication was required.
Password	pass	32	Password if authentication was required.
From user	frmu	128	E-mail address of user (obsolete).
Client address	addr	256	Domain name of client (or IP address if DNS lookups are disabled).
Server address	svnm	256	Domain name of server (or IP address if DNS lookups are disabled).
Server IP port	svpt	16	TCP/IP port server is listening on.
Script name	scnm	1024	The path of the CGI being executed. In the case of Actions, this parameter contains the file path portion of the URL.
Content type	ctyp	64	MIME type of post arguments, if present.
Referrer	refr	1024	URL of the page from which this CGI was referenced.
User agent	Agnt	256	The WWW client software name and version.
Action	Kact	32	The action being performed by the CGI, either the name of the user defined action or one of the strings: CGI, ACGI, PREPROCESSOR, POST-PROCESSOR, ERROR, INDEX, or NOACCESS.
Action path	Kapt	1024	Path to this CGI if it is executing as an Action (in which case, the script name parameter contains the URL file path sent from the client).
Post arguments	post	32,768	Arguments sent from WWW client as part of a POST request (for example, form arguments).
Method	meth	32	The HTTP method being requested (GET, GET_CONDITIONAL, POST, and so on).

Table 15.1 Parameters Passed to a CGI Application by WebSTAR *(continued)*

(Table 15.1 continued)

Name	Keyword	Max Size	Description
Client IP address	Kcip	32	The TCP/IP address of the client.
Full request	Kfrq	4096	The complete, unmodified HTTP request as received from the client.
Connection ID	Kcid	4	A unique long integer value identifying the TCP/IP connection the server is communicating to the client over. Used for sending the "Send Partial" Apple event to WebSTAR.

Once you have extracted all of the necessary parameters from the Apple event, your CGI application should use the parameters to perform whatever processing is necessary. This may be a small thing, such as checking the client IP address and logging it, or a large thing, such as processing form data being passed in the post arguments and sending it off to search a database and then formatting the returned results. Whichever it is, all of the processing has to be done at this point or stored in some intermediate form (such as a text file on disk) for later batch processing. When the processing is finished, your application needs to generate a reply and return it to the server.

Replying to an Apple Event

Replying to an Apple event is very straightforward. WebSTAR expects your CGI application to send back a single parameter in the direct parameter of the reply event of type **typeChar**. This parameter is a block of data representing the entire response that is to be returned to the WWW client. The server returns this data without modification to the client, which means that you are responsible for creating a legal HTTP header, as well as any content that your CGI has generated. Note that although the data type of the reply parameter is **typeChar**, you can also place binary data into the return parameter. This means that your CGI can return GIF images, for example, to a client, which is something that a CGI in AppleScript or HyperCard may not be able to do.

One important limitation on CGI applications that reply using the Apple event reply mechanism is that you should return only a maximum of 32K of data. Newer versions of the Mac O/S theoretically increase this limit to 64K, but it causes an inordinate amount of memory usage in the server to receive such oversized parameters. If you need to return more than 32K worth of data from your CGI application, you should either save the data to a file on disk and use a URL redirect header or use the new server-push feature. With server push the CGI application sends a "Send Partial" Apple event *to* WebSTAR to indicate that the data will be returned in several chunks over a period of time. This feature allows the CGI application to return arbitrarily large amounts of data at the expense of keeping the connection open much longer than usual. The "Send Partial" event is discussed later.

This example will show how to reply to an Apple event, assuming that all of the reply data will fit into 32K or less. So step 6 completes the processing of the Apple event as follows. At the end of your Apple event-handling subroutine, you should respond to the event:

```
    . . .
/* assumes that the string variable "out" contains your output*/
    if (reply->descriptorType != typeNull)
      err = AEPutParamPtr(reply, keyDirectObject, typeChar,
          out, strlen (out) );
    return noErr;
} /*end of the sdoc handler*/
```

This code checks to make sure that a reply is required. If the data type portion of the reply event descriptor indicates that a nonnull return value is expected, you should use the **AEPutParamPtr** call to copy the return data from your local buffer to the direct parameter of the reply Apple event. The reply variable is one of the parameters passed by the Apple Event Manager to your subroutine handling the WWWΩsdoc event. As a final step in processing the event, you should return the **noErr** return value to the Apple Event Manager, indicating that the event was handled successfully. If the event processing failed for any reason, you should return the appropriate error code. At a minimum, this should be **errAEEventNotHandled**.

Threading and Events

WebSTAR handles multiple incoming connections at once. It relies on the Apple Thread Manager to provide concurrent processing within the server application, allowing the server to use the same code to handle multiple connections in parallel. Unfortunately many ACGIs (asynchronous CGI applications) that are executed by WebSTAR become performance bottlenecks because they are able to process only a single incoming "sdoc" event at a time. Although this usually isn't a problem for ACGIs that perform their processing in a very short time, ACGIs that require longer processing time will be making later events wait in a queue for previous events to finish. This means that if your ACGI takes 15 seconds to look up some data in a database, perform some calculations, and return a reply, when five users are accessing your ACGI at once, the last user will have to wait more than a minute for a reply. On the other hand, if the ACGI is able to handle the multiple events in parallel, it could conceivably process all five requests in 15 or 20 seconds, eliminating the long delay experienced by users in the queue.

Using the Thread Manager requires a few tricks when the Apple Event Manager is involved. As far as the Apple Event Manager is concerned, an application can process only one Apple event at a time. If a threaded ACGI were to try to work on two threads for two different events at one time, nasty things might happen. In addition, the Apple Event Manager uses low-memory globals, which means that parallel threads of execution cannot do certain Apple event functions simultaneously or they will stomp all over one another's data. The companion CD-ROM includes some sample code for a threaded ACGI. You should spend some time studying how it works. The basic operation is the same as that for any threaded ACGI, except that the events are handled one at a time and then put to sleep so that the main processing, with a copy of the event data, can go on in parallel. The flow of processing goes something like this:

1. The main event loop, running in the main thread, receives an incoming Apple event.

2. The main thread's WWWΩsdoc handler begins processing the event, possibly extracting necessary parameters.

3. The WWWΩsdoc handler in the main thread suspends the Apple event, using the **AESuspendTheCurrentEvent** call, saving the Apple event and reply parameters for later use.

4. The main thread starts a child thread to process the event parameters and generate the reply, passing the appropriate arguments to the **NewThread** call.

5. The child thread performs the appropriate CGI function and places the reply data in a location (perhaps a queue) that the main thread can find. The child thread then terminates.

6. The main thread fills in the reply parameter for the appropriate, suspended event with the results from the child thread.

7. The main thread resumes the suspended Apple event by calling **AEResumeTheCurrentEvent** with the **kAENoDispatch** constant as the third parameter. This tells the Apple Event Manager that you have completed handling the event and that it is to return the reply.

There are variations on these steps, including resuming and replying to the event from within the child thread. If you choose to respond to the event in this fashion, you must make sure that two threads don't try to resume a suspended event at the same time, since the Apple Event Manager expects to be handling only one event at a time.

Extra CGI Functions

External applications can perform many other functions in conjunction with WebSTAR. CGIs can perform server-push functions to implement real-time interaction with WWW clients. Or, they can use the Send Partial Apple event to return large amounts of data to a client. Other external applications can register with WebSTAR to receive logging and status messages, performing logging and monitoring functions on a local or remote Macintosh. You can also implement custom administration functions that, for example, might monitor server performance and adjust server parameters in real time. Finally, with the implementation of several plug-in code interfaces in newer versions of WebSTAR, you can implement alternative security systems and high-performance CGIs that attach directly to the server as part of the server's code.

This section focuses on using the Send Partial event to return large amounts of data to WebSTAR as the result of a CGI operation. This same event can be used to return multipart MIME data to clients such as Netscape Navigator to implement server-push functions.

Using the Send Partial Event

The Send Partial event is one that WebSTAR receives rather than one it sends. ACGIs use this event to return data in incremental pieces to WebSTAR, rather than returning the data in the WWWΩsdoc event's reply parameter. An ACGI should use the reply parameter of the WWWΩsdoc event to inform WebSTAR that it should expect additional information to arrive via the Send Partial event. The WWWΩsdoc event handler should return the string **<SEND_PARTIAL>**, without any other information, in the reply parameter of the original event. The entire reply should consist of only 14 characters and is case sensitive. WebSTAR will use this specific reply as an indication that it should keep the connection open with the client for the ACGI. Once the WWWΩsdoc handler has completed processing the initial event, the ACGI needs to begin the process of returning the return data to WebSTAR. How your application handles this is up to you. The mechanics of sending the Send Partial event are described here.

The "connection ID" parameter that is sent to the ACGI (keyword **Kcid**) is used in the Send Partial event to tell WebSTAR which connection the ACGI wants data returned on. Sending a Send Partial event involves creating the event, addressing it to WebSTAR, placing the proper parameters in the event, and sending the event back to WebSTAR.

First, we want to extract the address of WebSTAR from the WWWΩsdoc Apple event so we can address our Send Partial event to WebSTAR. Then we need to reply to WebSTAR with the appropriate return value:

```
AEAddressDesc addr;
```

/*...inside the sdoc handler...*/

/*pull the Apple event address of WebSTAR out of the sdoc event*/

```
err = AEGetAttributeDesc(theAppleEvent,'from','****',
&addr);
```

/*save this addr variable along with the "connection ID" */

/*parameter (Kcid) that was extracted with a call to */

/*AEGetParamPtr. */

We now have a descriptor that contains the address of WebSTAR for future Send Partial events. When we use this address, we will have to duplicate the descriptor so the Apple Event Manager can have its own copy to play with, and we can retain this one for use in future events we want to send.

/*finish up replying to the sdoc event*/

```
if (reply->descriptorType != typeNull)
   err = AEPutParamPtr(reply, keyDirectObject,
typeChar,
      "<SEND_PARTIAL>", 14 );
```

/* set some flag or otherwise indicate that the ACGI */

/* needs to continue processing and returning info via */

/* the Send Partial event */

```
   return noErr;
}  /*end of the sdoc handler*/
```

Now, elsewhere in the ACGI you can begin returning data to WebSTAR. Here's what has to happen to create and send the Send Partial event to WebSTAR:

```
#define kMyAESendPartial      'SPar'

AEAddressDesc theAddress;
AppleEvent ourEvent,ourReply;
```

/* duplicate the address stored in the addr variable*/

```
err = AEDuplicateDesc (&addr, &theAddress);
```

*/*create the event*/*

```
err = AECreateAppleEvent(kWebSTAREventClass , kMyAE
   SendPartial, &theAddress, kAutoGenerateReturnID,
     kAnyTransactionID, &ourEvent);
```

*/*fill in the direct parameter with a chunk of return data */*

```
err = AEPutParamPtr(&ourEvent, keyDirectObject,
   typeChar,
     returnData, returnDataLen);
```

*/*put the connection ID we saved earlier into the event*/*

```
err = AEPutParamPtr(&ourEvent, kConnectionIDKeyword,
     typeLongInteger, &connectionID, sizeof
     (connectionID));
```

*/*put the "more" parameter into the event. "more" is a Boolean, */*
*/*if more is false, the server sends the data and closes the */*
*/*connection. If true, the server sends data and keeps the */*
*/*connection open.*/*

```
err = AEPutParamPtr(&ourEvent, kMoreKeyword,
   typeBoolean,
     &moreFlag, sizeof (moreFlag));
```

*/*Now send the event. If we get an error, the client has */*
*/*gone away and we should cease sending events to WebSTAR*/*
*/*for this connection.*/*

```
err = AESend(&ourEvent, &ourReply,
     kAECanInteract + kAECanSwitchLayer,
     kAENormalPriority, kAEDefaultTimeout,
     nil , nil);
```

This process repeats for as long as there is data to return to the
server for transmission to the client. The interval between sending
consecutive Send Partial events *must* be less than the timeout
value configured in WebSTAR, or WebSTAR will drop the client
connection. Each Send Partial event received by WebSTAR for a
particular connection resets the timeout timer.

There are many different techniques for performing the functions described here. You should experiment with the sample source code included on the companion CD-ROM. Writing CGIs in a high-level language like C can be a little more time consuming, but the high-performance results make the effort worthwhile.

16

Developing CGIs in Other Languages

CGI applications can be written in any language (or application, for that matter) that allows new Apple events to be accepted and replied to. Thanks to the popularity of the World Wide Web, there are now examples for almost every possible language or application as well. The companion CD-ROM has most of these examples and pointers to others. All I want to discuss here are some of the benefits and drawbacks of each language to help you decide where to start.

MacPerl

Perl is a very popular language on many platforms because it is very flexible and fast, especially for processing text files. MacPerl is a port of Perl to the Macintosh operating system by Matthias Ulrich Neeracher (**neeri@iis.ethz.ch**). It runs very fast, and an even faster PowerMacintosh-native 5.0 version should be coming out soon. In addition, Perl is available on almost every platform, so it is possible to write scripts that will work on both Macintosh and UNIX systems, which is a big bonus in some situations.

There are only a few drawbacks. First, MacPerl takes a good-sized chunk of memory, although that depends somewhat on the script as well. Second, it takes a while to launch the script, so Perl scripts don't have the same zip on Macintosh that they do on other systems unless you are doing enough processing to make the startup time negligible in relation. Finally, creating a CGI application in MacPerl 4.x is not a straightforward task, although it is not beyond anyone's skills. Instructions on this process, provided by Sandra Silcot, can be found at

```
http://www.unimelb.edu.au/~ssilcot/macperl-primer/
home.html
```

HyperCard

HyperCard can receive custom Apple events and reply to them, which makes it suitable for use as a CGI application. HyperTalk, the HyperCard scripting language, is very easy to learn, and several good books are available (and thousands of example HyperCard stacks) for beginners to learn from. HyperCard is also an OSA environment. As such, it can run AppleScript scripts or HyperTalk scripts with equal ease. Many prefer HyperCard for CGI application development because it offers better text-processing commands than AppleScript and has tremendous speed in searching text fields. It can be most effectively used as a small database or for quick text-processing jobs or best yet a combination of the two.

HyperCard has some drawbacks, though. The first is that usually only one copy of the HyperCard application is running on the server, so every CGI request for a HyperCard stack or card must go through the application. Since these requests are processed sequentially, every CGI request has to wait for all prior requests to complete. If you have several busy CGIs in HyperCard, the application will become a bottleneck for processing on your site. The second problem is that HyperCard is still not very fast for most processing compared to a compiled language, especially if the script accesses a file on disk or does a lot of text processing. Third, HyperCard requires a lot of memory (at least 1.5MB) to run. Many people think that HyperCard is the perfect CGI solution, but I recommend it only if you want to avoid any more difficult programming language and have a task calling for some database and text processing.

Frontier (Aretha)

Frontier began life as a commercial product from UserLand Software. It has always been a faster and more powerful scripting environment than AppleScript, but the higher price tag seemed to keep users away. After Apple began including AppleScript as part of System 7.5, Dave Winer (president of UserLand) decided to release Frontier 4.0 as free software to promote the product. As part of that distribution, he released the components and instructions needed to use Frontier as a CGI application. The package is called Aretha and is available at

http://www.hotwired.com/Staff/userland/aretha/

Mason Hale (**Mason_A._Hale@capmac.org**) made things even easier by creating a CGI package in Aretha and writing documentation for it.

Frontier (or Aretha) is far more powerful than AppleScript for CGI purposes. It allows threaded processing of CGI requests, has the ability to share variables between scripts and share scripts components, includes a central object database, and has hundreds more commands than AppleScript. You can even use AppleScript scripts within Frontier, since it is an OSA-compatible language. The only downside is that the Frontier scripting language looks to me like a cross between C and something else and therefore is not very easy to learn, especially for those without prior programming experience.

Prograph

Prograph is a completely graphical language that uses the data flow model for creating programs. It is a full-featured language, able to create any kind of application, and can be used to create

CGI applications as well. Unfortunately Prograph isn't cheap, and you need the CPX (more expensive) version and probably an extra library (the InterApplication Communication library) to create CGI applications. Still, if you already are using it, this can be a great environment for making CGI applications.

A sample CGI application written in Prograph is available from Michael Bjorn (**michael@wiz.sk.tsukuba.ac.jp**) at his Web site (**http://db.sk.tsukuba.ac.jp/**). In addition, it was recently announced that Prograph will be free (including the PowerMac compiler) to educational sites. For more information, contact **sales@prograph.com** or check out their Web pages at **http://www/pictorius.com/home.html**

FORTRAN/77

One of the first CGI applications I ever used was Mac-Imagemap, which is written in FORTRAN by Lutz Weimann (**weimann@zib-berlin.de**). As a language for creating CGI applications, there is not really a drawback to FORTRAN. It creates small, fast applications, and Lutz has provided some of his work as examples. The only negative is that use of FORTRAN is declining even in engineering, so fewer people are available to help if you get stuck.

Others

Many other languages can be used as well, such as FutureBasic and Macintosh CommonLISP, but they have smaller user bases and shouldn't be considered unless you are already familiar with the language, need some special feature of the language, or want some reason to learn it.

Part V

Advanced WebSTAR Topics

These topics cover areas that are of interest primarily to professional Web site developers. If you need to build a high-speed site or if you want to provide your own custom controls for WebSTAR, this is the place to look. Even if you never intend to tackle these areas, though, these chapters will provide additional insight into how WebSTAR Admin operates and how to tweak your own site for a bit more speed.

17

Superservers Using RAIC Design

If you plan to run a very busy site, you are looking at one of two options. The first and most common option is to buy the fastest machine you can find, with one or more network interfaces (Ethernet boards) and a high-speed disk interface. This is where many people will tell you that you have to have a UNIX machine, because "they're built for networking." This type of installation has a small problem, though. Everything is built on one computer, which means that a problem that affects one part of the site will affect the entire site. If your site is that busy, you can't afford any downtime, and yet any single server (SGI workstations included) is certain to fail at some time, leaving your users with their favorite "Server is unavailable" warning.

The second option is to take a tip from hard disk design, where the problems of high-speed access and redundant backups have been solved through the use of RAID (redundant array of inexpensive disks) design. With RAID disks, several disks are used as if they were one virtual disk. Data can be divided over several disks, which allows more data to be written or read at one time, providing higher-speed access, and data can be mirrored to several disks, providing an instant backup in case of failure. The same general method can be used to combine multiple Macintosh CPUs into one RAIC (redundant array of inexpensive computers) server. A RAIC system has three benefits over a single server:

1. RAIC servers will not only run faster than single servers but also have better average performance.

2. RAIC servers are much cheaper to build for equivalent power.

3. RAIC servers can be designed with hot-swapping capabilities (more on this later).

Processing can be divided among several servers in a number of ways, and they can be mixed and matched as needed.

Server Mirroring

The latest versions of BIND allow you to have a single DNS name map to multiple IP addresses, with connections being passed out in round-robin fashion to each machine in turn. This allows a cluster of computers to appear to be one computer to the outside world. This has obvious benefits in server design. By mirroring the contents of a WWW site across multiple servers, you spread the connection load across all of the machines relatively evenly, so no single machine has to handle a very high load. This allows several cheaper machines to provide the performance of one more expensive machine. As an example, 10 Macintosh SE/30 computers, each capable of handling 10 simultaneous connections easily, can be combined to create a virtual server that can handle 100 simultaneous connections without coughing with an absolute peak (theoretically) at 480 connections. These 10 older computers can also be had at much less than the cost of a high-end workstation.

Performance is not the only reason to go with a RAIC design, though. An additional benefit is being able to hot-swap the CPUs that make up your server. Since the DNS server takes care of connections, any single CPU can go down or be removed (for maintenance, update, or replacement) without shutting down the entire site. This gives your site a degree of fault tolerance that can't be matched by a single CPU. In addition, the CPUs do not all need to be identical. Any Macs that you have lying around and gathering dust can be used to create a RAIC server.

This technique is probably the single best way to speed up a site, although it may be overkill if your site is just slightly too busy for the CPU or if you just want something to help out during peak processing.

By the way, the new MacDNS software from Apple Computer has an easy way to designate groups of computers for round-robin name handling. MacDNS is by far the easiest DNS software to use and now has all of the features that you need for building a powerful site.

Application Isolation

Another method to consider is moving external applications and CGI applications to a separate server. CGI applications must reside on the same server as the HTML page that links to them, so you may not want to run another Web server just to handle them. External applications, though—by which I mean "applications called by a CGI application"—can easily be moved to another machine without running another copy of WebSTAR. As mentioned, if you are running a CGI that does database queries or that captures real-time images, or anything else that is processor intensive, you can greatly speed up both the CGI processing and WebSTAR performance by moving the external application to its own CPU. This allows the application to be in the foreground (control the CPU) on its computer and not continually be competing with WebSTAR for resources.

If you are providing a site for several computers (as many Internet service providers do), this technique can also be used to cut costs for your customers. By moving an external application to another computer, it can be shared by many different sites. Since the application is called by a CGI application, not by WebSTAR, there is nothing to indicate to the outside world that the application isn't entirely owned by the companies whose sites are on the computers, so their vanity is protected.

Server Distribution

Yet another way to improve performance with multiple CPUs is to divide your site up into discrete units that can each run on a separate machine. This is very useful for sections that have high traffic and cannot be easily mirrored, such as a Comments page where people use a form to leave their opinions about your site. This can also be used to give users the illusion of a faster site. A user's perception of your site speed is developed largely on the first connection to the site. By moving the site's home page or a single, very popular page to its own server, the user gets a very fast initial response, and that impression will last even if other pages are not delivered quite as quickly.

If you are planning to mirror pages across several servers, you may want to add one more server for some pages or sections that change content quite often, such as a chat section or archived e-mail. This can save a lot of the hassle of maintaining mirrored disk images across the front-end systems. Of course, this assumes that the isolated material is not in high demand, so that one computer can handle the request load.

Element Distribution

Most HTML files are very small (<10K). Even an older Macintosh can serve HTML files with great speed. If a page contains embedded graphics, though, it will take longer to download from the user's perspective, because separate connections are needed for each graphic. Newer clients, such as Netscape Navigator, can use multiple connections to retrieve the graphics in a page at the same time as the text, but this places a larger load on a single server. In addition, graphics files are generally larger and will take longer to download. By putting graphics onto a separate (and faster) server, you can improve the speed with which clients retrieve your pages. The same is true for other large files, such as movies, sounds, and file binaries. Moving these files to a separate server will prevent slow connections from tying up connections on the main server while they download.

If you move graphics and binaries to another server, you can speed the server up by reducing the configurations to a bare minimum. Removing any MIME settings that won't be used, removing Allow/Deny and Realm settings that aren't needed, turning DNS lookups off, and turning off logging will all reduce the amount of overhead processing required for each connection. Maxum Development has addressed this problem with a product called Image Monster (cool name!), a very basic HTTP server. All it does is pump data out fast—no logging and only minimal configurations. If your site has a large number of graphics, this can be the perfect solution.

Server Specialization

It might be a good idea for some sites to mix and match servers. Image Monster can be very useful for some specific needs. The secure version of WebSTAR is a separate server that is run only for pages and files that need to be encrypted. If you have a 4D database, you might also want to run one of the 4D HTTP servers specifically for access to the database. Many more options are likely to appear in the future as well.

Selecting the correct server for the job can improve site performance, especially for very large sites having a budget for purchasing more than four or five servers. This probably isn't as great an improvement as the other options, but there are sure to be a few occasions when it is just the trick to make things run smoothly and quickly.

Keep these techniques in mind the next time you wonder what to do with those older Macintoshes or when a UNIX user spouts off that you need an SGI workstation to get a really fast site.

Scripting WebSTAR

WebSTAR is completely scriptable and recordable. Every single server setting that can be changed from WebSTAR Admin can be set or read through an Apple event as well. In fact, WebSTAR Admin uses this Apple event interface to control WebSTAR servers. This can be very useful for custom installations where some event needs to take place regularly, such as saving out the log file for processing every day or adjusting the maxusers parameter higher if there have been refused connections. It can also be useful if multiple servers need to be kept coordinated, so changes to one are then sent to all of the others, or if you just want to make a mini-admin application to give restricted control of the server to a local administrator. I'm sure you will think of even more possibilities.

The Apple Event Interface

This suite is what you would see if you opened WebSTAR in a Script Editor or similar application to view its Apple event dictionary. Although the examples are all given in AppleScript, it is equally possible to send these events from Frontier, C, SmallTalk, or any other application that can generate Apple events. In general, any language or application that can create a CGI application can also be used to send Apple events to WebSTAR.

The following commands are used to change settings that toggle (are on or off) in WebSTAR.

- **Verbose Messages** *Boolean*

  Toggle Verbose Messages on or off

  Boolean: true=on, false=off

  Event code: fvrb

  Ex: `Verbose Messages true -- ` *sets WebSTAR to Verbose mode for logging information to screen.*

- **Hide Window** *Boolean*

  Toggle hiding status window in the background

  Boolean: true=hide, false=show

  Event code: fwin

  Ex: `Hide Window true -- ` *set WebSTAR to hide its Status window when it is not in the foreground.*

- **Refuse Connections** *Boolean*

  Toggle incoming connections on or off

  Boolean: true=refuse, false=allow

  Event code: fcon

  Ex: `Refuse Connections true -- ` *tells WebSTAR to stop accepting connections*

- **Suspend Logging** *Boolean*

  Turn logging on or off

  Boolean: true=off, false=on

  Event code: flog

  Ex: `Suspend Logging true -- ` *stops WebSTAR from logging connections*

The following commands set or retrieve information from Web-STAR. The commands for controlling password information affect only one password at a time. For security reasons, there is no interface for getting a list of all passwords in WebSTAR or for adding large blocks of passwords.

- **Status Report**

  Return status information about WebSTAR

  Result: *char*

  Event code: stat

  Ex: `set curr_status to Status Report -- ` *gets the status report*

- **DoMenu** *char*

  Execute the specified menu item from the WebSTAR menus

  char is "**<menu id>, <menu item>**"

  Event code: menu

  Ex: **DoMenu "4,1"** — *does menu item 1 of menu 4 in WebSTAR*

- **Add User** *char* **password** *char* **realm** *char*

  Add a user and password for a specific security realm

  char is a user name, password, and Realm name, respectively

  Event code: AUsr

  Ex: **Add User "Jon" password "x1*d9" realm "private"** — *allows the user Jon with password "x1*d9" to access the realm of all URLs with the string "private" in them.*

- **Delete User** *char* **realm** *char*

  Delete specified user from a particular security Realm

  char is a user name and Realm name, respectively

  Event code: DUsr

  Ex: **Delete User "Jon" realm "private"** — *user Jon can no longer access the realm "private". The password is automatically removed as well.*

- **Validate User** *char* **password** *char* **realm** *char*

  Validate a user and password for a specific security Realm

  char is a user name, password, and Realm name, respectively

  Event code: VUsr

  Ex: **Validate User "Jon" password "x1*d9" realm "private"** — *checks whether such a user/password combination exists for the specified realm.*

The following settings can be both read and set from AppleScript. For all of them the command is the same: **"get <setting>"** will put the value into **result; "set <setting> to <value>"** will change the setting. The changes should take place immediately, unless otherwise noted. The class code is **capp**.

- **dump_buf_size** *small_integer*
  Output buffer size for TCP/IP writes to clients.
  small_integer is a number in the range 256–10240
  Property code: Dbuf

- **pig_delay** *small_integer*
  Number of ticks to run WebSTAR before relinquishing control to other apps
  small_integer is a number in the range 0–120
  Property code: PigD
  Note: This property is ignored when the Thread Manager is used, so it is never used with WebSTAR 1.2 or later. It may still be used in earlier versions and in MacHTTP.

- **maxusers** *small_integer*
  Maximum number of simultaneous users
  small_integer is a number in the range 4–50
  Property code: MaxU

- **maxlistens** *small_integer*
  Maximum number of TCP/IP listens to queue up
  small_integer is a number in the range 4–50
  Property code: MaxL

- **no_dns** *Boolean*
  Toggle for domain name resolution by WebSTAR
  Boolean: true=off, false=on
  Property code: Ndns

- **time_out** *small_integer*
  Timeout value for idle WebSTAR connections and Apple events in seconds
  small_integer is a number in the range 5–600
  Property code: TimO

- **logging** *Boolean*
  Toggles logging on and off
  Boolean: true=on, false=off
  Ex: `set logging to true`
  Note: This is the same as `"Suspend Logging false"`.

- **verbose_messages** *Boolean*
  Toggles Verbose Messages on and off
  Boolean: true=on, false=off
  Ex: `set verbose_messages to true`
  Note: This is the same as `"Verbose Messages true"`.

- **refuse_connections** *Boolean*
  Toggles refusing incoming connections on and off
  Boolean: true=refused, false=allowed
  Ex: `set refuse_connections to true`
  Note: This is the same as `"Refuse Connections true"`.

- **default_mime_type** *char*
  Default MIME type for untyped files
  char is the MIME type with "text/html" as the default

- **port** *small_integer*
  TCP/IP port for WebSTAR to listen on
  Note: This doesn't take effect until the server restarts.

- **log_format** *char*
  Set message format. Send a single string of space-delimited keywords.
  The keywords (and their interpretations) are:
  - DATE (the current date)
  - TIME (the current time)
  - RESULT (the results of the request, which may be OK, ERR!, or PRIV)
  - HOSTNAME (the name of the WWW client's computer)
  - URL (the requested URL path)
  - PATH_ARGS (path arguments to the URL, text after a **$**)
  - SEARCH_ARGS (search arguments to the URL, text after a **?**)
  - METHOD (the HTTP method, usually GET or POST)
  - BYTES_SENT (the number of bytes transmitted)
  - TRANSFER_TIME (the number of ticks required to complete the transmission)
  - AGENT (the identity of the WWW client software (such as Mosaic or Netscape)

USER (the name of remote user if authentication was required)

FROM (from field in request, usually an e-mail address if present)

REFERER (the name of the document referencing this URL)

Ex:

```
tell application "WebSTAR"

    set log_format to "DATE TIME RESULT HOSTNAME URL
    BYTES_SENT"

end tell
```

The following settings will set special files to be used by WebSTAR or retrieve the current settings for these files. Changes to these settings take place immediately (unless otherwise noted). For each of these you can fetch the current setting with the line **"set <variable> to get <setting>"**, where **<setting>** is one of the following settings:

- **index_file** *char*

  Name of the default index file or home page

  char is just the name of the file, no path

  Ex: `set index_file to "Index.html"`

- **error_file** *char*

  Name of the error message file

  char is the path (relative to WebSTAR) and name of the file

  Ex: `set error_file to ":cgi:Error.acgi"`

- **log_file** *char*

  Name of WebSTAR log file

  char is the path (relative to WebSTAR) and name of the file

  Ex: `set log_file to ":WebSTAR.log"`

- **no_access_file** *char*

  Name of the "No Access" file

  char is the path (relative to WebSTAR) and file name

  Ex: `set no_access_file to ":NoAccess.html"`

- **pre_processor** *char*

  The ACGI to use to preprocess all connections

  char is the path and name of the preprocessor ACGI

  Ex: `set pre_processor to ":cgi:SecurePlus.acgi"`

- **post_processor** *char*

  The ACGI to use to postprocess all connections

  char is the path and name of the postprocessor ACGI

  Ex: `set post_processor to ":cgi:logAlerts.acgi"`

The following settings involve blocks of text. Each block is a series of statements, one per line, defining the setting. Generally, when you change these settings, you will first want to fetch the current settings (`set <variable> to get <setting>`), and then alter them or append new settings and update the server with the changed block.

- **suffix_mappings** *char*

  The suffix and MIME type mappings in text block format

  char must include the prefix SUFFIX and use this syntax:

  `SUFFIX <action><suffix><type><creator><mime-type>`
  `<action>` can be TEXT, BINARY, SCRIPT, CGI, ACGI, or a user-defined action.

  Ex:

  ```
  set suffix_mappings to "SUFFIX TEXT .html TEXT *
  text/html
  SUFFIX BINARY .gif GIFf * image/gif
  ....
  SUFFIX TEXT .hqx TEXT * application/mac-binhex40"
  ```

- **actions** *char*

  User-defined actions in text block format

  char must include the prefix **ACTION** and use this syntax:

  `ACTION <name> <path>`

  `<name>` is the Action's name

  `<path>` cannot contain spaces, so use URL encoding to convert any special Macintosh characters in the path. WebSTAR will decode the path before use. You can set multiple Actions just as you set multiple suffix mappings.

- **actions** *char (continued)*

  Ex:
  ```
  set actions to "ACTION OUTLOG :cgi:linklogger.acgi
  ACTION MAPS :cgi:MapServe.acgi"
  ```

- **access_controls** *char*

  The ALLOW/DENY statements in text block format

  char is the text block, with each line in the format:
  ```
  {ALLOW|DENY} <address>
  ```
  `<address>` is a full or partial IP address or domain name

  Ex:
  ```
  set access_controls to "DENY .edu.
  ALLOW .washington.edu.
  DENY .cac.washington.edu."
  ```

- **realms** *char*

  The security Realm entries in text block format

  char is a block of text, with each line in the format:
  ```
  REALM <text> <name>
  ```
  `<text>` is the text that represents the Realm
  `<name>` is the name of the Realm

  Ex: `set realms to "REALM private My_Pages"`

Sample Applications

Here are some examples of ways that the Apple event interface can be put to good use for remote control or automated maintenance tasks.

Daily Log File Rotation

One of the most common needs on a site for automation is log file processing. On even a moderately busy site, a log file can be as much as 10 MB per week (for a 10,000 connection/day site logging the standard data plus referer and client fields). This is too large a file to conveniently process on many servers. If you cannot afford a separate computer to process the log file, you need to process it more often, probably on a daily basis. Luckily this turns out to be a very easy task. Use the following line to change the name of your log file to reflect the current date:

```
set log_file to ":WebSTAR." & (current date) & ".log"
```

This causes WebSTAR to immediately close the previous log file and open a new one with the name provided. The old log file is now available to be run through ServerStat or another log data processor.

Server Monitor Application

WebSTAR Admin works fine over AppleTalk connections, but if you are far from home, you may want to check up on your server. With this CGI application, you can do that from any computer on the Internet that has Web client software. It doesn't even require forms support.

All this CGI application does is send a request to WebSTAR for the Status Report and then parse the report into a readable format and create an HTML page of it to return to the user. This is very little processing, so the script is pretty fast, even though it is in Apple-Script. A sample is provided in Listing 18.1.

Listing 18.1 Status CGI

```
property crlf : (ASCII character 13) & (ASCII
character 10)
property http_10_header : "HTTP/1.0 200 OK" & crlf ¬
   & "Server: WebSTAR/1.0 ID/ACGI" & crlf & ¬
   "MIME-Version: 1.0" & crlf & "Content-type:
   text/html" & crlf & crlf
```

— *This is the header that will begin your HTML page. Change it for your site.*

```
property html_header : "<HTML><HEAD><TITLE>Current
WebSTAR Status</TITLE></HEAD>" ¬
   & return & "<BODY>" & return ¬
   & "<IMG SRC=\"/Photos/TJPHeader.gif\">" & return ¬
   & "<H1>Current WebSTAR Status</H1>" & return
```

— This is the footer that will be added after the status information.
— Change it for your site.

```
property html_footer : return & "<HR>" & return ¬
  & "<A HREF=\"AboutTheServer.html\">[ Back to Server
  Page ] </A>" ¬
  & return & "<BR><A HREF=\"/cgi/Status.acgi\">[Check
  the Status again]</A>" ¬
  & return & "<P><I>Jon Wiederspan</I>" & return ¬
  & "<BR><I>June 6, 1995</I>" & return &
  "</BODY></HTML>"

on «event WWWΩsdoc» path_args given «class
kfor»:http_search_args

  try
```

— Get the report from WebSTAR.

```
    tell application "WebSTAR 1.2fc2 (bg)"
      set currReport to Status Report
    end tell
```

— Get the data out of currReport. This is hardcoded for WebSTAR 1.x.

```
    set AppleScript's text item delimiters to ","
    set totalCon to word 2 of text item 1 of
    currReport
    set maxCon to word 2 of text item 2 of currReport
    set currCon to word 2 of text item 4 of
    currReport
    set highCon to word 2 of text item 5 of
    currReport
    set busyCon to word 2 of text item 6 of
    currReport
    set denyCon to word 2 of text item 7 of
    currReport
    set byteSent to word 2 of text item 12 of
    currReport
    set tempUp to text item 19 of currReport
```

```
set tempVer to text item 20 of currReport

set AppleScript's text item delimiters to " "

set currVersion to (text item 3 of tempVer & text
item 4 of tempVer)

set upSince to text item 3 of tempUp

set AppleScript's text item delimiters to ","
```

— Format the data nicely.

```
set return_text to http_10_header & html_header ¬

  & "<B>Server Version</B>: " & currVersion &
  "<BR>" & return ¬

  & "<B>Running Since</B>: " & upSince & return ¬

  & "<P><B>Total Connections</B>: " & totalCon &
  "<BR>" & return ¬

  & "<B>Total Bytes Sent</B>: " & byteSent &
  return ¬

  & "<P><B>Maximum Connections</B>: " & maxCon &
  "<BR>" & return ¬

  & "<B>Highest Connections</B>: " & highCon &
  "<BR>" & return ¬

  & "<B>Denied Connections</B>: " & denyCon &
  "<BR>" & return ¬

  & "<B>Busy Connections</B>: " & busyCon &
  return

set return_text to return_text ¬

  & "<P><B>Current Connections</B>: " & currCon &
  "<BR>" & return ¬

  & "<B>Current Time</B>: " & (current date) &
  return

return return_text & html_footer

on error errMsg number errNum

  set return_page to OK_header ¬

    & "<HTML><HEAD><TITLE>Error
    Page</TITLE></HEAD>" ¬
```

```
                    & "<BODY><H1>Error Encountered!</H1>" &
                    return ¬
                    & "An error was encountered while trying to run
                    this script." & return
               set return_page to return_page ¬
                    & "<H3>Error Message</H3>" & return & errMsg &
                    return ¬
                    & "<H3>Error Number</H3>" & return & errNum &
                    return ¬
                    & "<H3>Date</H3>" & return & (current date) ¬
                    & return & "</BODY></HTML>"
               return return_page
          end try
     end «event WWWΩsdoc»
```

Sample Administration Interface via Web Page

Occasionally you want to not only check your server but also make changes to key settings. There are any number of ways to do this and dozens of scripts floating around as examples. They all come down to the same basic design, though. First, you design a form page that provides options for each setting that you want to change. The better ones will show the current value and allow you to select only from valid values. The form page could be a real HTML document or could be served from memory by the CGI application (I prefer the latter). After the user fills out the form with the changes to make to the server settings, the form is submitted to the CGI application, which determines what changes were made and sends the proper commands to the server.

Using this design, if the form page had a line that said "Verbose Messages" followed by On and Off radio buttons, when the user clicks on the **On** radio button and submits the form, the CGI application would send the command "Verbose Messages true" to WebSTAR.

Examples of this are included on the companion CD-ROM that approach the problem from different angles. One of them should be right for you.

Providing administrative functions in this manner is very dangerous for your server. Be certain to take proper measures to protect any form pages or CGI applications that provide these features so that only the Webmaster has access to them. It might be a good idea to build password controls right into the CGI application instead of (or in addition to) relying on a Realm for protection.

19

WebSTAR Data Interface

WebSTAR Admin provides a nice graphical interface to monitor and adjust your WebSTAR server. Perhaps you don't like its little strip chart, though, or perhaps you want to add some new features, such as having a pager notice set off when the Admin interface stops receiving data every 15 seconds. You could send mail to Chuck Shotton asking for these features and wait to see if they make it into the next version. Or, you can write your own Admin application.

This is not the daunting task that it would seem on many servers, because WebSTAR provides an interface so that any application can easily get all of the data that WebSTAR Admin receives on status information and log data (everything that shows in the WebSTAR Admin window). The interface is through Apple events, as with everything else, and therefore can be accessed from anywhere on an AppleTalk network through Program Linking.

To use this function, you need to create an application that can accept a custom Apple event that WebSTAR sends out. This is much like creating a CGI application (with a different event, of course). The main difference is that WebSTAR sends out a constant stream of these events, no more than 15 seconds apart, so your application has to be able to handle the data stream, or things will back up pretty quickly.

The first thing that your application has to do is to send a Request Reporting event (**WWWΩRqrp**) to WebSTAR. This lets WebSTAR know that the application wants to start receiving the data stream. It also specifies which parts of the data stream the application wants to receive. The application can elect to just get status information (total connections, connections denied, memory allocation, and everything else in the top part of the Admin window), or it can just get the log data (the line that describes the results of every connection), or both. In AppleScript the request would look like:

```
request reporting messages boolean status boolean id
long_integer
```

Here **messages** tells whether the application wants to receive log data, **status** tells whether the application wants to receive status information, and **id** is a long integer that is a unique identifier for the application. The **id** is used to keep track of which server is sending data, since a single application could log into data streams from multiple servers at once. Any number at all can be used for the **id** as long as it is unique for each server each time the application launches.

New Request Reporting events can be sent by an application if it wishes to change which data it is receiving. The Request Reporting event is also used to stop receiving reports by sending **false** for both **messages** and **status**. Whenever a new Request Reporting event is sent, it needs to use the same **id** that it originally did for the server that it is being sent to. This number is used by WebSTAR to determine which servers get which events.

Once an application registers with WebSTAR, it will begin receiving Receive Reports events from WebSTAR that contain the information requested. The events are of class and code **WWWΩRrep** and have three parameters:

Ksta—a char type that contains the status information

Kmsg—a char type that contains the log data

Kpid—a long integer that is the ID for the application

The **WWWΩRrep** event is sent out every 15 seconds with only the current status information (**Kmsg** is empty). It is also sent out with log data (but **Ksta** empty) whenever the log data buffer gets over 8K of data or when there is a high-priority log message. These, therefore, arrive at random intervals. When an event is received, you can test the **Ksta** parameter; if it has data, it is status information and there is no log data. If it is empty, you jump to **Kmsg** and get the log data. If both are empty, something is wrong.

The status information comes in a standard format that can be easily parsed. The general format is a repeating structure where each element looks like:

```
<ID><space><VALUE><comma><space>...
```

The comma-space combination is the delimiter for each element. You cannot simply look for a comma, because in some cases the value will contain a comma. Within the element, the first space encountered is the delimiter for the ID (the name of the data field) and its value. An ID will never contain a space, but its value might. The elements occur in a specific order that is always the same, so you don't need to test for an ID by name if you do not want to. As new elements are added in future versions of WebSTAR, they will be appended to the end of the status information. The overall structure and content of the status information is exactly the same as that you would receive if your application sent a Status Report request (**WWWΩstat**) event to WebSTAR.

The log data is almost the same as that displayed in the WebSTAR Status window. There are three types of messages that get displayed in the WebSTAR Status window: high, medium, and low priority.

High-priority messages are the lines that get saved to the disk log. These are the one-line summaries of the information selected to be logged for each connection. High-priority messages are sent out immediately by WebSTAR (instead of queueing up).

Medium-priority messages include the additional information that is shown when a server is running in verbose mode. Medium-priority messages are queued up until either they exceed 8K of data or a high priority message is sent. In the latter event the high-priority message is appended to the queued data and then is sent. Therefore, verbose mode data tends to appear in clumps instead of the continuous flow that the WebSTAR Status window has.

Low-priority messages are the startup notices, notices of changes in server settings, and connection error warnings (this is not the same as the one-line log entry that logs ERR! processing). Low-priority messages are not sent out by WebSTAR and can be seen only in the WebSTAR Status window.

The log data will arrive in exactly the same format that the server is currently set to use. If you plan to use your application to parse the log data, you can send a "get log format" request to WebSTAR to see what the currently selected format is and use that as a key to parse the data. The log data is tab delimited (for the high-priority messages), so the only big problem is determining which lines are part of the verbose-mode messages and how to ignore those lines.

Part VI

The Future

Where is the Web headed? What Apple technologies will be important in the Web? How will WebSTAR address these changes? These questions and more are answered here.

20

Preview of Coming Attractions

This chapter provides a short discussion of WebSTAR features that were added too late for more extensive coverage and where we see the Web heading in the near future.

The Most Recent WebSTAR Features

Several features came out to late too be covered in detail here. Two of them are worth noting, though, even if only in brief.

RAW! Files

WebSTAR 1.2 added the ability for the server to return "raw" files. A "raw" file is one that is returned by WebSTAR as the entire response to a request. No processing is done on the file; instead, the file contains its own HTTP header and data. This can be very useful to replace situations in which a URL redirect might be needed or in which a custom file type is to be returned. The "raw" file is a file of type **RAW!** with creator wwwΩ. When WebSTAR receives a URL request, it checks the file's type and creator. If it sees these two settings, it will completely bypass all other processing and simply return the contents of the file as a complete response to the request.

This is very useful for folders or files that have moved. You can leave a "raw" file behind that will automatically redirect users to the new file location or even to another server. The contents of a file like this would look like:

```
HTTP/1.0 302 FOUND<CRLF>
Location: http://www.webedge.com/<CRLF>
<CRLF>
```

The carriage return/line feed pair is required for line endings. If you do not have an editor that can be modified to put out UNIX-type lines, a utility is included in the WebSTAR distribution for making RAW! redirect files.

Another use for the "raw" file is to return multipart files. The WebSTAR distribution includes a utility for converting multiple GIF images into a multipart graphic file with a proper HTTP header, suitable for use as a "raw" file. When this file is returned to a Netscape Navigator client, each graphic will be displayed in succession, creating an animation effect without the need for animation software. Of course, the timing of the playback all depends on the transfer rate and how fast the client computer is, but it is a start.

SSL Secure WebSTAR

A new version of WebSTAR is available that supports secure connections with clients using the Secure Sockets Layer (SSL) standard. Previous chapters discuss SSL in some detail, but a few features need mentioning here.

This server runs only on port 443, which is the port that was designated for secure HTTP connections. This means that you can run this server on the same computer as your regular WebSTAR server. The Secure Server is a full-featured WebSTAR server (except that it can run only on one port), but you probably do not want to run it as your main server, because the overhead of negotiating secure connections will slow the entire site down. It is best to have it serve only those pages and files that require encryption.

The Secure WebSTAR server supports both DES and RC4 encryption. DES is allowed to be used only in the United States, and versions supporting that encryption method may not be exported. This goes for the client software as well. That isn't a problem, though. If your server is in the United States, you can run the U.S. version and it will support both DES (within the United States) and RC4 (international) connections. If your server is located outside of the United States, it will run only RC4, but even U.S. clients will be able to handle RC4. The main difference between the two is that the RC4 being provided (by all secure servers, not just WebSTAR) uses only a 40-bit key, which theoretically could be broken by brute-force methods in a reasonable period of time (a year or more). DES, on the other hand, and RC4 methods that use much larger keys (like 512 bits) are close to unbreakable for most purposes.

At this point Netscape Navigator is the only client software that supports secure communications, although by the time the book is released, there will probably be many more. Certainly Intercon's browsers, MacWeb/WinWeb, and Mosaic should add support for secure methods. If they do not use SSL, though (and it is likely that some of them won't), WebSTAR will need to add support for even more security options. The most likely alternative is S-HTTP, which Tradewave (makers of MacWeb) are pushing. Watch for WebSTAR to be adding new support options in the near future. If you plan to use one of these clients or have a variety of clients accessing your site, be aware that some of them may not be able to handle the secure connections and thus will not be able to reach certain pages. For a while, at least, you may need to offer alternatives for those clients.

Past, Present, Future: Chuck's Vision

The Internet is an interesting place. For the past 25 years, developments on the Internet have proceeded in fits, starts, and lurches. Occasionally a big leap forward happens. When the big paradigm shifts kick in, it usually takes between three and five years for the mainstream computer industry, computer users, and the popular press (in that order) to catch up. Such a huge leap was taken, beginning in 1993, with the explosive growth and adoption of the World Wide Web as an information delivery medium on the Internet.

The paradigm of user-driven "surfing" of the Internet is a successful one. The computer industry has finally adopted point-and-click as a user interface metaphor that the full spectrum of users can be comfortable with. The logical extension of this metaphor to the information-gathering methods used by computer users on the Internet was inevitable and was just waiting for the right application to pull all the pieces together. The Web does this in a way that even the most naive user can find approachable and useful.

But the huge leap is over for now. Advances on the Internet always seem to be followed by a plateau that lasts several months or years, while the user community assesses and assimilates the new technology. As with any technical advance, it takes time for the general public to become accustomed to new ways of interacting with information. Government regulations have to catch up, and the popular press needs time to understand how to convey the new technology to audiences. Technology takes several years to trickle down into mainstream business and entertainment activities.

This leap, the World Wide Web, happened to coincide with the wholesale commercialization of the Internet, and many would argue that the Web precipitated it. Although it's not clear how long the industry needs to pause to catch its breath, it's pretty clear that the third generation of Web tools is on the way and that commercial organizations will greatly accelerate the pace of Internet development, which was traditionally the province of academia.

So the big question is: What will the World Wide Web and the Internet be like in the next few years? Just as the commercialization of the Internet has brought rapid change to the way users perceive it, it seems that the "personalization" of the Internet and the WWW will be the next big leap. Tools that enable the individual, rather than the corporate entity, will become the norm. The rapid pace with which high-speed networks are being extended into homes and offices, coupled with some impending advances in Web tools, will bring the next leap forward.

Currently the intelligence behind Web browsing is the person driving the mouse. Web client software consists of monolithic applications that provide a myriad of built-in tools for a human to manipulate data with. What's more, the data is oriented toward electronic representations of paper publications intended for human consumption. Very few online resources are intended to convey information from one software application to another. Typically the server providing information is relatively oblivious to the content it serves, and the assumption is that the data will be rendered in a way that makes sense to a human reader. This is about to change.

Although it will take many more years for the majority of WWW services to shift from the "electronic paper" metaphor for information delivery, the time will come when sites on the Internet will provide their information in a form that is more easily manipulated by other computer programs. These intelligent agents will roam the Internet, doing the bidding of their human masters and retrieving information that the agents can understand. The agents will be responsible for rendering this in a human-usable form.

To clarify, let's look at a simple example of information on the Web. Take the Weather Machine at the University of Illinois, for example. Currently weather information is provided in the form of image data that can be viewed by humans as pictures. Imagine instead that this information were provided as tables of pressure, temperature, precipitation, and wind data. Instead of retrieving an image of the current conditions for the person to view, an intelligent agent could obtain this data and return with it to the user's computer. There the agent would feed it into a weather-forecasting application on the user's computer that would predict tomorrow's weather by running a weather simulation and displaying much more information than a simple GIF image.

Of course, many other examples can be drawn. The proliferation of online catalogs is amazing but virtually useless to a busy consumer. One would have to visit literally hundreds of Web sites in hopes of doing anything resembling comparative shopping for computer software. Imagine, instead, if all online malls made their pricing information, product descriptions, and shipping information for their software products available online in a standard format. Rather than forcing a user to wade through dozens of HTML pages written by a human for a human, intelligent agents could surf the Internet, comparing prices and returning with information on the best buy to the user. In short, the Web needs to take the next big leap from human-oriented content to agent-oriented content.

How will this happen? The short-term trend is toward bigger and better Web clients for human users. But while this technology is being produced and focused on by large Internet-oriented corporations, many advances are being made in parallel in areas critical to the development of intelligent-agent technology. Programming languages for agent development, like Java, are in the works. Web server software is migrating from the realm of the centralized IS department into the hands of individuals. This same server software is being repurposed as a "home base" for agents to operate from. Rather than having your WWW server online to provide information to users on the Internet, your server will become the "in-basket" for your agents, with data they find on the Internet being sent to the "home" Web server for storage. Your Web server will become the provider of information for you to view locally. Of course, you may choose to republish some of this information or provide your own content to other users or agents. But the trend is definitely going to be toward a Web server running on every workstation. Just as your answering machine is online, listening for information from phone calls while you are away, your Web server will be online, listening for data being sent to your site by your agents for your perusal.

A majority of the pieces of technology necessary for this next paradigm shift already exist on the Macintosh. Technologies, such as Apple events and AppleScript, and environments for agent development, such as Java and Frontier, are here today. WebSTAR servers are already being used as receivers of information in many information applications. There are several examples of WebSTAR-to-WebSTAR transmission of scripts or small programs that roam from server to server, executing searches for their owners, with the results eventually being returned as post arguments to a CGI running on the home server.

New technologies, such as OpenDoc, are going to make it possible to develop component frameworks that will allow agents tailored to do specific tasks to be tied into Web servers. They'll retrieve data in formats specific to viewing or analysis programs. Client frameworks, such as Apple's CyberDog project, will have plug-ins that will work with these agents to display and analyze the information. When standardized agent languages become widely deployed, it will greatly simplify and secure the process of passing an agent from site to site while it performs its searches and queries.

The technology is already here, by and large, for the next leap. The difficult part is the paradigm shift from human-readable content to agent readable-content. Users have to be comfortable with understanding how they manually browse the network for information before they will be comfortable with the concept of an intelligent-agent application doing it for them. Content providers have to develop standard ways for representing information to agents. Once this paradigm switch is made, Macintosh users will be at the head of the queue to take advantage of the new opportunities that become available.

Site Administration Tools

The information in this section refers to software that may change or become unavailable in the future. Much of it is shareware or freeware and although very useful, it has no guarantee of support from the various authors. For the shareware software, please be sure to pay the fees for any software that you use, so the authors can continue to support and improve the products.

General Utilities

The following utilities are difficult to both classify and do without.

ServerStat

- **Kitchen Sink Software (Forsythe.14@osu.edu)** *commercial*

  `http://1165.247.199.177`

  ServerStat will process HTTP or Gopher logs to produce useful reports of daily activity totals, by file, by site. There are many options for filtering information, customizing the look of the report, and more. A Lite version is available as shareware.

WebSTAR Link Checker

- **David Habermann (habermann@dow.com)** *freeware*

  `http://www.dow.com/~haberman/`

  The Link Checker is a set of scripts (now in both AppleScript and Frontier) that will check the links on your site and report on those that seem to be nonfunctional. This is a problem on sites once they get more than a few dozen pages and will result in many irate user messages if they are not tracked down.

Pounder

- **Chuck Shotton (chuck@starnine.com)** *freeware*

    `http://datapig.concom.com/`

    Pounder is an automated HTTP client (Web browser) that can simulate being up to 20 clients at once. The configuration file (yes, a text file) allows a URL to be specified, and it will randomly select from the list and try a URL. The delay between new URLs can also be specified in the settings. The URLs can point to HTML files, binaries, or even CGI applications, so you can get a "real-world" test of your site's performance.

Running Remotely

The following will help if you are running servers in a location that you cannot reach in minutes. If any of the software does not have a download location specified (with the exception of commercial software), it can be downloaded from my FTP site at

`ftp.comvista.com.`

Timbuktu Pro

- **Farallon Computing, Inc. (sales@farallon.com)** *commercial*

    `http://www.farallon.com/`

    Timbuktu Pro is a combination application and system extension that allows one computer to completely control another over AppleTalk or TCP/IP network connections. If you install it on your server and your work computer (that requires two copies), your work computer can display the screen of your server. With that you can use the menus, drag files, launch and quit applications, and do whatever else you want—all on the remote computer. There are also Windows clients available and it includes settings to give users everything from the ability to exchange files to the ability to completely control the remote computer.

AutoBoot

- **Karl Pottie (karlp@macbel.be)** *shareware*

    AutoBoot is a combination system extension and control panel that will reboot (restart) your Macintosh when a system error occurs or when the computer "freezes up." In these situations you would not be able to access the computer using Timbuktu Pro. AutoBoot watches the computer processing to see whether it ever halts. The amount of time to wait before considering the system halted is configurable, and a log of reboots is kept. AutoBoot will not reboot the server if an application has crashed but the system is still operating in the background. Then, you need something like KeepItUp to watch specific applications.

KeepItUp

- **Karl Pottie (Karl.Pottie@uz.kuleuven.ac.be)** *shareware*

  KeepItUp watches certain applications to see whether they are still running. If an application no longer runs because it "unexpectedly quit" or because the user quit it, KIU will attempt to relaunch this application (and open certain documents assigned to the application) or restart the computer. This will ensure that your application is always running and available. The control panel interface allows the user to specify which applications will be watched. KeepItUp can also restart your Mac at certain scheduled moments in time.

Okey Dokey

- **Dan Walkowski and Brent Pease (walkowsk@apple.com and brent@apple.com)** *freeware*

  Okey Dokey is a control panel and system extension that automatically chooses the default button in a modal dialog box after a specified amount of time. The control panel lets you set the time and specify whether you want a little countdown display in the lower-left-hand corner of the modal dialog box. It affects only modal dialog boxes that use the system trap ModalDialog, which means that it won't work if the software uses a different (unrecommended) method for putting up notices. Okey Dokey will not reply to the Standard File dialog because there is no single obvious choice to use (the first file?).

Automated Processing

Cron is an application that runs as a daemon on UNIX systems and launches processes or scripts at preset times or time intervals. It is often used for daily renaming of files or folders, running system cleanup routines at regular intervals, or producing weekly reports. Several applications for Macintosh computers will provide similar capabilities.

Crond

- **Mark Malson (markm@xetron.com)** *freeware*

  Cron (often called "Crond") is a basic implementation that consists of two pieces of software. Crond is a faceless background application that is the equivalent of a daemon process on UNIX. CronMgr is a control panel that allows configuration of Crond. The interface for launching processes is not very good. The time for launching is specified in the name of the file to be run.

Cron

- **Chris Johnson (chrisj@mail.utexas.edu)**

  `http://gargravarr.cc.utexas.edu/cron/cron.html`

  This version of Cron includes a Cron application and dozens of commands that it can implement. It can use a standard Cron file as you would have for a UNIX system, or you can write your own, using the many extensions that Chris has added just for Macintosh (such as running after so much idle time). Instructions are included for creating new commands or altering an application so that it can be used as a command.

  An application called CronX10 by Jerry Gatlin (`jerry@hipark.austin.isd.tenet.edu`) lets the Cron application control hardware through an X10 module. X10 modules allow software control of power to other hardware, so this module can be used to cycle power on a computer to force a reboot. X10 modules are available from Leviton, Radio Shack, and most other electronics stores.

Chronograph

- **John A. Schlack (John40@aol.com)** *shareware*

  Chronograph is the most complete of the three options. It also is distributed as two applications: a faceless background application and a manager. The manager provides a very easy-to-use interface for creating new events to be launched. If you are familiar with the Crontab structure, a Crontab file can also be used, or single lines from the file can be entered by using the "advanced" mode. Chronograph has excellent logging features and is available as a PowerPC-native application.

TCP Utilities

These utilities are useful for monitoring or troubleshooting your TCP/IP connections and activity.

MacTCP Monitor

- **Chris Johnson (chrisj@mail.utexas.edu)**

  MacTCP Monitor provides a graphical view of TCP/IP activity on your computer. One panel shows all 64 available connections in an 8X8 grid, with different colors used to indicate the state each connection is in (idle, read, write, and so on). The other panel provides a strip chart of activity, displaying the amount of data sent and received in two-second intervals. MacTCP Monitor requires System 7.1 or later, Apple's Thread Manager extension (which is built into System 7.5), Color QuickDraw, and, of course, MacTCP.

MacTCPWatcher

- **Peter Lewis (peter.lewis@info.curtin.edu.au)** *freeware*

  MacTCP Watcher displays the internal data of MacTCP. It shows the IP address, DNS name, and other internal information that MacTCP provides about the computer. It will also list all of the currently open TCP connections and information on each of them. It allows you to test MacTCP and your network, using the ICMP Ping protocol and the UDP and TCP Echo protocols, and it tests out the DNS by looking up the name of a given IP or IP of a given name. If you are having problems with your server and suspect MacTCP, this is the place to start.

ZapTCP

- **Steve Falkenburg** *freeware*

  ZapTCP is a system extension that works by installing a systemwide patch that takes control when an application quits (or is quit by a forced MacsBug "es"). When it runs, the code scans through all of the currently open MacTCP streams and connections, looking for those that have their stream buffers allocated within the heap that is about to disappear. When ZapTCP finds a stream whose buffers are in that heap, it forces the connection closed and releases the stream, posting a notification to the user. This is extremely useful if you are writing or testing MacTCP software. ZapTCP *requires* MacTCP, or nasty things could happen.

MacTCP Switcher

- **John Norstad (j-norstad@nwu.edu)** *freeware*

  `ftp://ftp.acns.nwu.edu/pub/jlnstuff/mactcp-switcher/`

  MacTCP Switcher switches on the fly among presaved MacTCP configurations. If MacTCP is already in use, it will warn you that the computer needs to be restarted to install the new configuration. It includes the source code.

MacTCP NetSwitch

- **David Walton (David.Walton.10@nd.edu)** *freeware*

  `http://www.nd.edu/~dwalton1/`

  MacTCP Netswitch is a control panel designed to automatically reconfigure MacTCP for those who move their Macintoshes from network to network. It loads in new MacTCP Prep files to be used the next time the computer reboots, so you can keep dozens of different configurations on hand by keeping a Prep file for each. It is not able to switch the network configuration on the fly, though.

GetMyAddress

- **Mahboud Zabetian (mahboud@aggroup.com)** *freeware*

  This application provides a quick report on general TCP/IP information about the computer, such as its IP address and Ethernet address. It can also query a DNS server for the machine name. The information can be appended to a text file, which makes it very useful for gathering information on several computers at one time.

Other TCP/IP Services

These services are commonly run in addition to an HTTP server, often on the same machine. There are obviously going to be many that I will not list that could be useful (such as anything to do with electonic mail, mailing lists, or Gopher). These are the ones I have found good uses for, though.

Script Daemon

- **Peter Lewis (peter.lewis@info.curtin.edu.au)** *freeware*

  Script Daemon listens to port 23 (the Telnet port), accepts logins, validates them by using the Users and Groups AppleScript extension, and then compiles and executes scripts. The external interface uses the ISO-8859-1 character set. It supports only the English dialect of AppleScript, and the interface is still pretty rough. It can be very useful, though, when you're stuck on the road with access only through some poor student terminal or a 9600 bps modem.

MIND

- **The Jourvian Group (webmaster@josaiah.sewanee.edu)** *freeware*

  `http://josaiah.sewanee.edu/mind/mindInfo.html`

  MIND (Macintosh Internet Name Daemon) is a free DNS solution that runs under the Macintosh OS. The interface is very minimal ("About" wasn't even in yet), and it still requires UNIX-style text files for configuration. On the other hand, it can be a secondary as well as a primary server, which is all that matters.

  MacDNS, the DNS server from Apple Computer, has a much better interface and easier configuration, as well as an easy way to assign names for round-robin matching. It is not able to be a secondary server, though (although this should be addressed quickly), so it is likely that the two could be used well in combination.

QuickDNS

- **Men & Mice (sigurasg@menandmice.is)** *freeware*

  `ftp://ftp.menandmice.is//pub/quickdns/`

  QuickDNS is a caching-only Internet Domain Name Server that runs on Macintosh computers. It keeps the cache in RAM and so can be a very fast nameserver that will speed up any servers that need name resolution. If you like to have DNS lookups on with your WebSTAR server (I do), this will boost the response speed a bit.

EasyTransfer

- **Christopher Reid** *shareware*

  `ftp://mac-ftp.cs.strath.ac.uk/macstuff/EasyTransfer/`

  EasyTransfer is a file transfer utility, somewhat like FTP, that works exclusivly on Macintosh computers. It knows Mac applications, so you don't have to BinHex or MacBinary encode files to transmit them. It does compression on the fly to speed transfer. An accompanying EasyDrop application will allow users to simply drop folders or files on an icon and have them automatically uploaded to a remote site without allowing the user to browse the site at all. Installation and configuration of the server and client are very easy.

Daemon

- **Peter Lewis (peter.lewis@info.curtin.edu.au)** *freeware*

  Daemon is a general TCP server, implementing several simple UNIX daemons, namely, Finger, Whois, Ident, Daytime, and NTP (time). It runs as a background-only application and answers queries to those services. The NTP (time, not news!) is very useful for keeping servers in time synchronization.

Anarchie

- **Peter Lewis (peter.lewis@info.curtin.edu.au)** *shareware*

  Anarchie is an FTP and Archie client in one. It can do several downloads simultaneously and is scriptable, which makes it very useful for automated work with FTP sites.

FTPd

- **Peter Lewis (peter.lewis@info.curtin.edu.au)** *shareware*

  FTPd is an FTP server that uses the Users & Groups settings on a computer to control access to files and folders. The interface for configuration is not daunting, but it is also a bit confusing, and it may take some practice to get things just right. In general, though, installation is pretty easy, and it coexists well with other services. This is very useful when you need a way to upload files to a site.

FTPShare

- **About Software Corporation (sales@ascus.com)** *commercial*

  `ftp://ftp.ascus.com/`

  FTPShare is another FTP server for Macintosh computers. It allows up to 20 simultaneous sessions and uses its own settings for file and folder protection. It is very fast and works well with other services on the same machine.

Information Management

These products help you manage the overwhelming number of items of value that you will find in your Web travels. It's debatable whether this is a development or administration tool. Luckily, it's my book, and I'll put it where I want to.

GrabNet

- **The ForeFront Group (800-867-1101)**

  `http://www.ffg.com/download.html`

  GrabNet is a tool designed to easily collect and organize information while browsing the Internet. GrabNet stores information intuitively in folders and subfolders on the local desktop. Users can casually grab snips of information, including images, text and URLs, for reuse, navigation, and organization within a customized collection of folders. GrabNet works in conjunction with your World Wide Web browser. At this time Netscape Navigator™ version 1.1 or later is required for full GrabNet capability. Use of this browser with GrabNet enables drag-and-drop and retrieval of current browser page information for images, text, and URLs captured while surfing the Internet. Some GrabNet features will not work with older versions of Netscape. ForeFront Group is currently in the process of testing GrabNet with additional World Wide Web browsers, and several features will work with any browser.

  GrabNet requires System 7.1 or later. It makes heavy use of drag-and-drop, which is part of System 7.5, or will be added by the GrabNet Installer if you are running System 7.1.x. GrabNet also provides AppleGuide help, if AppleGuide is supported by the system.

CyberFinder

- **Leonard Rosenthol and Victor Tan (cyberfinder@aladdinsyscom)** *freeware*

  CyberFinder extends the Finder to allow the creation of files that are aliases to Web sites. Double clicking on the files sends your Web browser to the site specified. This was first released at MacHack '95. CyberFinder is *not* an Aladdin Software product.

Cyber Link

- **RTZ Software (rtz@netcom.com)** *shareware*

`http://www.rtz.com/`

Cyber Link is a utility that allows you to use the Finder and its icons to keep track of and organize all the places you visit while you are surfing the World Wide Web. Cyber Link files aliases to Web sites. When you double click on one, your Web client is directed to go to that site. There are also shortcuts to ease access to company and educational sites.

URLKey

- **City Net Express (http://www.city.net/)** *freeware*

`http://www.city.net/cnx/software/urlkey.html`

URLKey is a control panel/extension that allows you to load a URL with your preferred World Wide Web browser from any application on your Mac that supports the clipboard. Just select any text that contains a URL, copy it to the clipboard, then type your HotKey (command-shift-u by default). The URL will be loaded by your Web browser; the browser will be brought to the foreground if you have that option checked in the Settings dialog. It doesn't matter how much text you select or whether the text contains multiple URLs; URLKey will parse the text and use the first URL it finds, based on the order of the URL types in the Settings dialog.

Index